THE ANALYSAND'S TALE

THE ANALYSAND'S TALE

Robert Morley

KARNAC

First published in 2007 by
Karnac Books Ltd.
118 Finchley Road, London NW3 5HT

British Library Cataloguing in Publication Data

A C.I.P. for this book is available from the British Library

   ISBN-10: 1 85575 437 1
   ISBN-13: 978 1 85575 437 9

Edited, designed and produced by The Studio Publishing Services Ltd,
www.publishingservicesuk.co.uk
e-mail: studio@publishingservices.co.uk

Printed in Great Britain by Biddles Ltd., King's Lynn, Norfolk

10 9 8 7 6 5 4 3 2 1

www.karnacbooks.com

CONTENTS

ACKNOWLEDGEMENTS

I acknowledge with thanks permission to use extracts from the following: *An Autobiographical Novel*, by Marie Cardinal, published by Pan; *Tribute to Freud*, by HD, published by Carcanet; *Folie à Deux*, by Rosie Alexander, published by Free Association; *The Wolf-Man and Sigmund Freud*, edited by Margaret Gardiner, published by Penguin; *Jung, My Mother and I*, by J. C. Reid, published by Daimon Verlag; *Final Analysis*, by Jeffrey Mouisaieff Masson, published by Random House; the Masson Family Trust.

My special thanks are owed to Brett Kahr, who enthusiastically supported my presentation to Karnac. Even more particularly, my loving thanks are due to my wife, Elspeth, who read and re-read every word, sometimes challenged my grammar, and encouraged me to complete the book. We share all our work, and the ideas from that sharing might not otherwise have seen the light of day. Such errors as remain are all my own.

ABOUT THE AUTHOR

Robert Morley, after war service, graduated at Durham University and joined the Probation Service, where he was introduced to psychoanalytical thinking by Dr Hyatt Williams. His subsequent career included training as a couple and individual therapist, which he combined with full-time jobs. In the 1970s he designed and taught a degree course in Social Work while a Principal Lecturer at the Hatfield Polytechnic. He followed this with an appointment on the staff of the Institute of Marital Studies (now TCCR). He subsequently became Director of The Family Welfare Association until he retired. He now works in private practice with couples (with his wife, Elspeth) and individuals. He has published a number of papers about couple and individual therapy, and his book, *Intimate Strangers*, was published in 1984.

Introduction

"The principle is that it is the patient and only the patient who has the answers. We may or may not enable him to encompass what is known . . ."

(Winnicott, 1971)

If the analysand and the analyst were each to write a separate account of the therapy in which they had both participated, and if they seemed to differ, whose account would be more likely to be authentic? Which of them would be most able to identify the important moments in the therapeutic process that had led to a successful outcome? Are psychoanalysis and psychotherapy like medicine, where the doctor's diagnosis and the treatment flowing from it are the important factors in the recovery of the patient? Or is it quite different from medicine in that the analysand's belief about what was therapeutic is as likely to be as correct as the therapist's? Published accounts by analysands themselves are very uncommon compared with those by therapists. In this book I have assembled a number of such accounts where analysands and patients describe their experiences, with both eminent and less well-known analysts

and therapists, with the intention of providing material to examine
these and other questions. Because these accounts have not usually
been part of any research programme, where the research protocols
may unconsciously influence the way the material is recalled, they
have a freshness and directness not usually to be found in the
detached findings of an outcome study.

Many of them are book length. In the daunting task of summa-
rizing them I have tried to preserve as far as possible the
analysand's way of describing the experience. Unfortunately, there
is only one example where both the analyst and the patient have
published their accounts (the Wolf-Man) and they differ significantly. Freud (1918b) seems to be claiming that his penetrating
insights of the Wolf-Man's infantile phantasy world cured him,
though in fact he was really demonstrating the validity of his theory of infantile sexuality rather than the curative power of the therapy. It is also apparent that in so far as there was any change in the
Wolf-Man's psychopathology, it may have had quite a different
cause than Freud claimed in his famous paper. So is Freud's account
of the analysis of the Wolf-Man definitive, or does the Wolf-Man's
own story have an equal claim to validity? Although there are no
other separate accounts by therapist and analysand, I think that the
differences between the accounts of the Wolf-Man and Freud might
be characteristic of what happens in other analyses, that the analysts and the analysands may have very different, *discordant agendas*. It follows that there may be a struggle between the two to
establish control of the situation, with the power firmly on the side
of the analyst, who determines the terms of engagement and whose
authoritative and suggestive influence may be fundamental. I
believe that this struggle, plainly demonstrable in the case of the
Wolf-Man, may be dimly discernible in the singularity of the
patients' accounts collected here. I think that it can be shown that
the patients' discordant agendas are as likely to be the root of resistance and defensiveness as the idea that painful unconscious fantasies are being warded off. Both may occur, but it is not always
evident which is the more determining. Carotenuto (1886, p. 13)
makes a similar point when he links failure in therapy to the
absence of the convergence of mutual destinies. One of the important aspects of psychoanalysis, and psychotherapy, is its interactional nature. Unlike other forms of treatment for mental disorders,

it claims that its effectiveness depends upon the relationship between the psychotherapist and the patient, a joint creation of the interpenetrating subjectivities of the analyst and the analysand (Gabbard & Lester, 1995, p. 53), differing from any other kind of intervention. This effect has been conceptualized as the interaction between the transference from the patient (i.e., the emotional reaction to the therapist, as if he were a historical figure from the patient's life, or as if the therapeutic situation was an unconscious repetition of the past) and the psychotherapist's countertransference to the patient (i.e., the therapist's emotional reaction to the patient's transference). For some contemporary forms of psychoanalysis, drawn largely from Kleinian tradition, the work of therapy depends almost entirely upon this factor. In the more classical forms of analysis and therapy the interaction between transference and countertransference was thought of largely as a consequence of defences, hindering the focus on the story being told by the patient (Couch, 1995). The interactional aspects of the process in this tradition are concerned with helping the patient to work at those elements of the narrative that are being unconsciously expressed by the transference manifestations. While successful work on those issues enables the patient to disclose painful material that, it is believed, advances the process of recovery, the therapist may not always correctly identify what is occurring in that interaction, and may fail to notice something about it not falling within the theoretical concepts he or she uses. Whatever the particular theoretical stance of the psychotherapist, it is common ground that the process differs from medical practice in that the patient is not simply the object of the "treatment" flowing from the diagnosis, but is an active participant in it.

Jung (1945) went so far as to claim that, while the work of psychotherapy should be in the hands of doctors, it differed from medical practice in important ways, notably that the diagnosis could not be made until the treatment had been completed. Moreover, he also asserted that each patient required the reformulation of the theory to make it relevant to that patient's particular circumstances. Communicative psychotherapists (Ferro, 1999; Langs, 1976) claim that there is a special characteristic of psychoanalytic treatment, i.e., that the unit of treatment is the therapeutic pair, with neither the therapist nor the patient having greater significance than the other. To extend Erikson's (1958) comment that the evidence is not all in until the therapist's associations are taken into account, it may be that the evidence is not all in until the thoughts and associations of both the therapists *and their patients* are taken into account. In other words, perhaps the patient's contribution should be given equal weight to that of the therapist.

In view of that special interactive characteristic of psychotherapy, it might be expected that accounts of the analysis or the therapy would differ in presentation from the description of other medical treatments. However, the surprising thing is that they do not, and usually case presentations consist of the psychotherapist's story of what happened, just as the medical story consists of the doctor's diagnosis and the consequential treatment. Strachey (1934, p. 142) published his paper claiming that the important factor in the analysis was the "mutative interpretation", or, to put it another way, that it was the psychotherapists' agendas and interventions that mattered beyond anything else. The patients' accounts of their therapy, in this study, do not on the whole confirm that claim.

If the patient is heard at all, it is through the mouth of the therapist. Psychotherapeutic case studies are often presented as a vindication of the work done by the psychotherapist; or, more especially, of the analyst's theoretical stance; or of the way the concepts may be adapted to meet new problems. Whatever the purpose of the accounts presented in this way, they undermine the intersubjective nature of the psychotherapeutic process, and substitute the traditional subject–object stance of standard medical practice. A discussion about the presentation of case reports in clinical practice (Ward, 1997) at the Freud Museum in 1995 demonstrated the problems about such reports, and drew attention to the many conscious and unconscious factors that might influence the way in which they were presented. Spurling (1977, p. 65) went so far as to claim that it might be a fundamental feature of the psychoanalytic profession and its methods of public case presentations that nobody could really know what "each of us gets up to with our patients". It might also be added that neither do the therapists really know how their patients have experienced the treatment, nor what their patients might believe had been most helpful. However that may be, patients' accounts of their therapies are often disparaged by professional critics In referring to Godley's (2001) account of his experience with Masud Khan, Willoughby (2005, p. 96) describes Godley's story of what happened in the sessions as uncorroborated without noticing that, in every case, so is the analyst's report.

If the therapeutic effect is actually a consequence of the interaction between analyst and patient, rather than the therapist's magisterial interventions, what is it that gives the therapist's account such exclusive authority? Spence (1997, p. 79) refers to the case report as a one-time event with only one witness, the patient, "who is not normally permitted to speak or publish", although who might prohibit him from doing so is far from clear. Eissler did, however, succeed in preventing, until after the Wolf-Man's death, the publication of Obholzer's conversations with the Wolf-Man, revealing a perceptible gulf between patient and analyst (Obholzer, 1982). Eissler thought that anything the Wolf-Man might have said ought not to be made available to unsophisticated members of the lay public who would not be able to understand the psychoanalytic implications of those conversations. So the analyst's claim to authority rests on the ownership of esoteric knowledge not available to those outside the enchanted circle of the cognoscenti, but which has never been cognitively substantiated.

Recently, in recognition that there are several different theories in the field, none of which can demonstrate its superior therapeutic effectiveness, it has become the practice in one of the professional journals (*Journal of the British Association of Psychotherapists*) to provide an extract from a therapeutic session and to seek commentaries from psychotherapists with a different theoretical stance from the presenter. In this situation it is not clear what is being claimed for the effectiveness of the treatment offered by the presenter, or, indeed, for the effectiveness of any of the alternatives discussed. Since only the presenter has any contact with the patient, it may be very difficult to decide what the outcome of the interventions offered by the other commentators might have been. Would any of the alternative formulations have made any difference? Since they were not offered to the patient during the therapy, who can tell?

The claim that the contributions of the therapists are definitive by virtue of their specialist knowledge and of their special comprehension of unconscious processes is undermined by the admission of alternative conceptual formulations. It may be that there is no uniquely authoritative theory of unconscious processes sanctioning the account of the particular analyst, and his idiosyncratic theory, above all others. Moreover if, as postmodern and hermeneutic theories claim, there can be no single authoritative interpretation of a text, then none of the various interpretations of the content of a therapeutic session can be more authoritative or authentic than another. Each is simply another way of understanding the same material.

What is missing is any account from the *patient*, whose views might be expected to be equally authoritative if the process is supposed to be about the interaction between therapist and patient. So why are the stories of the patients mostly absent from the records? It may be that it is too difficult to persuade patients to record their impressions of each session so that they could be compared with, and considered alongside, those of the psychotherapists. Many psychotherapists might be very wary of such records since it might be that what the patient believed had happened, or was therapeutic, would differ too markedly from what the therapist thought about it. The struggle between the different agendas might then become too apparent. It has been suggested that the patient's story would be too inaccurate to be a valid account, a view likely to be more favoured by therapists rather than others. It is not, however, clear why the therapist's case report should be considered to be any more accurate than the patient's story. Spence (1982, pp. 26–30) has drawn attention to the "narrative polish" and other forms of distortion that are feature of most case reports. Additionally, Bollas & Sundelson (1995) have argued that the requirement to create records that may be made available for use in courts of law is not simply a breach of therapeutic confidence but also inevitably distorts the account to provide an impression of evidential authority, which they describe as "false expertise" (*ibid.*, p. 136). So it may be assumed that the edited account of the therapist for presentation to colleagues, or for publication, is no more likely to be the unembellished truth about the process than the patient's unpretentious record.

Christopher (2002) has described the difficulties of attempting to write a paper with a patient about the treatment. For her and the patient the problem lay in their being unable to relive the distressing material that had been worked through in the treatment. Those difficulties led her and the patient to give up the struggle to write the combined story. Her account of her own issues in choosing to write about this patient, rather than another, is described very frankly and honestly in her chapter. I wonder how it might have been if each had written their respective accounts independently of each other. There are, however, at least two accounts of therapy written by both patient and therapist (Barnes & Berke, 1991; Caine & Royston, 2003).

At least four more of Freud's patients—Kardiner, Blanton, Wortis, and HD—have published accounts of their experiences in analysis with him. Wortis (1954) recorded his impressions of each session after he had left the consulting room. It is not clear whether he presented them to Freud, but it seems unlikely, and Freud's case notes have not been published. A comparison would have made very interesting reading. The Wolf-Man wrote his assessment of his experiences in psychoanalysis with Freud independently, and offers some thought-provoking material about the struggle between their discordant agendas. Another, HD, both kept a diary for part of her analysis and also wrote letters daily to her lesbian partner, describing graphically what had occurred in the session on that day. She wrote two memoirs (1944, 1948) of her work with Freud. Those memoirs have been supplemented by a literary critic's review of her accounts of what happened in her psychotherapy (Friedman, 1981), and by the publication of her letters, edited by Friedman, in 2002. It is claimed that HD's story is an account of her subversion of Freud's phallocentric theory in favour of her own feminist ideas; a discordant agenda, indeed. Another of Freud's patients, Blanton, kept an intermittent diary of his analysis (Blanton, 1971), describing his impressions of that work. Over the years, a number of other accounts by patients of their experiences in psychotherapy have been published, although they have not usually been contemporaneous with their therapy, or never written in conjunction with any account by their psychotherapists. None of the psychotherapists' case notes has been available for comparison.

If the accounts of Freudian patients have been sparse, there have been even fewer published accounts by Jung's patients (or by patients of other Jungian analysts). One very extensive and detailed story of her analysis with Jung has been written by Catherine Cabot Rush, complied from shorthand notes made by her during her sessions and published in full after her death (Reid, 2001). A comparison with the stories of Freud's patients is very thought-provoking.

The argument of this book, then, is that the stories told by patients are as valid as those told by therapists in their case presentations; and they may be just as illuminating for understanding the process of therapy. They frequently stand as an *ex post facto* attempt to re-assert the patients' agendas as being as important as those of their therapists. In the ensuing chapters the voice of the patient, whether well-known or unknown, will be the focus. How the patients have told their stories will be significant, and as far as possible in the first instance, will be presented in an unvarnished form. All the accounts have been published separately, and some have been commented on by the psychoanalytical community, but there has been no opportunity to think about them collectively. Although it cannot be claimed that the collection, or any conclusions which may be drawn from them, has any scientific validity, their collective presentation may allow for some common themes of interest to emerge. As Bollas & Sundelson point out, psychoanalysis has been unable to establish itself scientifically without its being diminished thereby. There have been some studies of outcomes, almost exclusively defined by the therapists without consultation with patients; so that they, too, are themselves part of an expert narrative that may be no more significant than the unembellished material from the patient.

I begin with two very contrasting accounts by two patients of different psychoanalysts. Why the experiences of these two patients were so different, although both their analysts were fully qualified by their Institutes, poses some interesting questions about the patient's contribution to the process, as well as about the analyst's expertise. One of the analysts is unnamed, and the significance of his anonymity and unobtrusiveness contrasts very powerfully with the named colleague of the second patient, whose therapeutic approach could hardly be described as unobtrusive. Both patients had very decided views about their treatment and its consequences, and in neither case would it have been appropriate to dismiss their opinions as irrelevant

Other accounts fall into a number of different categories and they are considered in subsequent Parts of this book. Part II consists of stories published by patients of Freud and Jung. That there are very few published accounts by Jung's patients, or by patients of other Jungian analysts, seems to have been largely a consequence of Jung's views about the inviolability of the privacy of the consulting room, even after both participants had died. These two eminent, founding theorists offer contrasting theoretical ideas about analysis and therapy, but their patients' accounts, although respectful, suggest that their therapeutic influences, and sometimes their practices, may not have been concordant with their theories. Both the theories and psychotherapeutic practices of Freud and Jung are strikingly different, and they diverge over the issues of whose ideas are truthful descriptions of the contents of the unconscious, as well as their relative therapeutic effectiveness. It has not been possible to find an objective way of determining these matters. But for the patients of both, evidence of the attempt to establish the patients' agendas over those of their analysts can be demonstrated.

Part III considers stories of analysts and psychotherapists in the process of training, so their stories cannot be so easily dismissed as being by unsophisticated subjects. In view of the fact that all psychoanalysts and psychotherapists under training have to undertake a training analysis with an experienced training psychotherapist or analyst, it is surprising that there are not many more. Most provide a very respectful narrative, and what is not reported by them may be as interesting as what is included. At least one, by Jeffrey Masson (1992), is highly critical. He has been attacked on the grounds that he had not been properly analysed, which seems quite unfair as his analysis must have been validated by both his analyst and the training institute. Both believed that his analysis had been successfully completed. After he had published his account, he withdrew from the profession of psychoanalysis in disgust. It is of particular interest that in several of these accounts from these quite sophisticated individuals, differences between what their analysts were doing and the interests of the analysands are evident, despite there being a significant pedagogical element in all of them.

Evidently, the motives for these various accounts may differ greatly from one patient to another. Some were clearly grateful for a gratifying outcome, and their account was a way of publicly acknowledging their gratitude, as well as offering support, from their own knowledge, of the concepts that underlay the treatment.

The Wolf-Man seems to have been one of these, and adopted the *nom de plume* as part of his identity, having apparently made both narcissistic and economic gains from that identity. However, towards the end of his life he also had some grave criticisms of the process, as well as rejecting some of the important constructions Freud had made in his account of the analysis. Others were more critical, and rejecting of both their therapists and the treatment. In this connection, Masson has already been mentioned, but among others are Sutherland (1987) and Wolpert (1999), who were particularly rejecting of the practice of psychoanalysis and psychotherapy. This collection ends with the accounts of those patients who have been gravely critical of their treatment which, in at least one case, may have been malpractice. Although patients' accounts are rather few in comparison with the multiplicity of those by their therapists, bringing them together in this book may highlight some important issues and provoke some significant questions about psychoanalysis and psychotherapy, even though it cannot be claimed that the stories presented here form a representative sample of all those who have experienced psychotherapy over the past 100 years. If therapists can learn from their patients, the stories written by these patients may provide an important contribution to that process.

PART I
TWO CONTRASTING STORIES

CHAPTER ONE

Prelude

I begin with two very different experiences of therapy and analysis. Both patients were relatively unsophisticated about psychotherapy and psychoanalysis, although Marie Cardinal had attended some academic lectures about psychoanalysis, and had sought her therapist because she was aware of some Freudian concepts. She thought intuitively that analysis might be more helpful to her than other physiological treatments to which she had been subjected. Rosie Alexander tried two other treatments before being referred to her analyst. Her lack of sophistication appears to have been taken advantage of by her first two therapists, and her experience with analysis was no better. So this exploration of patients' accounts can begin with these two stories, unencumbered by much technical knowledge or previous experience of psychotherapy.

Marie Cardinal, who suffered from a chronic psychosomatic symptom that had been exhaustively investigated and treated physiologically without success, had abandoned that treatment and sought psychoanalysis. It had not occurred to her that her chronic symptoms might be psychological in origin until many other medical interventions had failed. To her great surprise, the psychotherapy brought an immediate relief from her physical symptoms, and over a period of seven years with a very unobtrusive analyst she was able to work through the underlying unconscious bases of that symptom. The treatment enabled her to live more happily and productively than ever before, as she was able to acknowledge. Her account, written in the form of a novel, makes a most enthralling story, while remaining true to the experience she describes.

Rosie Alexander's title for her story, *Folie à Deux*, succinctly sums up her experiences over several years with three therapists, one of whom was a psychoanalyst. None of the three was able to help her deal with the intense feelings of love and hate that she felt their respective treatments unleashed in her. She blames them all for their imposition on her of the process that evoked such powerful transferences, so that she felt trapped within them in a way that failed to give her any understanding of, or relief from, what she was suffering. Indeed, the analysis apparently made her distress and anxiety significantly worse. She experienced the therapies as being only immensely painful and damaging to her. Her inability to escape from these feelings appears to have arisen from the work of the therapy having been carried out entirely within the context of the present. Or, to put it another way, the work was done in the "here and now". For the first two therapies, which were not analytical, this was perhaps inescapable. For the final one, conducted by a qualified analyst, the understanding of the transference, in terms of the repetition of the past, might have been thought to be a fundamental aspect of it. Even if the transference had not been interpreted directly in those terms, then it might at least be expected that the analyst would take opportunities to help her explore memories and associations related to her history, as Marie Cardinal's analyst did with her therapist without his interpreting the transference at any point. None of that appears to have occurred in Rosie Alexander's case, even though there were occasions with the analyst when the opportunity arose but was not taken. Her account makes a startling contrast with the work done by Marie Cardinal.

It might be asked, "Why are there such differences in the experiences of these two women in their respective therapies and analyses?" Are they to be found in the differences in the techniques and skills of their various therapists? Spinelli, in his Afterword to *Folie à Deux* (Alexander, 1995, pp. 153–165), indicates that he felt that none of her therapists was sufficiently respectful of their patient, and this lack of respect lay at the heart of their failure. Alternatively, are there significant and important differences between the two patients that might account for the success of one and the failure of the other? Or, more subtly, were there significant differences in the interactions which each of the therapist and patient pairs were able to establish, thus determining the outcome in the same way that such interactions may be seen to determine the outcomes of marital partnerships? For Marie Cardinal, her difficulties with her doctors before she went into analysis arose from their failure to consider more than the physiological symptoms, seeking to apply treatment on those terms which Marie could intuitively understand were inadequate. Although all Rosie's therapies were psychological, none of her therapists was capable of finding a psychological explanation for them, nor a context into which her symptoms could be fitted. Their psychotherapeutic agendas as experienced were irrelevant to her needs, and she was unable to present them in a way to which they could appropriately respond.

CHAPTER TWO

Marie Cardinal

Introduction

Marie Cardinal's account of her therapy with an un-named analyst, whom she called "the little doctor", was written as an autobiographical novel (Cardinal, 1984), with the account of her life told as it had been recounted in the analysis. So her life story is not told consecutively, and recollections of different periods emerged as they became relevant to her current preoccupations in the analysis. As an account of the way free associations may lead to appropriate recall of past events it is completely realistic. This is not to suggest that the emergence of recollections in this way provides evidence for the challenged hypothesis of the "recovered memory syndrome". Many of her memories had clearly not been repressed, but were appropriately remembered, and related to the stage she had reached in her treatment. One very significant memory did seem to have been repressed, and it was produced in response to the therapist's request for her free associations to the word "tube". The recovery of that memory proved to be a turning point in the analysis, and it will be described more fully when the analysis is described.

Marie Cardinal was born in 1929 in a French colonial family in Algeria. At the time of Marie's birth her parents had separated, her mother having discovered that she was pregnant only after she had left her husband. Her father, who suffered from chronic tuberculosis, was despised by her mother and blamed for the death of their first-born daughter, who had died aged eleven months, and for their son's curvature of the spine, resulting from infection by TB. This history was very significant in the development of Marie's psycho-somatic symptom and its resolution in a long analysis. Although subsequently divorced, her parents carried on a very acrimonious relationship centred on the support and care of Marie.

Marie's mother's love was focused on her deceased daughter, and Marie felt that *she* had her mother's love only when she was sick. At other times, her mother's treatment can only be described as sadistic, although it was often ameliorated by the attention of her Spanish nanny. Her mother's resentment of her birth and attempts to abort her were revealed to Marie when she was entering puberty, and those revelations had a determining effect on later symptomatology. In her analysis she wrote that of its immediate effect on her, "There on the street, in a few sentences, she put out my eyes, pierced my eardrums, scalped me, cut off my hands, shattered my kneecaps, tortured my stomach, and mutilated my genitals" (Cardinal, 1984, p. 102).

Happier experiences were with the Arab boys who were the children of the local families working on the farm. With them she developed an envy of their penises, trying to replicate them with paper cones she called spigots, feeling despised as a "squat pisser". This idyllic period was ended in puberty when her mother forbade her to play with boys.

Sometime after the Second World War, Marie and her mother moved to Paris. Marie enrolled in the University, where she studied psychology and some psychoanalysis. She had, therefore, some inkling about what might have been the origins of her first overt anxiety attack, which took the form of panic while listening to a Louis Armstrong concert. She thought she was going to die and felt that neither her mother nor her doctors were taking it seriously as they tried to reassure her. She knew that she had always been very concerned about her inner bodily sensations, and being possessed by something she called "the Thing". She was aware of her parents' sexual difficulties, and how her mother resented her birth. She felt that these may have led to her decision to remain a virgin. She then decided that she would have sex with somebody she did not love. She wrote of her gratitude to the young man who deflowered her, although she did not have an orgasm. However, she did have another anxiety attack, comparing herself to the women who had visited her father.

Over the following years, she felt gnawed at by what she described as "the slow gestation of the madness" (*ibid.*, p. 40). This was despite maintaining an appearance of normality; passing her exams, marrying and having three children. She developed a flow of blood when she was twenty-seven years old, which was treated by a variety of drug and other treatments and hospitalization, against which she eventually revolted, absconding from hospital and seeking psychoanalytic treatment.

The analysis

She had, abruptly and surreptitiously, left the hospital, where she was about to have a radical operation on her uterus, deciding to seek psychoanalysis. She wrote that although she could not remember the physical surroundings of her analyst's house at that time, she did recall her first impressions of him. He was dark-skinned, lightly built, and formal in his appearance. She began by telling him of the illness and her escape from the hospital. She felt afraid, and ashamed of her condition, which she felt separated her from him and others. He asked her to tell him about the treatment she had been receiving, and she described in graphic detail the symptoms of her uncontrollable, bloody flux, the humiliating treatments she had received, and the increasing limitations her condition imposed on her. She felt herself to be mad and sick, and that the mad person seemed to be split off from her self, and that she was inhabited by something she called the "Thing". The analyst listened attentively without any apparent reaction, and asked what she felt apart from her physical malaise. She replied that she was afraid of death, but it was not so much that she was afraid of a particular thing, but that she was full of fear. She went on to think about her past treatments in detail, and she told the analyst of her refusal to take the pills recently prescribed. He approved of her refusal of the drug treatment, and told her that the pills were very harmful. She at once relaxed and felt grateful to him, hoping that he would prove to be somebody she could talk to freely.

He offered to begin psychoanalytic treatment at once, three sessions per week for forty-five minutes each, at a fee of forty francs per session. She was not to take any medication of any kind. He warned her that psychoanalysis might be very disturbing, and would last for at least three years. She should not make any use of what she knew of psychoanalysis. Although she felt reassured by his offer, she was concerned that she could not afford to pay him. He told her that she would have to go to work and earn it, but that he would wait for three to six months while she made the arrangements. She had to realize that payment from her own resources was important. She agreed, and left after she had asked what she should do if she had a haemorrhage. He said that she should do nothing. Before she left she asked what he thought was wrong with her, a query he seemed to dismiss, but replied that she was tired and troubled, but he believed that he could help her (*ibid.*, p. 28).

During the night, after this session, she lay awake, but took no medication to help her sleep as the analyst had instructed. However, "The Thing was rumbling inside me", she wrote (*ibid.*, p. 29). She felt very disturbed, but finally fell asleep, only to awake drenched in her own blood. It had soaked the mattress, and was dripping on the floor. She felt that in bleeding she had surrendered to the blood; she was left exhausted, with her defence against the "Thing" now removed. She went to her session bundled in cotton wool pads. As she entered the consulting room she said, "Doctor, I am bled dry." His reply shocked her. He said, "Those are psychosomatic disorders. That doesn't interest me. Speak about something else." (*ibid.*, p. 30). It felt like a slap in the face; that she had been struck by lightning. Without the blood only the "fear" remained, and she could not talk about it in the session. She spent the rest of the session in tears. Returning home she was astonished to discover that the bleeding had, indeed, stopped. Later, she realized that there was nothing wrong with her physically, and the analyst had somehow caused the bleeding to stop. She understood that the "Thing" was the essential element, and that she had been made to face it (*ibid.*, p. 33). It was only much later that she had been able to tell her husband that the bleeding had stopped. The important thing about these sessions was that the analyst was clear about what he required her to do, establishing firm boundaries, and he was confident in his belief that her problems were psychological.

For the next three months she went to her sessions regularly on Mondays, Wednesdays, and Fridays, fearing that the cessation of the bleeding might only be a reprieve. The weekend breaks were difficult, but the sessions were a source of hope and joy. She could only refer to her fear of the "Thing" as an anxiety, rather than as split-off madness. In the analysis she began to feel able to explore aspects of her life more freely, starting with her first anxiety attack at a Louis Armstrong concert, and the aftermath of her first sexual experience. She told him how she had felt as if she were suffering "the slow gestation of madness", although she had been able to lead an apparently normal life; how she had he passed her exams; had other sexual experiences; taught in lycées; had got married and had three children.

The memories of her life with separated, and then divorced, parents only emerged slowly in the analysis, but related to the issues she was dealing with in it. So memories of her father's illness, death, and funeral came first and accounted for a sense of solitude and an inexplicable void (*ibid*., p. 49). The recollection of his absence opened up a kind of hidden sore and infections, which were the germs of her illness. Other memories of him seemed to rekindle a forgotten love for him. Remembering the analyst's instructions about free association (to say whatever came into her head; not to choose or compose her sentences, every word was important) she began to relish the freedom it gave her, and to realize that it was a weapon against the "Thing". She began to talk about her mother, "never stopping until the end of the analysis" (*ibid*., p. 53). She wrote that the gap between the woman her mother had wanted to be and the person she was had allowed the "Thing" to lodge itself in her. Although, at that point in the analysis, she was not conscious of what her mother had done, she was aware that she had loved her mother to distraction in childhood and adolescence, and then hated her. Finally, she had abandoned her mother just before she died, and her death brought the analysis to an end.

Despite believing that she had loved her mother profoundly in childhood, her memories revealed a rather different story. Her mother was anxious about dirt and being soiled, and this gave rise to bizarre behaviour over toileting when they were travelling. Marie described her mother's appallingly sadistic acts when eating problems arose, and on one occasion when she got into a serious conflict with her elder brother, who had been teasing her unkindly. She wished to give her mother presents but could not afford the priceless things her mother enjoyed. She wrote sadly, "The door to her happiness was, therefore, closed to me since I thought it could only be opened with presents. My love was not, apparently, the right key" (*ibid.*, p. 56). She had to create a sense of her self-esteem alone, and she filled her life with imaginative activities of all kinds. She did not share her mother's religious devotion, and the idea of swallowing the Body of Christ was abhorrent to her. She had anxieties about the inside of her body and what went into it. Her mother had told her that, if she swallowed a cherry stone, a cherry tree would grow inside her. If she thought she had done so, she became frightened that the tree was growing inside her, and had to vomit before she went to sleep. Her mother would then come and comfort her, cleaning her up and holding her in her arms until she fell asleep.

Later, she remembered, in adolescence, walking to church with her mother, and the rituals of Confession and the Mass, and praying for Grace so that she would be loved by her mother. Her mother would, however, find fault with her and her school work, calling her a slattern. However much Marie prayed she could not identify with her mother's Christian virtues, as her mother wished. She split the inner unconformity from the outer conformity, perhaps adding to the split that she had described earlier in the story of her analysis. Happier memories were of being with her mother in the garden, and on their farm during the war years, when they were unable to go to France during the hot summers in Algeria.

Algeria was very important to her. She felt particularly distressed by the revolution against the French occupation, by the torture of Algerian partisans, and the Army's attempt to wipe them out. She wrote,

> It seems to me that the Thing took root in me permanently when I understood that we were to assassinate Algeria. For Algeria was my real mother. I carried her inside me the way a child carries the blood of his parents in his veins. [*Ibid.*, p. 69]

Her happy memories of Algeria and of her Spanish nanny, whose love may have offset the primary indifference of her mother, were recounted in the analysis.

Marie noted how, in the analysis, she would alternate small measures of her anxieties and fears with happier memories. Although she does not say so, the contrast between mother and nanny was repeated in her transference. The unobtrusive, but attentive, doctor was somehow like the nanny, who was there and whose love could be taken for granted. At other times she would feel he was like her mother, and she then felt compelled to be less free with her associations. It was, however, some time before she was able to disclose the full horror of her condition; the hallucination of herself as the corpse (her dead sister) lying between her and her mother, which she feared would result in her being taken back to the hospital. Her analyst's unobtrusiveness was sometimes total, with nothing important to say to her between "Bonjour, Madame" when she arrived and "Au revoir" as she left. Sometimes he would pick a word from the jumble of her monologues, saying "Such and such a word, what does it make you think of?" (*ibid.*, p. 73). Her associations would lead her to new insights, and gave her confidence that he knew his job. At the beginning, she wrote, he never intervened. Sometimes she left feeling very agitated because she had not said all she had to say in the time allotted. He could not be seduced into giving her extra time, leaving her feeling full of murderous rage as the session ended. By the time she got to the end of the cul-de-sac she felt better. She wrote about how she later came to understand the process:

> ... the mind doesn't just present itself at the gate of the unknown. It isn't enough merely to want to penetrate the unconscious so that consciousness can enter. The mind procrastinates. It goes back and forth. It delays. It hesitates. It keeps watch. And when the time has come, it stands motionless in front of the gate like a setter, paralysed. Then the dog's master has to come and flush the game. [*Ibid.*, p. 74]

In a session further on in the analysis she made "an imperceptible but important departure". She remembered that she had observed their chauffeur's son with an erect penis, masturbating. She referred to the penis as a spigot. She at once wished to have one herself, feeling inferior because of "the smooth fruit at the base of my stomach". She described how she made herself a penis with a cone made from stiff paper, with which she was able to piss like a boy. She also called it a spigot, the name she had given to the penises of her boy playmates, who also masturbated publicly. She realized that the fumbling she had to do to fit the cone to her body was the same as that she had later used to check on the flow of blood. She was flooded with urine in the same way that she later was flooded with blood, and the feelings of shame were the same. She promised Jesus that she would never masturbate again, but she had been unable to keep that promise. At that time she had not known that what she was doing was called masturbating, and had never made its connection with the paper spigot when she did learn what masturbation was. She was left with a feeling of deep disgust and, at this stage of the analysis, was unable to understand how she had come to choose being abnormal and ill.

In the following session she spoke about what she called her mother's villainy (*ibid.*, p. 80). She remembered in detail the circumstances on a day in 1943, when she was sitting with her beautiful mother, feeling that she loved her wholeheartedly. It was unusual for them to take tea together, and on this special occasion something about her mother's attitude made her feel that she was to be treated as an equal. Mother referred to their recent visit to the doctor. In the analysis this led to free associations about her liking to behead her dolls, as if in a surgical operation, but realizing that the operation had failed she would feel that she had to kill her children. Parenthetically, there may have been links in these associations with the dead sister, and also with something of which, at that time, she was completely unconscious, i.e., her mother's death wishes for her, about which she had not yet been told. Her mother told her that she was approaching the menarche, and informed her of the biological consequences, and the possibility of pregnancy. Marie wrote that she felt paralysed by the situation and by the revelations being made, although she was aware, through observations in the farmyard, of the facts of pregnancy and birth of animals. She recalled the discussion in detail (*ibid.*, pp. 83–88); there was something about hearing it from her mother that distressed her, and especially her mother's prohibition of any association with boys once her periods had begun. The conversation continued, and

Marie was told the history of her parents' courtship and unhappy marriage.

The account is interspersed with Marie's own recollections of her father, and of her parents' interaction. After the eldest child's death, her mother had a horror of her husband, feeling that he had killed their dead baby: if she had not been away from home with the baby when it died, she told Marie that she would have killed him. That horror intensified after the birth of Marie's brother, whose TB condition had made her mother wish to leave her father, but she seemed unable to do so because of the scandal it would have caused. There was also a problem about the factory on which their income depended, and her mother's dowry was at risk. Four years later she did pluck up courage to leave, not realizing that she was pregnant with Marie until three months later, after she had begun the divorce proceedings.

In Marie's written account it is not clear whether she then told the doctor that what she had just said was not quite true, because the discussion, which she thought had taken place over tea, had actually occurred while walking in the street. She thought that her mother had preferred telling her these things in a place not conse-crated to their life (*ibid.*, p. 99). Her mother had gone on to tell the most devastating part of these confidences when she told Marie the villainous thing that she had wanted to abort her, but could not do so because of the church's prohibition of abortion. Her mother had then told her that she had tried to miscarry, because that would be an accident, not a sin. Marie wrote of her mother's account of her attempts to miscarry:

> I [Marie's mother] went to find my bicycle, which had been rusting away in the shed for I don't know how long, and I pedalled off into the fields, into the land being cultivated everywhere. Nothing. I rode horseback for hours: jumping, trotting. Nothing happened, believe me. Nothing. When I was through with my bicycle or got down off my horse, I went to play tennis in the hottest part of the day. Nothing. I swallowed quinine and aspirin by the bottle. Nothing. [*Ibid.*, p. 102]

She gave up after six months. All this was on the pretext of warning Marie against sexual relationships and unplanned pregnancies.

When Marie was born, her mother felt that the very painful birth process, worse even than the two previous births, was God's punishment for her attempts to miscarry or abort. She remembered how pretty Marie had been at birth, and that recollection impelled her to laugh and lean forward to kiss her. Marie, who had been devastated, recoiled, feeling that she had fallen into an earth fissure. The hatred for her mother did not bloom immediately, but she felt estranged from her, as if in an emotional desert, throughout her adolescence. When she herself became pregnant in her twenties, having her own baby in her womb made her mother revolting to her. The signs of life inside her, as the baby quickened, brought the realization that her mother, experiencing the same signs, understood them as meaning that she had failed to kill Marie. She had a series of associations to her mother's murderousness towards her, and to her eventual birth. She did not blame her mother for wanting an abortion, but for not carrying it through. She felt that her mother continued to hate her in the womb, and then expressed it now in telling her of the attempts to murder her.

> And yet [she wrote], it was thanks to her beastliness that, on the couch in the little cul-de-sac, I was more easily able to analyse the malaise of my entire former life, the constant anxiety, the perpetual fear, the self-disgust, which finally blossomed into madness. Without my mother's acknowledgment I might never have succeeded in going back to the womb, returning to that hated and pursued foetus, which, without knowing it, I had found when I curled between the bidet and the tub in the obscurity of the bathroom. [*Ibid.*, p. 106]

She felt that this discovery in analysis had been a turning point in her life.

In general, she wondered how her analyst remembered what she had told him. Did he have a recording machine, or keep handwritten notes as she talked to him? He just listened, and she felt able to tell him the truth, even after she may have dissembled, to avoid the pain of remembering her feeling of failure and guilt for not being able to gain her mother's love. This had been the generator of the "Thing" that had pursued her.

One day she plucked up the courage to tell him of her hallucination of an eye looking at her. The analyst had asked her what the word "tube" meant to her, and she remembered her father's eyes. Further associations led to a memory of an eye looking at her through a tube, and the anxiety and fear that it generated, more shameful than from all the rest of her illness. She felt that she had come to an important moment in her analysis, and had to find an explanation for the hallucination. But when the analyst asked her to associate to the word "tube" she became angry, calling him many derogatory names. He simply repeated his request for associations. She related her associations, which were about holidays and travelling, with her mother's anxiety about cleanliness and the toilets on the train so that she always carried a pharmacy bag containing materials to cleanse the toilets before Marie could use them. Germs had to be got rid of; Marie associated to the germs, which she believed were eating away in her father's lungs. The preparations for Marie to use the toilet in the train were so elaborate that she ended up with her nanny holding her pants up so that she wouldn't wet herself, and at the same time supporting her back. She recalled looking between her legs and seeing a large round pipe and its contents. Below it the ground sped by; she felt afraid of being sucked into the hole and falling through the tube on to the track.

While telling this incident, occurring, she thought, when she was four years old, she began to hear an incessant tapping sound in the present that was giving her a physical pain, like a headache. This grew worse until she felt at she was going crazy, and cried out to the analyst for help, but the noise continued, and she had to find its source. Further associations and memories led her to a scene in the woods with her nanny when she needed to go "peepee" behind a bush. The tapping continued, and she turned to see her father with a film camera, looking at her through what she thought was a tube in front of one of his eyes. He mustn't see her bare bottom. She got up, went towards him, starting to kick and scratch him, feeling a terrible rage about his eye in the tube. The nanny and her father tried to pacify her, and when she calmed down she felt naughty, ashamed, wicked, and crazy. As she recalled this scene she suddenly felt at peace, and realized that now she had understood the hallucination it would never return. She said this to the analyst, who replied, "Of course. The session is over now."

With great relief, she felt that somehow she had been made perfect, and reborn. She nevertheless needed to ask her mother if she remembered the incident. Although her mother had not been there, she did remember and had seen the film. In response to a question, her mother told Marie that she had been between fifteen and eighteen months old when it had occurred. Her father had just left the sanatorium, where he had been treated for his TB, and, wishing to get to know her, was making a movie with a film camera.

This recollection, which had been completely repressed and recovered in the analysis, made Marie feel euphoric. "The dead end", she wrote, "had become the road to paradise . . ." (*ibid.*, p. 115). The reference to the dead end perhaps referred both to the cul-de-sac and to the breaking of the barrier to the repressed memory. The euphoria was acted out by her becoming promiscuous, and voracious in a number of ways. However, it was short-lived.

She began to feel guilty and regressed, experiencing the return of the "Thing". She became deeply anxious and depressed, wishing to die, to become nothing. She became angry with the analyst, accusing him of making her worse, of brainwashing her to make her more mentally ill than she had been when she began analysis: a negative transference in spades. Leaving the sessions she went drinking, getting dead drunk as if to destroy herself. She wrote,

> In deciphering the hallucination I had believed that I was putting myself in the world, I had really believed I was being born. Now it seemed to me that by putting out the eye at the end of the tube I had aborted myself. That eye was not only my mother's eye, and the eye of God, and of society, it was my own eye as well. Everything I was, was destroyed, and in its place was zero, this beginning and end, this point from which everything vacillates between the more or the less, the zone of living death and of dead life. Could one be zero and thirty-four years old at the same time? I was a genuine monster. [*Ibid.*, p. 121]

Although she continued to go to her sessions three times a week, she had nothing to say. She was mostly silent and sometimes slept on the couch. She experienced herself as empty, impoverished, and in danger of dying. Sometimes she missed sessions, and on other occasions went at the wrong time, either too early or too late. She often felt confused, angry, and in considerable distress. The analyst remained imperturbable throughout, from time to time making brief remarks that Marie felt might be germinating within her, although she stayed powerfully resistant. This was, indeed, the dark night of the soul.

Relief came imperceptibly, beginning with a dream that she had dreamt almost every night as a child, but not for a long time until now. She was in a pleasant place on soft, sandy ground. A horseman arrived who harmonized with the scene, and could have been either a medieval knight in full armour, or a modern day horseman in tweeds. She felt he was very seductive as he cantered around, like a dressage rider, in ever decreasing circles, until he was turning on the spot. She wanted to jump up behind him, but could not do so as the ground had become soft and she sank into it. Before the analysis she could understand nothing about this dream, and had woken in terror wishing to repress its memory. On the couch she realized it represented two worlds; the world of her mother from which she wished to escape, and the adventurous world of men and sex that she could not reach. She also realized she did not like to be watched while making love; and, as she became more ill, she fantasized that she was making love with a dog. As she spoke of that fantasy she appreciated that it was because the dog could not judge, hurt, or humiliate her. She learned, in the analysis, and through her associations to the dream, that what was unconsciously terrifying her were infantile fears of a big cockroach; of her disturbance at being filmed by a gentleman "while she was doing peepee"; of being paralysed by the horseman's visits; or being frightened by a paper spigot. These were childish fears, she thought, and not appropriate for an adult woman. The dream and its interpretation seemed to mark a turning point in the analysis, and she wrote that the first part of the analysis had helped her to win health and bodily freedom. Now she was slowly beginning to discover her self (*ibid.*, p. 129). It took another four years to complete the process.

She wrote of the way her confidence in the analysis had grown, slowly but surely. At first, she was not convinced that mere words would drive away her illness, expecting all the time that the physical manifestations of the flow of blood would return. However, she felt that the analyst, and the analysis, were safety nets. She had regressed to childhood memories, hoping to find a healthy embryo that would be the basis of her recovery. She found instead her mother's dangerous personality. She then recounted a horrific scene at the dinner table when she had refused to eat and was forced by her mother to do so in a most sadistic way so that she regurgitated it, and then was compelled to eat it. She then felt ill and her mother relented. She could appeal to her mother only through sickness. As soon as she was well her mother would leave her, to attend to the sick and poor in the community.

Soon after this memory, Marie seems to have recalled in the analysis the visits to the cemetery to attend to the grave of her dead sister. She was evidently ambivalent about these annual visits on All Saints Day (*ibid.*, p. 142), but they left her with the feeling that the dead were always the object of her mother's affection and interest. She knew that her mother, even sixteen or seventeen years later, continued to talk to the dead child, and to weep at night. She thought that her mother had again begun to grow the dead child within her, and that it would live there forever. At the cemetery her mother would embrace the tombstone tenderly, and Marie wished that she could be that stone, to be dead, so that she could be loved as much as her dead sister.

As these memories arose in the analysis, helping her to realize that although, on the surface, she had tried to be obedient to her mother's wishes and to gain her love, she also knew of the hatred her mother had for her, and her awareness of the "Thing" inside her mother which had also invaded her. Marie was both the dutiful daughter and the rebel, from birth. She felt that there had been a struggle between her mother's wish to love Marie in her way, and Marie's wish to be loved by her mother in *her own* way. There had been moments of harmony (*ibid.*, pp. 148–149). When her mother was pointing out to her the grandeur of the stars and the cosmos they had got on well; why had she forgotten them? Had her recollection of those moments of accord brought the realization that she felt happy only when participating in a greater whole?

In the following phase of the analysis she became less resistant, and seemed freed from her negative transference. Her anxiety attacks had disappeared, and she was able to work productively with her analyst on her difficulties, shortcomings, and symptoms. She became both actress and spectator in the analysis, while the analyst was spectator and director. She discovered an important reason why she would cry so easily. Sometimes she cried if the telephone rang during her sessions, or when she felt the end of the session had come before she had completed what she wanted to say. Apart from enjoying the feel of her deprived tears, she realized that they were often inappropriate, but also expressive of what she described as her greatest shortcoming.

The understanding of her greatest shortcoming arrived by way of an incident after she had bought herself an old car; the first she had ever owned. She had parked, briefly, illegally and returned to find a policeman issuing her with a ticket. She pleaded tearfully with him, but he was unmoved. She had been on the way to her analysis, and began by telling the analyst the story of her distress, and her feelings of violent rage with the policeman. It seemed to go to the heart of her sense of always being scapegoated, of being denigrated by her mother about her appearance and her personality. She remembered a scene when she was two or three years old, and the recollection caused her to choke and to have difficulty in breathing. She was in their playroom with her brother, who often tormented her. She would retaliate if she could. She had many dolls, which she hated and never played with, but on this occasion had given him one of them, a boy doll called Phillip, to ingratiate herself both with him and her mother. She did have a favourite toy, a monkey on roller skates, which would move when she pulled a loop at its back. She and her brother got into a fight, and he threw her monkey into the fire. She flew into a murderous rage, which she displaced on to the doll, Phillip, that she had just given her brother, dragging it from its cradle and stamping on its face. Her mother came in and slapped her, which had the effect of making Marie even more enraged. Mother told Nanny to put her under the shower to calm her down. At that she became even angrier, jumping up and down and shouting. Mother and Nanny held her down in the bath under a cold shower, with her brother looking on. She felt overpowered by all three of them, and had to summon up an enormous power to overcome her violence and rage. She was left breathless and tearful. In the session recalling this scene, she rediscovered the repressed violence that had begun to be evoked by the exchange with the policeman. This sudden revelation she thought was the most important single moment in her analysis (*ibid.*, p. 155). Its repression, she felt, had been the greatest source of nourishment of the "Thing", and her memory of this scene had come at the right moment. She could not have tolerated it before, and it was counter to the non-violent person she had consciously believed herself to be. She could see the way in which the analysis had enabled her to make this discovery gradually, between the unravelling of the hallucination and the recollection of the scene in the shower. She felt that she could now make use of her newly discovered violence to create rather than destroy, and that it accompanied the recovery of her vitality, gaiety, and generosity.

These developments were followed by others in her daily life with her children and her husband. The illness had caused a rift between her husband and herself, and, although they had not formally separated, he had spent much of the time abroad with his job and was home for only short periods. Divorce had been men-tioned once, when he had been unable to cope with the manifesta-tions of her illness any longer. He had found another woman, accepted a post abroad; but they did not divorce. As the analysis progressed her husband saw that she was getting better, and spent more time at home. She had begun to write, and eventually she showed her husband what she had been writing. To her surprise her work moved him to tears, which at first she misunderstood, until he told her how good he thought her book was. It had the effect of rekindling their love: they began to form a unit again. Both were able to change, and she attributed their new life to the discov-eries she had been able to make in her analysis.

Although there had been such a transformation for her, she and the analyst both knew that their work together was not complete. She had, however, been able to reduce her sessions to twice per week, and had begun to dream more after the dream of the horse-man. Often, she was able to interpret them for herself, bringing her interpretations to the analysis. They had worked out together a kind of vocabulary in which certain words would contain a wealth of meaning that they both understood. There was one dream she had been unable to understand, but realized that its meaning would hasten the progress of the analysis. The dream replicated a visit she had made in Provence to some artistic friends. One of them, André, collected discarded fragments of all sorts and incorporated them into paintings. With him she had visited a dovecote, in the form of a tower, at the top of a barren hill. Inside lush, colourful vegetation was growing, fertilized by birds nesting in blue and yellow rows of niches. The tower was open at the top. The beauty and peace of the whole scene evoked a feeling of being part of a "Whole" (*ibid.*, p. 172). In the dream she was alone in the tower when suddenly clear, bright, and beautiful water sprang out from the walls, isolating her in the vortex of a whirlpool. She was neither soaked nor dirtied by the water; she felt that her distress had vanished. Then she noticed that the water was carrying along some silver objects, each one more beautiful than the last. They proved to be silver boxes containing excrement. Without shock or distress she realized that, in the dream, she was in the middle of a lavatory bowl. She woke full of joy and satisfaction.

Telling the dream on the couch, she found it impossible to utter the word "turd". She asked herself why this word was so unacceptable, and understood that when she was able to pronounce a word it led her to a domain that was acceptable to her. A word she was unable to say concealed a domain she was unwilling to enter. So, she had found harmony acceptable and excrement rejectable. How was it that, in the dream, harmony and excrement went so well together? The answer came when she discovered that for the whole of her life she had never accepted her anality. Her acceptance was accomplished through remembering a visit to the circus, where the clowns' rear ends were lit up by a little red bulb. With this memory she also rediscovered laughter, with its healing qualities. She had lived in the world of bourgeois values where those things whose proper names were unmentionable did not exist, except as objects of laughter. These things included incidents and memories from the past:

> ... worn out lungs of the glass blower, the great-aunt's swollen feet, the seamstresses eyes which were destroyed, the lacerated wombs of women and my asshole, such things were in the lowest ranks along with other objects of pity, commiseration, or charity, about whom one made amusing remarks or vulgar, derisive comments, because they signified the minimal, the negligible, the poor, the small, the wretched, the ridiculous, the empty, dirty, or meaningless. [*Ibid.*, p. 176]

So, with that lovely dream, she understood that everything was important, even excrement. That realization helped Marie to understand that her mother had been just as distressed as she had been herself, but that there was nothing Marie could do about it. Her distaste for her mother's ageing body remained.

Now that she was going to her analysis only once weekly, Marie was beginning to feel that she had to terminate it. Her life was proceeding happily and actively. Two nightmares heralded the ending of analysis. The first involved the recall of a childhood home in Algeria. As she arrived her mother came out into the hall and told her that three partisans had come into the apartment. Marie was unafraid because she supported their cause, so she went into the room where they were, but was unable to make contact with them. Her mother and other women dragged her back, and she found herself sharing the fear of the women. Marie then decided to get away to warn neighbours on the floor below, who had a telephone. One of the partisans discovered her escape, chased and caught her. She struggled, dragging him towards the neighbour's door, trying, but failing, to kick it. She felt the breath of the partisan on her neck, and felt paralysed by his grip. He took out a knife, a penknife, and she thought he was going to cut her throat, but felt, at the same time, that it was too small for that purpose. She woke with a start, sweating and feeling completely destroyed (*ibid.*, p. 182).

She then recalled an occasion, aged ten, when she had been the subject of an attempted sexual attack from a man who had followed her home from school. She remembered the man and his approach to her in detail, and the way he had grabbed her, as the partisan did in the dream. While he was fumbling with his flies she managed to escape, and ran up the stairs. He followed her, shouting abuse at her, and caught her at the door of their apartment, trying to pull her clothes down while she banged at the door. He succeeded in getting his finger into her anus, to her absolute terror, and she feared that he would kill her. As they heard footsteps approaching from the inside he let go of her, and ran away down the stairs shouting obscenities at her. She fell into her nanny's arms in terror. On the couch she realized that the man, and the partisan, could not have killed her; and questioned this fear of death that was not merely physical. The relationship of the nightmare to the memory of the attempted sexual assault emerged on the couch.

She apprehended that her mother had been afraid, like the fear in Marie's nightmare; but of what? She and her mother were both women, with feminine genitals, vulnerable, as all women were, to masculine sexual aggression. "What woman", she wrote, "can oppose a man, who really wants to, from penetrating her and depositing in her his alien seed?" (*ibid.*, p. 188). In her associations she wondered why she had selected some things rather than others, and she realized that it was because she was now making those associations that would lead to the unconscious. The motif of the dream appeared to be the "vision of a woman having an opening, a way in". She had discovered the repression of her knowledge of the existence of the vagina, and with it had come the awareness that to use this knowledge she needed to terminate her analysis. She could now live with the totality of her physical and psychological self. She wrote,

> Now I had discovered my vagina, and I knew henceforth, as with my anus, we were going to live together, in the same way as I lived with the hair on my head, the toes on my feet, the skin on my back and all the parts of my body. I lived with my own violence, deceit, sensuality, authority, capriciousness, courage, and high spirits. Harmoniously, without shame, distaste and discrimination. [*Ibid.*, p. 189]

With that sense of wholeness, and complete acceptance of her femininity, she began to end the analysis after seven years.

Interestingly, at this point, she recorded a flash of anger with her analyst for having enabled her to escape from bourgeois thinking and conformity, only to submit her to another: that of psychoanalysis. At least she was aware of it, he had said, and she realized that was true; she was free to leave the analysis if she wished. But how could she be sure that she had overcome the fear of the "Thing"? A nightmare of being terrified of snakes, and of being able to get her husband, in the nightmare, to destroy the snake she felt threatened by, helped her to deal with her residual fear, not of the penis, but of male power. With that she became able to enjoy her life with her husband and children, with her work as a writer, and her life in the community and her wider family.

She had been unable to forgive her mother, who was by this time dying and losing control of her bodily functions. Marie was quite unable to deal with that, and made her brother care for their mother in her final days. She refused to attend her mother's funeral. After her mother's death she felt compelled to visit the grave of her grandmother, whom she had loved, and at the graveside she recovered some happy memories of her mother, and her love for her as an infant. Finally, the analysis could end. She announced her departure, thanking her analyst, telling him that her mother had given her the "Thing", and that his gift of the analysis was in balance with it. He replied that she need not thank him, that he could not have done anything without her, that he would be there if she needed him again, and that he would be happy to hear about her if she felt it necessary to tell him. She thought he had maintained his role to the end.

This is a story of a highly successful treatment, conducted in a classical style, with the analyst maintaining a firm but containing boundary. It is noteworthy for the very unobtrusive stance of the analyst, who was highly effective in his interaction with Marie despite, as far as can be told from this narrative, having made no transference interpretations. She did not report any of his interpretations, and he apparently eschewed interpretations of the classical Freudian kind, yet allowing Marie to explore for herself their relevance to her sexual development. The significance of the central trauma of her mother's murderous wishes towards her might never have emerged so powerfully had he not refrained from imposing on her the classical formulations. Whether he was aware of the significance of both the timing of her traumatic symptom and its meaning, discussed by Bettelheim in his Afterword, was never made clear (*ibid.*, pp. 216–219).[1] He had told her, in the final session, he believed that her contribution to the success of the analysis was as much due to her as to his own psychoanalytical skill. The statement "I could not have done anything without you" (*ibid.*, p. 212) was both a truism and a tribute to the important contribution that any patient makes to the success of his or her treatment.

Note

1. Bettelheim draws attention to the emergence of the symptom of continuous bleeding when Marie was twenty-eight, the same age as her mother when she was pregnant with Marie. The identification with her mother was also indicated by other matters, such as that they both had given birth to three children. The identification was also

with her mother's death wishes towards her, but also to her mother's wish not to have been pregnant at all. The continuous bleeding was an expression of her identification with this wish, i.e., her mother, with whom she had identified, was not pregnant with her.

CHAPTER THREE

Rosie Alexander

R osie Alexander wrote her account of her three therapies in her book published in 1995 (Alexander, 1995). While it contains full descriptions of them, it includes almost nothing about her history, making it very difficult to understand the material in the therapies. None of her therapists, including her analyst, who was the third and final one, seems to have made any attempt to help her recover her early memories, which might have assisted in understanding the traumas she experienced with all of them. So her life before, and up to, the beginning of her first therapy remains a mystery. All that she discloses about her past is that she sought treatment in her mid-forties when she was living in France; that she had lost her job as a translator and technical writer for a journal; that she had a older brother. She tells nothing of her life in London before she went to France, or of her life in France before seeking therapy. We learn nothing of her parents, or of the history of her relationship with them in childhood. A note on the back cover of her book simply adds that she now lives in London. Her stories about the first therapy and the analysis are told under the forenames of the first therapist, and of her analyst. The story of her work with the second therapist, a psychiatrist, is given under his surname and medical title. She prefaces them all with a complaint that they all addicted her to what she describes as a non-chemical counterpart to a drug, administered by "a process known as transference". In addition to its addictive qualities it was intoxicating, hallucinogenic, and destructive (*ibid.*, p. 1).

Marion

Rosie first sought treatment when the company she was working with went out of business. She had no job, had recently given up smoking, and these factors, together with the loss of income, triggered a mid-life crisis. She went to a Neuro-Linguistic Programme workshop that was conducted by Marion. While she found the group and Marion's technique helpful, Rosie felt that she needed more individual treatment to help her with her feelings of low esteem, and her emotional oscillations between over-aggressiveness and timidity. She arranged for individual sessions at Marion's home despite Marion's rather dowdy, middle class, middle-aged appearance. A highly charged relationship quickly developed (*ibid.*, p. 2), and Rosie felt she had been sucked into an emotional whirlpool. Marion's somewhat disparaged image seems to have been transformed in Rosie's mind after she began her individual treatment. Marion began to use other methods with which she was familiar. As a result Rosie found herself in a visceral bond, so that Marion had become the centre of her life. It was infatuation without sexual desire, although Rosie wondered if she might have had some remnants of homosexuality. However, she felt that she could not do anything to please Marion, resulting in a tussle in the relationship. Despite that she found herself in what she describes as "a state of rhapsodic communion with Marion" (*ibid.*, p. 6). She regressed to feeling like a very young child, felt jealous of the other patients (something which was to become a feature of her subsequent treatments with other therapists), and acted this out in the sessions, wishing to fling herself on the floor and scream. Curiously, this jealousy did not extend to Marion's twelve-year-old son. She wrote, "I could burn inside with rage thinking about her relationship with other clients, but the fact that this child was bound to her in the most intimate relationship of all didn't touch me" (*ibid.*, p. 7).

Marion was not experienced in dealing with transference, and could not manage this intensity of interaction. After more than 166 hours (one and a half hours once weekly) Marion decided to refer Rosie to another therapist, a psychiatrist, Dr Weissmann. Marion suggested that Rosie could continue to see her at the same time as working with Dr Weissmann, if she wished. Rosie was reluctant to be referred but one day, as she contemplated the possibility of seeing this unknown psychiatrist, she felt such an upsurge of hate for him that it gave her a sense of relief. She phoned him at once (*ibid.*, p. 8).

Dr Weissmann

Dr Weissmann was the very antithesis of Marion. Although he, too, was middle-aged, in contrast with Marion he was handsome and elegant in appearance and dress. Rosie never felt comfortable in his consulting room. He began the consultation by saying that he was listening, so she told him of her problems in life and her obsessional feelings about Marion. He stopped the session after twenty-five minutes because he had a train to catch, and arranged to see her again before deciding whether to begin treatment. This surprised her, but she had no other feelings at that stage. At the end of the second session he arranged to see her once weekly for thirty minutes, and she was already beginning to feel attracted to him.

Soon after the treatment began she suffered what she describes as a personal catastrophe. A minor operation on her nose was bungled; she was left with what she felt was a serious disfigurement (*ibid.*, p. 10). She could not look at herself in a mirror; she raged against the surgeon, fantasizing about throwing acid in his face to blind him. These feelings preoccupied her for many sessions, turning them into a stagnant pool of negative feeling, into which the psychiatrist occasionally dropped a lazily ironic comment. She found herself becoming increasingly attracted to him without desiring a physical relationship with him, believing that her disfigurement would make her unattractive to him. She noted that most of his patients were women, forming a harem in which she was the most insignificant member. She enviously thought that they were talking endlessly about their exciting sexual experiences and wishes with him. He claimed to have a special rapport with women, but she felt excluded from it, feeling sexless, unseductive, and unerotic (*ibid.*, p. 11). This was accompanied by the ending of her relationship with a lover with whom sex had not been a problem.

In the therapy she felt compelled to discuss with Dr Weissmann her relationship to him. She had asked him if he liked her, but he did not respond until the next session when he admitted that he was finding her likeable because she was intelligent, and a rum character. Later, he interpreted that she must have been an impudent and tiresome child, which she thought referred more to the present rather than the past. Neither of them took up this opportunity to explore how her history might have been relevant to the present.

She was evidently becoming bored by the therapy, which had been conducted alongside some occasional meetings with Marion, for whom her previous intense feelings had subsided. So she decided to terminate her work with Dr Weissmann and left. Five days later she was overwhelmed with her wish to return to therapy. When she met him again she attacked him for his claimed understanding of women; she thought he was an arsehole but was addicted to him (*ibid.*, p. 12). He responded by saying that things were becoming interesting. This pattern of relating continued for the rest of the therapy with Rosie becoming increasingly angry and aggressive. She chided him about his relations with his other women patients, of whom she was intensely jealous. She was especially angry about his habit of taking phone calls in the session. When, after she had protested, he did it again, she became so furious that she threw her shoe at him while he was talking on the phone. The shoe missed him and hit a valuable porcelain lamp, which, he angrily claimed, was the most precious object in the room. That behaviour was unacceptable, and she would have to see somebody else. She whimpered that she needed him, and he relented enough to say that she could come again the following week.

The relationship continued in what she called this sadomasochistic way that she did not feel was helpful. She did not know how it could change; how could she have other thoughts and feelings when she was with him? Her solution was to get very drunk at a pre-Christmas lunch when she was to see him in the evening.

Unsurprisingly, that session was a disaster and, after some drunken burbling, he terminated it prematurely, saying that he had had enough. At the next session he told her that drunkenness made sessions impossible. She accepted this, but wondered why he had not enquired why she had found it necessary to come to the session drunk. Similarly, although the therapy continued for several more months, during which her mother died, he did not enquire why she did not discuss the loss of her mother with him. She did try to discuss with him why the therapy was so unsatisfactory. He told her it was because she did not tell him her fantasies. She replied that she had none. After this the sessions petered out because she knew that she was to be sent abroad for twelve months in her job, and he took a month's holiday before she went.

While he was away she wrote to him expressing her concerns about the therapy, and her rage that she had been deprived of treatment that might have been helpful and cathartic if he had been more available to her She wrote that her unexplored rage would stay with her like an emotional cancer until it destroyed her. At the same time she realized that she had been increasingly in a state of sexual arousal about him. She ended,

> ... I'm in a dreadful mess, as if you'd picked me up and smashed me on the floor and hadn't bothered to put me together again. It makes me wonder if you can have any conception of the emotional maelstrom stirred up by "therapy". But this is an otiose question: of course you do. [*Ibid.*, p. 17]

She wanted him to explain, and in the final session he told her that he had kept things superficial because she thought that she was too fragile. While that judgement may have been correct, it seems unlikely that Dr Weissmann understood anything about her condition and that he was really preoccupied with himself and his image.

Although Marion had given up the neuro-linguistic programming it is not clear what the nature of the therapy she practised individually was, but it may be guessed, since she did not understand about transference, that it was concerned with current issues. While Marion recognized the inadequacy of her approach in choosing Dr Weissmann for Rosie as an alternative to herself, she found someone whose practice did not include a fundamental element of psychoanalysis: making links between the present and the past. So, Marion's and Dr Weissmann's work with Rosie was stuck in such a way that progress could not be made, despite the evocation of such powerful transferences crying out for understanding in terms of her early history. Rosie was aware that these therapies had left her in a very vulnerable state, so almost immediately after her final session with Dr Weissmann she found another psychiatric service in the phone book, which contained a psychoanalyst who responded to her call and was able to see her half an hour later.

Luc

Luc was at the beginning his professional practice, but she felt quite secure with him from the beginning, despite his youth and inexperience. She learned that he was both a medical doctor and a classical Freudian psychoanalyst, and although she had doubts about his Freudian allegiance she decided to ignore them. He quickly interpreted her need to have someone to look after her. Although she was very shortly going to Africa because of her job, by the second week she was besotted, and wanted to stay and have all of him. She thought that she would be able to return to him when she came back from Africa, and felt that their last session was like two lovers agreeing heroically to part because of some *force majeure*. He agreed that he could see her again when she returned, responding to her concern by saying that he would not abandon her, and that she could write to him. It felt like a lifeline, she wrote. He had, however, failed to tell her that he would not feel obliged to reply to her letters, as Spinelli points out in his Afterword. As with her other therapists, Rosie seems to have developed very powerful loving feelings about Luc almost immediately. That they were so quickly and so strongly evoked appears to have been independent of the technique that Luc was using. This was similar to her response to her two other therapists. Rosie's repetitious reactions to her different therapists were perhaps a way of communicating to them what her psychological problem was about. None was able to decipher the code.

Luc, however, also proved to be a disappointment quite quickly. It seems to have been characteristic of her that she could experience feelings of disappointment and fury simultaneously with desperate feelings of dependency and love. In Africa, she realized that wherever she was she always felt alienated. The sense of alienation she then experienced may have determined her need for such an intense loving experience as that which she expressed so powerfully and early in her treatments. As this sense intensified, she felt the need to write to Luc, although she did not know what to say. She eventually wrote quite briefly saying that she needed him. There had been no reply after a long wait, so she wrote to him again, telling him she was coming to Paris soon, and asking if he would he be able to see her again, and why he had not replied to her earlier letter. There was still no response for two months, so she wrote again telling him how needy she was and she would be in Paris two weeks later. She felt that she "was coming back to Luc, to throw myself in the arms of my father/lover, to retie the umbilical cord with my mother" (*ibid.*, p. 27). (A significant insight which never surfaced in the subsequent analysis.) These hopes were disappointed when she phoned Luc shortly after arriving in Paris; he thought another patient, Karen, was calling him.

She began therapy again, but could not forgive him for his failure to reply to her letters, or for mistaking her for another patient. She wrote that for a month they fought like stags, and characteristically, she felt the incompatibility between her desire and her rage. She was to return to Africa for three months and it was agreed that she should continue her therapy when she was back in Paris again. She remarked that neither the nature of the therapy, nor the reasons for it were ever defined. She wrote,

> But it was a relationship riddled with cancer. I knew that he'd behaved badly over the letters. He'd done wrong—both professionally and at a personal level. In a way it was understandable, the kind of thing that happens all the time in non-therapy situations . . . Only this wasn't a non-therapy situation. [*Ibid.*, p. 30]

At this point, given this degree of understanding, it may be permissible to wonder why Rosie did not terminate the therapy, and seek another analyst when she eventually returned from Africa. It may be that this insight was *post hoc* when she came to write the book, but, answering her own question about how she could trust someone who had exposed her to such vulnerability, she wrote that she felt that she had no choice; she only wanted him.

Three months later she returned from Africa, arranged an appointment, and went to it filled with sexual desire and excitement. The session was a disappointment; nothing happened. Her lover had proved to be impotent, she wrote. The following sessions were concerned with his abandonment by not replying to her letters while she was in Africa and her increasingly obsessive desire for him. As the sessions progressed the floodgates of her rage opened and she attacked him verbally on personal and professional grounds. She arrived at his flat in a state of depression. Her account went as follows:

R. . . . I turned the chair so I was facing the wall and began silently to cry.

L. Are you sulking? he asked.

R. No, I sobbed.

L. Are you crying?

R. Yes.

L. Why?

R. Because you abandoned me.

L. And what does that remind you of.

R. Nothing.

L. What do you feel, then.

(Silence for a while.)

R. I feel completely crushed, I admitted finally, in a snivelling heap. [*Ibid.*, p. 33]

It might have been possible for Luc to have made his penultimate comment differently if he was trying to evoke some memories, or unconscious phantasies, about the past. But Rosie did not take the opportunity to respond to it, beyond commenting, post-session, that she felt that their relationship had been spiritually consummated. How it had been was not clear.

She began to feel jealous of others, and the thought that there might be a woman in his life was intolerable. The furnishings and decoration of his flat that she was able to see while waiting to go into his consulting room made her feel that he might be a playboy, and that his sex life would consist of many brief affairs. On one occasion while she was waiting she was startled to hear the front door open. When an old woman, evidently the cleaning lady, came in she felt relieved. But she continued to obsess about whether he was married or had a woman living with him, and felt she would rip him to shreds if she learned that he was not a virgin. She must not allow herself to discover any trace of his sexual activities. These concerns were accompanied by an increasing preoccupation with sexual thoughts, even sexual hallucinations, about him. "His presence in my head", she wrote, "was so powerful that he was also there in my bed and in my body" (*ibid.*, p. 37).

These feelings were intensified when, on one occasion while she was waiting, she saw that his bedroom door was open and she could see his bed, and felt that she had seen him naked in bed, with his genitals exposed. She was unable to tell him about these continuous fantasies, although she was able to talk abut her wish to have sex with him. She told him that the "reality" of the feeling of her sexual experiences about him were like those she had known with LSD. Although she sat in a chair for her sessions, she found that the couch in his consulting room was an object of sexual stimulation and fantasy about him, as well as of her jealousy of his other women patients who did lie on it. If she heard one of his women patients in his waiting room while she was with him she would fall silent and, later, leave the session without another word.

Her sessions continued in much the same vein, with her feeling great distress because of her jealousy of the woman he lived with, as well as of his patients, and rage about his lack of responsiveness to her sexual wishes. She made obsessive attempts to find out about the woman he lived with, on one occasion passing her as she came, and on another watching the flat to see if she was there overnight. She wrote of physical fighting and contact between herself and Luc, often with an erotic aspect over which he appears to have had no control, even if there is no evidence, at first, of his initiating or encouraging it. Later, as the intensity of their physical interaction increased, Luc did initiate some physical contact by stroking her hands or her hair, and by allowing her to lie on the couch in such a way that she could, and did, touch him. She felt torn between her intense wishes for him, which she felt were driving her mad, and her wish to escape from him, which she was unable to put into effect. She wrote, "I realised that if I wasn't going to end up in an asylum or a coffin, I was going to have to look elsewhere" (*ibid.*, p. 71).

She even went as far as to advertise in a national newspaper for former patients of other analysts who may have had better experiences than her, but was unsuccessful in finding any. She pursued other professional avenues, including consulting the Institute of Psychoanalysis, but these, too, were ineffective in enabling her to get free of the obsessional and destructive relationship with Luc. The professionals all advised her that she should work out this problem with Luc, and none was willing to take her on in his place. She was unable to do this because the intensity of her feelings invaded her whole life, and in every session she felt smashed to pieces. She felt that all she could do would be to commit suicide on his doorstep. Although her interview at the Institute of Psychoanalysis had not helped her to escape from Luc, she believed that it had helped her to give up the idea of dying. In a sense it had made it even more difficult to leave him, despite her complete despair combined with a feeling of impotence and fear that she might fragment under the intensity of her powerfully ambivalent attachment to him. Worse still, as time passed without the possibility of terminating her therapy or of resolving the impasse within it, she again began to wish to escape from the intolerable turmoil in her life, and from the analysis, by dying. Getting through each day without killing herself seemed like a miracle. One of the other medical therapists she consulted suggested that she might go into a clinic, but then was unable to find one suited to her needs.

Without hope, she continued meeting Luc. Feeling deeply disturbed, she phoned his flat to talk to him about her psychotic state, knowing that he would not be there as it was the day he worked at a hospital. His girl friend answered and she was shattered emotionally, and put the phone down without speaking. She felt demented with grief as she went to her session the next day. She sat on his knee, put her arms round him, and whispered "*Je vais faire la mort avec vous.*" He asked what she meant, and she told him she meant to kill herself in his flat, and it would be his fault. He asked her if she knew the expression "*la petite mort*"; she did not. He said,

"It's sometimes used when referring to an orgasm. Perhaps that's what you mean when you say that's what you want to do with me" (*ibid.*, p. 101). She said nothing, but that thought had not occurred to her. He tried to resume a more analytic mode, saying that she had never identified whom he represented for her. She replied that she could not do so because their relationship was swamped with his identity as the lover of "that woman". His reality was too present. He interpreted this response as resistance because she was afraid of what he might represent for her. Reflecting silently about his intervention, she realized that he reminded her of the golliwog she had as a child. It reactivated the intensity and desperation of the love she had felt for the golliwog, and her distress at its loss. She dreamt that night of her brother Jack: and remembered his use of the golliwog as a hostage, threatening to hit it when she was being tiresome. She relived her intense love for it, and her sense of total powerlessness when Jack said he was going to hit it. This seems like the only authentic analytic moment but she did not bring it to the therapy, so sadly it led nowhere.

Hostilities were resumed even more intensely in the ensuing sessions, with more physical struggling leading to physically intimate incidents, such as feeling his penis with her heel while she was lying facing him on the couch, and discovering that he had an erection. In the verbal exchange that followed, he justified his allowing her to act out in that way by saying that this was the way she was able to express and recognize her feelings, since she had difficulty in verbalizing them. She continued to act out, belittling his masculinity, and feeling more and more like an infant in a tantrum. She wrote that she was like a child, sulking, having tantrums, shrieking with rage, writhing all over him and sinking down into his arms. Her final sessions were frequently concerned with her erotic wishes combined with her fury about his actual sexual relationship with the woman living with him in his flat. She wanted to smash the flat up and destroy the belongings of his partner. She derided him for his lack of masculinity, being unable to gratify a woman sexually because his penis was too small. He interpreted this as her penis envy, which she denied while recollecting silently that, as a small child, she had wished to be able to urinate like a boy. She had dreams about Luc that she felt he was not very interested in, perhaps because she was unable to report them truthfully. She told him that the next time she came, if he was still with another patient, she would go into his bedroom, undress, and wait for him to come and fuck her.

On the next occasion she was able to see into his bedroom and saw that it had several mirrors. She accused him of narcissistically wanting to see himself having intercourse with his partner. An almost psychoanalytical moment occurred in relation to this incident as she had a fantasy of being in bed and having sex with him. He asked if they were naked; she replied that they were, but with bodies like children. She realized that this fantasy belonged to the past, but couldn't tell him. She began to feel that her longings for Luc, although expressed sexually, and sometimes acted out physically, in the sessions, might really be infantile longings. It is evident that she understood that her distress in the therapy might have been a result of regressive, infantile wishes. However, she had to deny anything as infantile as that, so she claimed that she really wanted adult sex with him. She wrote,

> ... I clung to my sexual desire for him. I didn't want to lose it: perhaps because it was something that could always be satisfied by orgasm whereas there was no possible means of satisfying all the other types of desire I was beginning to glimpse in me. Recognising their existence could only lead to frustration. [*Ibid.*, pp. 117–118]

Luc could not make any use of this because she did not tell him, so another opportunity to gain some insight into her distress was lost.

In the last session before a break in the therapy, she demanded a cigarette from Luc that, when he gave it to her, instead of smoking it she chewed into fragments and spat them out into his hands. This is very likely to have been have been some acting out of an oral fantasy that may have been an aspect of her intense, conflictful feelings that had been so evident in all the therapies. Again, no use was made of this incident, and perhaps it was too late, because she was contemplating not returning to the analysis after the holiday.

After the holiday she sent Luc a note enclosing a quotation from Maud Mannoni that she hoped he would understand as meaning that she would not be returning. She was not able to keep her resolution and began to feel desperate again, so she phoned him asking if he had had her note. He had understood her meaning, and this caused her to burst into a flood of tears saying that she could not come to a session because seeing him would be worse than not seeing him. Nevertheless, she phoned the next day for another appointment to which he agreed. When she got to his flat, the anxiety about whether she would overhear his girlfriend was so powerful that she could not speak, and felt like throwing herself through the window in his consulting room. Finally, she wrote him a note, during the session, saying that she should not have come. He asked her if she was upset because he was going away in the following week. She shook her head. He asked if she wanted to attack him, or for him to take her in his arms. She again shook her head, and a few minutes later passed him a note saying she wished to go. He escorted her to the door and told her he would see her in two weeks. She knew she would not.

In the days that followed she felt dazed with misery, and wrote, "My mind was slowly overcome by a kind of paralysis. I carried on living mechanically" (*ibid.*, p. 123). It was a bleak and sad ending to her struggle to get relief from her debilitating condition.

Reading this graphic account of Rosie's various therapies, there can be no doubt that she suffered grievously, and never experienced any relief from the painful emotional conflicts she endured. She attributed it to the pernicious and detrimental consequences of the transference. Transference is not just a phenomenon of psychotherapy or psychoanalysis, but manifests itself in any personal interaction. Although there is no evidence that any of the therapists deliberately fostered the transference in any of their transactions, none seems to have understood or made any attempts to interpret it within the therapeutic encounter. All seem to have either warded it off, or, in Luc's case, acted out his countertransferences to the condition from which Rosie suffered and had brought to therapy for treatment. It is very sad that none of the therapists, and Luc in particular, was able to trace it to its source so that insight and understanding could have replaced the acting out that became ever more frantic and uncontrollable. It may have been a repressed, encapsulated, psychotic state focusing on her intense jealousy of the other patients of her various therapists, but for which none of them had sufficient resources to deal. As I have suggested, they may all have been preoccupied by their own agendas, which were discordant with Rosie's wish to be relieved of her painful distress.

CHAPTER FOUR

Discussion

W hat was the reason for such a marked difference between these two experiences? Both had previous unsuccessful treatments for their conditions. In Marie's case they were all physiological and inappropriate to the psychosomatic condition from which she suffered, as she knew intuitively, despite being shocked by her analyst's affirmation of it. In Rosie's case she correctly identified it as a psychological problem but failed to find a therapist who could understand it. Despite her flashes of insight she could not communicate them to her analyst.

In the case of Marie Cardinal, was the successful outcome a result of the classical correctness of her analyst, or due to some other reason? At the beginning he did three important things: he set firm boundaries in terms of time and money; he gave clear advice about the meaning of free association; and he affirmed his strong belief that he symptom was psychosomatic and could be helped by psychoanalytical methods. He held to this structure steadfastly throughout the whole analysis. He appears to have made no powerful interpretations, or, if he did, they made no impact on Marie since she reported none. Despite his classical stance, Marie reported no basic interpretations of the instinctual drives, oral, anal, and phallic, although she made independent mention of penis envy, and of the anus and vagina in psychological terms. So the "little doctor's" unobtrusiveness included refraining from imposing on her the classical elements of the Freudian theory. It is likely that the freedom he gave her, within the staunch dependability of the boundary he prescribed in their first session, was concordant with her wish to be cured. His stout confidence that he could understand her psychic enigma, and the resulting cessation of her somatic symptom from his firm dismissal of it as unworthy of his attention, must together have created a feeling of safety for her so that she could explore her unconscious fantasies without fear. Illness need no longer be the path to love, as it had been with her mother.

In the terms I have used about the possibly discordant agendas of therapist and patient, it seems as if there was no such conflict between them. He had nothing to prove to himself or others about his understanding of the psyche, and he could unite with her to understand, in her own terms, the cause of her troubles. Further evidence of this concordance between them is Marie's comment that they had constructed a common language that they could use together to advance their understanding of her unconscious problems (Cardinal, 1984, p. 170).

There were occasions when there were powerful negative transferences, but the structure he had established, and his confidence in his capacity to survive any attack she made, was enough to contain her until she was able to give them up. Her discovery of her mother's murderous wishes towards her in the womb, replicated in her physical symptom, erupting when she was twenty eight, the age when her mother had been acting out death wishes for her, was perhaps the fundamental revelation of this treatment. It cannot be described as the discovery of a repression since the foetus has no ego to provide the repressing impulse. It was a deeply unconscious sense enveloping Marie in the womb and at birth. The undogmatic stance of the analyst allowed this to emerge in its own time when Marie could then attack him, in the transference, with her primitive anger for her mother, which he could contain.

In addition to the concordance of the two agendas of the patient and analyst, affirmed by his comment in the last session that he could not have done it without her (*ibid.*, p. 212), there was creation of the safe container in which positive and negative could be held without danger. Having set the boundaries at the outset, the analyst kept to them, some might think rather rigidly, and ensured that Marie felt safely held in a way she had not experienced as an infant and child. This must have helped to create the feeling that, come what may, they were working together in pursuit of a common goal.

How different it had been for Rosie Alexander. Her first two therapists were interested in their own methods of psychological treatment, even though those methods did not enable them to understand her powerful unconscious wish for exclusive primitive love and mothering. Marion at least recognized her own inability to cope with the demands that Rosie made on her and referred her to Dr Weissmann, in the hope that he would be a better therapist for Rosie than she was. Her second therapist not only did not understand her, but his narcissistic priorities, e.g., his failing to tell her that her first assessment meeting would be ended prematurely without notice because he had a train to catch, made her feel that the most important thing was his time rather than hers, and effectively diminished any progress. His narcissism needed continual refreshment as he consistently failed to understand her, and it prevented him from making an appropriate referral to another therapist who might have done better. Rosie may have been correct in her fantasy that his other patients were all women who gratified his narcissistic need for worship and adoration, of whom she would not be one despite her intense, psychotic demand for his love.

Luc, her final therapist, was an analyst who had only recently qualified and was in the early stages of setting up his practice in his own, rather small, flat where there was no room to separate his private life and space from his professional practice. So, while waiting, Rosie was sometimes able to see into his bedroom, and occasionally meet his woman partner. She was also very obtrusive into his private life, sometimes spying on him at night, trying to learn more about his sexual partners. However, Luc also failed to set other kinds of boundaries. He did not make clear to her the fundamental rules of analysis. Nor did he tell her that he would not respond to her letters in the earliest stages of the therapy, when it was going to be interrupted by her residence in Africa. His inexperience may have been pertinent here, in that he may not have realized the importance of not beginning an intensive analysis that was to be interrupted so early, and he may not have been confident about whether it was appropriate to agree to her wish to write to him. Her urgent and intense feelings about him, and her intense psychotic jealousy of his other relationships, must have overwhelmed his neophyte professionalism, so he got into difficulties from which he was never able to extract himself. The basic conflict was between Luc's need to establish himself in professional practice and gain confidence in his analytic role, while hers, which clearly failed, was to discharge in therapy the intense, primitive relationship with her mother. Because there is so little information about her history or of her infantile fantasies, this conclusion has to be speculative, but she had one or two flashes of insight, never communicated to Luc, which suggest that this might be the case. Her dilemma was that her desperate need to be loved and wanted always led to her being warded off, or was met by an inappropriate response. Luc could have gained no professional gratification from his work with her, and was continually being trapped into very inappropriate, erotic behaviour, about which he must have felt some anxiety for his professional reputation when Rosie attempted to find other analysts. They were concerned about Luc's lack of professionalism but declined to do anything about it.

It was not simply the sense of having different goals in all of the therapies, but the failure of any of the therapists to create with her a secure container within which her distress could be safely held and understood. From the beginning her analyst completely failed to define what the therapy required, and the lack of boundaries led her to act out around the sessions in a most destructive way. Moreover, he was unable to maintain his own role as an analyst and also allowed himself to act out in an unprofessional way, perhaps reinforcing her own need to act rather than to try to explore the sources and meanings of her powerful need to be loved.

Rosie left in distress, feeling that all her therapy had made her condition worse, which certainly seems to be true. Her behaviour, particularly with Luc, was almost psychotic, and perhaps he unleashed in her the encapsulated psychosis that, before therapy, may have been contained, while leaving her feeling anxious in an undefined way. Her complaint that therapy had damaged her was in part correct, because she had the misfortune to meet a succession of therapists whose own narcissistic agendas made it impossible for them to feel secure enough in the face of her primitive demand and rage. She left looking for other former patients whose experiences had been similar to her own, seeking solace from them that she had not found in the various forms of psychotherapy she had received.

.

PART II

PATIENTS OF FREUD
AND JUNG WRITE

CHAPTER FIVE

Prelude

By contrast with the patients in the first section, whose analysts were anonymous or relatively unknown, in this section I bring together patients analysed by Freud and Jung. Both were charismatic founders of important, rival schools of analysis, resting on different concepts about the contents of the unconscious and its relationship with other parts of the psyche, and also with very different ideas about what was therapeutically effective.

The three patients of Freud considered here were not formally in any kind of training as psychoanalysts, although Dr Wortis presented himself for an educational rather than a therapeutic experience. Accounts by patients of Jung and other Jungians are far fewer than patients of Freud and other psychoanalytic practitioners. According to Bair (2004), Jung took a very pronounced view about confidentiality and privacy, believing that what happened in the analytic session was sacrosanct and never to be revealed even after the analyst and analysand had died. The Wolf-Man is unique as the only one about whom Freud himself had written publicly, so that it is possible to set his views in contrast to those of the Wolf-Man. Freud's paper, entitled *From the History of an Infantile Neurosis*

(1918), also makes the Wolf-Man the most well known of the three. His associations to the famous Wolf Dream were used by Freud to demonstrate that his theories of infantile sexuality and, in particular, his theory of the primal scene, were validated by the reality of the patient's repressed unconscious memories of early and significant events in his life. Those unconscious memories, Freud believed, could be recovered by the technique of free association. He thought that he had demonstrated this most effectively in his paper. That view was endorsed for many years by the developing psychoanalytic community, which kept the Wolf-Man under its wing until his death. The Wolf-Man himself, although adopting the sobriquet in his daily life, began to resile from Freud's view as his life proceeded, and before he died he had rejected the complex interpretation that Freud had made of his dream. In fact, the long resistance that the Wolf-Man displayed for the first three years of analysis may have been a consequence of the discordant agendas between himself and Freud, rather than from resistance to the return of the "repressed memories".

HD (Hilda Doolittle) is well known for her poetry and other writings, many of which seem to have been a continuous reworking of her psychoanalysis with Freud. The details of that analysis were not known widely until the publication of her *Tribute to Freud* in 1945. It is a retrospective account of her work with Freud in two periods in 1934 and 1935. Although drafted ten years after the first of her two sessions of analysis, it reads as if it was a contemporaneous record. There were such records in the shape of a diary of the first month in March 1934, and her letters to her very close friend, Winifred Ellerman, known as Bryher. Those letters were written daily during both periods of the analysis, but they also contain material other than her interaction with Freud. The diary was not available to her when she was writing *Tribute,* and it is not known if she made use of the letters at that time. The diary was later published in 2002 as part of *Tribute,* and the letters under the title *Analyzing Freud,* edited by Friedman. Friedman claimed that HD's letters showed that she had subverted the position of the woman patient in analysis, having clung to her own understanding of her problems while apparently submitting to Freud's concepts.

In 1954 the third patient, Dr J. Wortis, published his notes, made at the time of his analysis with Freud in 1934. They had been edited for publication and some of the material was removed, so they are not a complete account of what occurred. However, they convey the flavour of the interaction between them as Wortis experienced it. Wortis's resistance to Freud's attempt to analyse him seems to have arisen from his different purpose in seeking to work with Freud.

All three accounts give rise to the question of whether they can be veridical or objective records of what occurred. The issue arises most acutely in respect of the Wolf-Man, since he is the only one of the three about whom Freud had also written. It could be asked if either Freud's or the Wolf-Man's stories were objective accounts. There seem to be reasons for believing that both are not. Freud, in fact, disclaims that his was a complete history of Sergei's illness and treatment, since that would be "technically impractible and socially impermissible" (Freud, 1918b, p. 8). Freud's account of the Wolf-Man was plainly used to demonstrate the validity of Freud's theories of infantile sexuality and to combat the "twisted reinterpretations which C. G. Jung and Alfred Adler were endeavouring to give to the findings of psycho-analysis" (*ibid.*, p. 7, fn.1). In a sense it is Freud's *experience* of the analysis in the light of his theoretical concepts. In some cases it differs from the Wolf-Man's recollection in terms of the facts of his history. Does the use of the theory in Freud's account invalidate the objectivity or veracity of the story as told by the Wolf-Man? In so far as he reported his own subjective experience it might not accord with an objective reality, if that could ever be established. It might also be argued, and is indeed argued by some psychoanalysts, that the Wolf-Man could not give a truthful account of himself and his analysis because of the problem of repression of unconscious phantasies that could be understood only by those psychoanalytically sophisticated. I argue that because he was familiar with Freud's published material about him, he is unlikely to have repressed salient material in his own account. He might also be regarded as being moderately sophisticated in the understanding of psychoanalytical matters. Moreover, his recollection could have been kept alive by the continuing interest of the psychoanalytic community in him, as well as by the psychoanalytically orientated conversations with Eissler during the last decades of his life. So, his story is no more likely than Freud's to be a distorted account of his experience of the analysis.

Different considerations apply in respect of HD and Dr Wortis. Both, in different ways, wrote contemporaneous accounts of their interactions. Each kept diary notes for all or some part of their analyses. HD also wrote daily letters to Bryher, some of which were concerned almost exclusively with her analysis, and all contained references to it. Additionally, it is evident that she continued to work at the issues raised in her interactions with Freud, both in other analyses with other analysts and in her poetic and artistic writings. This may account for the freshness of the first part of her Tribute to Freud, entitled *Writing on the Wall*. All her writing, whether as letters or diary notes, has the ring of truth. So far as can be told, they do not suffer from the repression of salient matters, but it is evident that she often understood them in a very different way from Freud.

Equally, the same might be said of Wortis's record of his rather sad experience with Freud, which left him respectful, but almost untouched by his experience. His *post hoc* ruminations are quite rejecting of both Freud's theory and technique. Reading his notes about his work with Freud, it is possible to understand why. In his subsequent professional experience he seems to have turned his back upon psychoanalysis and thought of it as no more than a possible preparation for psychiatric therapies of quite a different kind.

Turning to the conspicuously few of Jung's patients who wrote of their therapeutic experiences, Henderson, an experienced analytical psychologist writing in the *Journal of Analytical Psychology* (1975), describes his discomfort at being asked what it was like to have been in analysis with Jung himself. He wrote of the private nature of such an intimate process of analysis, the real essence of which could not be easily conveyed to those not part of it. Additionally, as his analysis had been so long ago (1929), if written many years later he might not be able to reproduce an authentic account rather than some kind of myth. He resolved those concerns by realizing that myth in analytical psychology is a certain kind of reality. The issue of confidentiality is also referred to in the Preface to the story of Catherine Rush Cabot, where it is suggested by her daughter, who edited it, that the material would not have been appropriately published when it had been written at the time of the analysis.

Henderson's paper does not, in fact, describe his own analysis in detail, a story that was to be confined to the collection of taped interviews gathered by Gene Nameche and filed in the library of Harvard University, with all access embargoed until twenty years after Jung's death in 1961. Although that time embargo has long elapsed, few if any of the stories have been published to make them accessible to the public. Henderson wrote only briefly in his paper about his own experiences with Jung in 1929. Jung himself could not be put into any frame, he wrote, and would both personally and technically burst out of any frame. Henderson described how, during his sessions, Jung would pace up and down, gesturing and talking about what ever came into his mind in response to the patient's associations. He might also sit quietly, but close to the patient, which Henderson found too close for comfort. Sometimes, in response to a patient's anxieties, Jung would quote a classical story illustrating the dilemma and offering a way of resolving it; or a quotation from his personal understanding of classical history seeming to suggest a solution. Henderson wrote that despite Jung's very free and open attitude, there was always a sense of reserve, like a curtain covering a secret truth (Henderson, 1975, p. 115).

Yet, Jung's many worldly interests came into the work with patients. Henderson describes an occasion when he had dreamt about a house where he was trying to think of how he could create a style of architecture appropriate to his family history, combining traditional and contemporary features. In the course of the session devoted to interpreting the dream, Jung took him on a tour of his own house in Küsnacht, showing him the mixture of traditional styles he and his wife had chosen. Responding to a criticism that this may have been too personal in terms of the transference, Henderson comments that Jung had also been criticized for being too impersonal, or too shaman-like. This, he claimed, demonstrated Jung's flexibility, and more technically, illustrated his principle of amplification, imaginatively bringing together all the material relevant to the dream or fantasy (*ibid.*, p. 118).

On occasions he would send his analysands to Toni Wolff (his analysand, colleague, and lover)[1] when the transference to himself seemed too powerful. She was Jung's opposite, so that while Jung could not be put into a frame, she was most comfortable in one and had a talent for putting the analysands into *their* frames. Henderson

seems to have experienced this himself, and wrote that her interpretations often took the form of, "You are the kind of person who
..." (*ibid.*, p. 117).

Henderson continued his account by moving away from his
personal experience as an analysand to describing, and making a
critique of, the early stages of analytical psychology and its later
development at the time of writing in 1975.

In a collection of memories of Jung, published after his death
(Fordham, 1993), a number of the contributors evidently had been
in analysis with Jung, or had had therapeutic analytic experiences
with him not formally identified as analysis. Although all the
contributions are necessarily brief, the accounts of these two different types of experience show that there is a remarkable similarity
between them. It is as if Jung did not make a precise distinction
between occasions when analysis was formally on the agenda and
when it was not, although it perhaps depended as much on what
the individual was seeking as upon the formal designation of the
occasion. As will be seen from the account of Catherine Cabot, the
therapy was often accompanied by other modes of relationship. It
may be that in Jung's system the therapeutic element was as much
the responsibility of the analysand as of the analyst. In the case of
the informal discussions this may have been entirely so. It may also
be that the very individualistic nature of both formal and informal
contacts with Jung makes it difficult for those individuals to write
of their experiences as if they are examples of a system. Jung, in
fact, protested that nobody could know what his method was
simply from their experience in analysis with him. In so far as there
was a system, it was different with different individuals. However
that may be, it remains the case that very few, if any, full accounts
of analyses with Jung, or with other Jungians, have been written.
Only one has been published: the analysis of Catherine Cabot Rush
(Reid, 2001).

The question of the accuracy of Catherine's account does not
arise because she kept shorthand notes taken during many of her
sessions with Jung. Taking notes during a psychoanalytic session,
since both analyst and patient would be aware of the fact, is
distinctly unusual. Jung seems to have made no objection, nor did
he enquire about the purpose of the note-taking, despite his firmly
held objections to the possible violation of the privacy of the

sessions. Those notes were later transcribed, first in handwriting and later typed. They were published after her death by her daughter, Jane, who had become a Jungian analyst herself. Such verbatim published accounts by other patients of Jung, or other Jungian therapists, have not been found and may not exist.

Note

1. Henderson described her as Jung's assistant.

CHAPTER SIX

The Wolf-Man

Introduction

The Wolf-Man, whose real name was Sergei Pankejeff, was born on Christmas Eve 1886 according to the Julian Calendar (6 January 1887 according to the Gregorian Calendar). He was the son of a wealthy Russian landowner. As a child he suffered from a severe psychological disturbance from the age of three and a half, the details of which are described in Freud's paper about him. He had an elder sister, Anna, who had a very prominent role in Freud's account of the analysis, as well as in his own recollections, although they were rather different from Freud's. For example, his depressive breakdown after his sister's suicide is made little of by Freud, apart from saying that the depression was a result of a gonorrhoeal infection causing him to be completely incapacitated and dependent on others. Sergei denied the latter, and did not ascribe his depression to the sexual infection. Sergei's relationship with his sister, Anna, had been most important to him and he wrote that he had always had a deep inner relationship with her, regarding her as his only comrade (Gardiner, 1973, p. 40). One consequence of Anna's death was that while alive she had been father's favourite, but after her death he became intensely interested in Sergei. Although he had always longed for a better relationship with his father, the change now left him cool. He felt that his father had just transferred his feelings from Anna to him, rather than valuing him in his own right. Partly as a result of that feeling, and partly through having developed gonorrhoea, he fell into a deep depression His depression was exacerbated by his father's death, and fluctuated until he went into analysis with Freud. It has been suggested that Sergei had not really mourned his sister and had been cool towards her death. This appears to be a misreading of his memoirs when he wrote that his father's change towards him after Anna's death left him cool (*ibid.*). He did, however, find it difficult to grieve for his sister and displaced it on to a long deceased Russian poet, whose grave he visited and wept over. His father, who had been becoming increasingly depressed from a much earlier time, died (and may have committed suicide) the year before Sergei began analysis with Freud in 1910. The loss of his father made him feel even more bereft, and his search for a substitute found its goal when he met Freud and was an important factor in his entering analysis with Freud in 1910.

Before meeting Freud he spent some time exploring various treatments for his condition, some of which involved treatment in German sanatoria. While in St Petersburg he overheard his father, in conversation with the doctor, saying that the best thing for Sergei would be that he should really fall in love (*ibid.* p. 55). Perhaps it was not surprising that when he later arrived at the sanatorium in Munich he met and fell in love with a nurse on the staff, Therese, who had a child by a former marriage. Although of a lower social class than Sergei, a wealthy young Russian aristocrat, she did not fit the image, in Freud's analysis, of the degraded women who aroused Sergei sexually. When Freud met Therese towards the end of the analysis he was very impressed by her, said she was beautiful and not at all like the impression he had first formed of her. She was the daughter of a businessman who had lost his fortune. She had married a man from the same social background as herself, but that marriage had ended in divorce after her daughter, Else, had been born. During the years 1908 and 1909 Sergei's alternate depression and euphoria fluctuated with the state of his relationship with Therese, who herself seemed torn between Sergei and her daughter.

When he met Freud to begin his analysis in 1910, he was emotionally preoccupied with Therese, who had symbolically taken the place of his sister. Freud's approval of Sergei's relationship with Therese was an important factor in his decision to be analysed by him. He did not marry her then because he understood from Freud that during analysis he should not make any material change in his life. It is difficult to understand why living with Therese was not considered to be a material change in his life, although marriage would have been. Therese's daughter was left with her uncle during this cohabitation, and was perhaps evidence of Therese's emotional difficulty of being with her daughter and Sergei together. As soon as the analysis ended, and problems arising from the hostilities between Russia and Germany were resolved, they were married in Odessa, continuing to live there with Sergei's family until the end of the war. Therese did not get on with Sergei's family and particularly not with his mother, and she left the family at the end of the war to be with her daughter, who was seriously ill. Soon after the couple were reunited in Freiburg, Therese's daughter died After the Revolution had made it impossible for Sergei to live in Russia he and Therese lived in Vienna, partly supported by gifts of money from Freud, even after he had independently found a job. Additionally, Freud paid for his re-analysis with Ruth Mack Brunswick. Those gifts were continued by the Freud Archive after the Second World War until Sergei died in 1979.

Freud's analysis and the Wolf-Man's memoirs

The story of the Wolf-Man first made its public appearance in 1918, when Freud published his renowned account (Freud, 1918b). In it, Freud sets out to demonstrate the truth of his theories of infantile sexuality and their influence on childhood development and mental illnesses of both children and adults (Gardiner, 1973, p. 34). It seems to have been very carefully crafted to ensure that it confirmed Freud's theory of infantile sexual development, and had been written, in 1914, for those who were already convinced about the theory (Freud, 1918b, p. 13). The story was regarded by his psychoanalytic colleagues as a *tour de force*, and for many years held the psychoanalytic world in its thrall. More recently, some studies

(Esman, 1973; Kanzer & Glenn, 1980; Mahony, 1984), while still respectful, have been more critical of some very questionable elements of Freud's account. There has been a tendency to re-analyse the Wolf-Man using the material in Freud's and Ruth Mack Brunswick's accounts as a basis. There seems to be a certain omnipotence and grandiosity about these "re-analyses", and, perforce, none involves much input from Sergei himself. Many of these stories confirm the implication that analytical treatment is really an objective, medical enterprise to which the patient's views are irrelevant. Kanzer (Kanzer & Glenn, 1980) is an exception to this, writing that the patient's contribution would add a further dimension to the analyst's account.

In a footnote, Freud described how the study came to be written in the winter of 1914–1915. It was intended to supplement the polemic he had published previously against the views of Adler and Jung (Freud, 1914d), but, because of wartime conditions, it was not made public until 1918. Of course, although intended as an objective presentation of the psychoanalytic material, it could not escape the polemical intention of the original. Many asides directed at Adler and Jung betray its contentious character. As an objective, scientific account it suffered as a result. It is a very persuasive attempt to show how Freud's views of infantile sexuality could be constructed using incidents believed to have occurred in the childhood of Sergei as he recalled them in the analytic sessions with Freud some twenty years later. To that extent, it falls short of a critical examination of the concepts themselves, since they appeared to have been taken for granted, and criticisms of them, such as those from Adler and Jung, were dismissed by reference to Freud's constructions of the story drawn for the analysis of the Wolf Dream. In relation to that dream Freud proposed an agenda for further exploration. It was "A real occurrence—dating from a very early period—looking—immobility—sexual problem—castration—his father—something terrible" (Freud, 1918b, p. 34).

This, then, became Freud's agenda in the analysis. Freud established to his satisfaction, in Chapter Four of the account of the analysis, that the primal scene and his construction of it was an actual event, describing all the realities: the time of day and season of the year; the state of undress of the parents; their position in the intercourse and the number of times that it occurred; and the observation of their genitals, by way of confirmation. It then comes as something of a surprise in the following chapter when Freud wrote that such scenes, related in exhaustive analyses, were not reproductions of real occurrences but products of the imagination in mature life and ascribed to an earlier time (*ibid.*, p. 62). Freud contradicts himself later in the same chapter by writing that the primal scene could be nothing other than the reproduction of a "reality experienced by the child" (*ibid.* p. 49). In the final pages of his paper, Freud said that it was a matter of indifference whether it was regarded as a primal scene or a primal fantasy (*ibid.*, p. 120, fn.1). Whether the primal scene was reality or fantasy was not resolved in Freud's paper; it remains unresolved to this day in psychoanalytical discussions. Freud offered as incontrovertible evidence for his theory the claim that intercourse *a tergo* offered especially favourable opportunities to view the genitals of the participants, which simply suggests that he had never seen such intercourse himself. It may also have been a product of his own imagination in adult life, ascribed to infancy. Mahony contended that Freud's main conclusions from the Wolf Dream were *a posteriori* justifications of *a priori* concepts (Mahony, 1984, p. 62; see also Magid, 1993, p. 167). It is evident that Freud was always seeking confirmation for his theories, and sometimes adjusted the "evidence" to deal with problems that might arise. Examples of this will be found in Sergei's story.

Freud's account of the way that Sergei's prolonged resistance to his interpretations of the Wolf Dream, and other concepts, was overcome is revealing. He decided that, when Sergei had become strongly attached to him, after three years, he would set a date for the termination of analysis a year ahead so that he would be forced to give up his resistance. Sergei then capitulated and the analysis produced all the material that Freud was seeking. Magid writes,

> Freud's use of the forced termination seems to have been a last-ditch effort to force the facts of this difficult case to conform to his expectations about the centrality of infantile sexuality in neurogenesis. Only under pressure of this deadline will his patient accede to the reconstruction of the primal scene as the key to his illness and of the famous dream. [Magid, 1993, p. 162]

So Freud's agenda triumphed over Sergei's, but did not heal Sergei's distress. The relationship with, and subsequent marriage to, Therese seems to have provided the relief from the depression he had brought to the analysis, rather than the triumph of Freud's interpretations of the Wolf Dream, but not, however, from his other symptoms, to which both Freud and Brunswick refer in their analyses of him, and which on the whole remained unresolved.

Other detailed criticisms of Freud's constructions can be found in Mahony (1984), and in Kanzer and Glenn (1980), but I do not propose to comment further on Freud's account, as I wish now to turn to Sergei's own story.

The Wolf-Man according to Sergei Pankejeff

His own accounts fall into at least three parts. There is, first, an autobiographical story, providing his own memories of occurrences in his life, and particularly of his childhood, in chronological order. These memoirs were written at different times, although they are presented chronologically, in reverse order of their writing, in Muriel Gardiner's (1973) book. The first, entitled "Recollections of my childhood", was written in 1970 when Sergei was eighty-three years old. The section called "Unconscious mourning" is attributed by Gardiner both to 1958, and to between 1961and 1968. The section entitled "Castles in Spain", about the year 1908, was written in 1957 when Sergei was sixty. The period of his analysis with Freud is called "Shifting decisions" and seems to have been written between 1961 and 1968. Three sections, entitled "1914–1918 After my analysis", "1919–1938 Everyday life", and "1938 The climax", appear to have been written in or about 1958, when he was in his seventies, although Gardiner also says that he had written several sections of his memoirs before 1956. Second, there is his brief account of the analysis called "My recollections of Sigmund Freud", written in 1952, and, thus, the first of all his writings, an account he later claimed was first written for a celebration of Freud's sixtieth birthday. This must have been a mistake, as that would have placed it in the middle of the First World War, in 1916. It is more likely that it was written in 1926, when Freud was seventy. He wrote that Freud would not allow it to be published in 1926, which perhaps confirms that it was written for Freud's seventieth birthday. Third, there are extracts from letters that he wrote to Muriel Gardiner from 1948; and, additionally, there are two letters published in 1957 under the title "Letters pertaining to Freud's 'History of an Infantile Neurosis' (The Wolf-Man in the Freud Archives, 1957). Although it is not available to the public, there is also a long record created by Eissler who, according to Mahony (1984), spent several weeks nearly every summer from the mid 1950s to 1979 seeing Sergei daily for "analytically directed conversations". Additionally, Obholzer (1982) published, after his death, her recorded conversations with Sergei, in the course of which he made some very interesting comments about the Wolf Dream and other matters reported by Freud. It is significant that Eissler, through some kind of legal process, succeeded in delaying the publication of these detailed conversations until after Sergei's death. It is perhaps an indication of the lack of respect for the analysand's story by the more purist part of the psychoanalytic community. It also displayed similar contempt for the general public, who were considered to be unable to understand the mysteries of psychoanalytic theory and practice.

The timing of the writing of these memoirs is quite important, because there are surprising differences between them and Freud's account of Sergei's childhood. Those differences in the later writings might be ascribed to the faulty memory of old age, but Sergei had read Freud's writings avidly and he must have been acquainted with the contents of Freud's paper about his own analysis. Evidence for that knowledge can be found in some of his comments, especially in "My recollections of Sigmund Freud" (possibly written when he was thirty-nine), as well as in his adoption of the soubriquet, the Wolf-Man. Additionally, he had had further analyses with Freud and other analysts, as well as analytically directed conversations with Eissler while he was writing some of his memoirs. In 1957 he had received a letter from the Freud Archives enquiring about a letter about the Wolf Dream he had written to Freud in 1926. The original letter and his response to the enquiry were published in *Psychoanalytic Quarterly* in 1957. Both contain references to the Wolf Dream and the castration complex and were written when he was beginning to compose some of his memoirs. So the decay of memory with old age seems to be an unlikely explanation for those differences.

Sergei's "Recollections of Freud"

As an account of his analysis, Sergei's "Recollections of Freud" are disappointing because they say nothing about the story that Freud had written so eloquently. What they do portray was his powerful transference to Freud from their very first meeting in 1910. This was relevant to the death of his father, who had died unexpectedly, and prematurely, a year before his analysis with Freud began, leaving him with some very ambivalent feelings subsequently explored in the analysis. Sergei confirmed this in a letter to Muriel Gardiner in 1970. He described how Freud, by his very appearance, "won his confidence immediately" (Gardiner, 1973, p. 103), and gave him the feeling that he was encountering "a great personality", and that he had found a new father in Freud (*ibid.*, p. 104). He also wrote that he would not have begun analysis with Freud unless he had agreed to his returning to Therese (*ibid.*, p. 103). Some of his ensuing comments suggest that Freud might have been captured by this transference. So, for example, he reported that Freud had told him ". . . it would be good if all his pupils could grasp the nature of analysis as soundly as I" (*ibid.* p. 158). This comment may have provided an early indication to Sergei that he was the first among Freud's analysands and students.

In his conversations with Karin Obholzer he frequently referred to his transference to Freud, claiming that it had never been resolved and that it had been quite damaging to the rest of his life. Sergei's relationship with his father had been very disappointing to him. His father had preferred his sister, Anna, who had been very tomboyish and apparently took up the role of the son with their father, even to the extent of being dressed as a boy. His parents sometimes said that Sergei should have been a girl. It was not until his sister died that his relationship with his father changed. It was as a replacement for Anna, not for himself, that his father was interested in him after her death, Sergei said. Thus, the first significant thing for Sergei, in the analysis, was the need to find in Freud that love he had not had from his father in infancy. Hence, Sergei's agenda to find a father in Freud who valued him for himself, and to deal with the depression following the suicide of his sister, was discordant with Freud's agenda to seek for confirmation for his theories. Sergei's need to maintain Freud's love was also significant in his capitulation at the end of three years, when Freud set a date for the termination of the analysis. It was that ultimatum which produced his acquiescence to Freud's construction of the dream, and thence to become Freud's, and the psychoanalytic community's, favourite son for most of the rest of his life. (Anna Freud, in the Introduction to Gardiner's (1973) book, calls him "our Wolf-Man".)

Throughout his account he seemed keen to demonstrate his understanding of psychoanalytic theory, referring particularly to *Beyond the Pleasure Principle* (Freud, 1920g), claiming that he added some ideas to it. Here and elsewhere in his memoirs he described Freud as commending his "breakthrough to the woman" as a great achievement for neurotics as well as a sign of the will to recover, but Freud made no reference to that in his paper. By contrast, Sergei made no reference to the famous Wolf Dream, or to any of the constructions which flowed from it. He, in fact, dismissed the need to make any recollections of his analysis in this memoir for the birthday celebrations. He wrote,

> This is not the place to speak of all the phases of my treatment. I can only say that in my analysis with Freud, I felt myself less as a patient than as a co-worker, the younger comrade of an experienced explorer setting out to study a new, recently discovered land. This new land is the realm of the unconscious, over which the neurotic has lost that mastery which he now seeks, through analysis, to recover. [Gardiner, 1973, p. 158]

This idea of being a kind of preferred junior colleague to Freud is evidence that he felt that he had received from Freud what he had not had from his father even after his sister had died. His powerful wish for Freud's love made him susceptible to gaining it through becoming Freud's apt pupil and colleague. Freud's approval of him in that role was highly significant for Sergei.

It is not evident that Freud ever discussed the basic concepts of psychoanalysis with Sergei. Many of Freud's interpretations, however, may have conveyed the significance of infantile sexuality and its phases, which may have been *experienced* by Sergei as concepts. Freud, in fact, referred to them as "constructions", and it is far from clear how they were conveyed to the patient, since Freud's report offered very little in the way of verbatim interactions between himself and the Wolf-Man. For example, a very careful reading of the first reference to the castration complex (Freud, 1918b, p. 9) leaves the reader quite unclear as to what Freud may have said. He wrote of two interactions with Sergei's English governess, Miss Oven, that they "might permit of a construction being made" (*ibid.*, p. 19). He went on to make an apologia about the harmlessness of making an interpretation too soon, but that overlooked the possibility of suggestion, particularly to somebody like Sergei, who had made such a powerful transference to Freud.

Although Sergei reported (Gardiner, 1973, p. 159) that Freud believed that the friendly relationship with the patient should not overstep a certain (undefined) boundary it seems from his own story, if correct, that Freud allowed himself considerable freedom from the strict boundaries that later characterized classical psychoanalytic practice.

Sergei described Freud as talking about one of his sons in an analytic session, almost as if Sergei was one of the family, as discussing issues of technique, and also referring to another patient (*ibid.*, p. 160). Additionally, he is reported as commenting on criticisms of the concepts of psychoanalysis, as interpreting a dream in Dostoevsky's novel *The Brothers Karamazov*, of conveying information of his views about art, and about his favourite authors. Some of this may, of course, have been discovered by Sergei during his long association with Freud and the psychoanalytic world. Langs (1980) describes this exchange of information as a misalliance that then subverted the rest of the analysis.

The publication of *From the History of an Infantile Neurosis* may have later perpetuated the message that he was Freud's most important patient, confirmed by the later response of the psychoanalytic community to the story. Added to that, Freud not only treated him without fee after he lost his fortune when he returned to see him briefly in 1918, but for many years he also from time to time gave him money to support himself. Freud conveyed the idea that difficulties in the transference might increase if the patient thought of the analyst as a father substitute. There can be little doubt that Sergei himself did feel that Freud was such a substitute, influenced by his father's preference for Anna, and his premature death in the year before Sergei began analysis. His wish for a substitute may have been added to by the death of his much loved Uncle Peter, also in the year that his father died (Gardiner, 1973, p. 95). Freud may have inadvertently fostered such wishes, although the danger of becoming "stuck in the transference" after the treatment had ended had been discussed before the termination of the analysis. Freud's apparent acting into the transference, and its continuance by the psychoanalytic community for the rest of Sergei's life, may have been important in such improvement as there was in mental health. Was this one of the very important factors in the analysis as seen by Sergei, but of which Freud himself made little?

"Castles in Spain" and "Shifting decisions"

These two accounts cover the years up to and including the analysis. The former was concerned with the beginning of his relationship with Therese, whom he married after his analysis had finished. The latter covered the whole period of analysis between 1910 and 1914. The recollections of his relationship with Therese in the eighteen months leading to his work with Freud were important since the psychiatrists who were treating him then advised him against his relationship with her. His thoughts about that relationship had formed an important part of the first months of his analysis. It seems possible that Therese, whom he met while he was still suffering from the depression following Anna's death, was a replacement for her. He recorded telling Freud of his "stormy courtship of Therese" and its fateful (but temporary) ending in Berlin, which inadvertently had led him to Freud. He reported that Freud approved of his passionate courtship of Therese (Gardiner, 1973, p. 98), but called his ending of it a "flight from the woman". Asking Freud if he would agree to the resumption of the relationship with Therese, he wrote that Freud had advised him that he could return to Therese, but only after several months of analysis. After much frustration, in February or March 1911, Freud gave his permission for him to see Therese again. With difficulty he found Therese in Munich, where she was living in straitened circumstances and poor health with the daughter of her first, failed, marriage.

After resuming their relationship, Therese moved to Vienna to live with him in a flat with a view over the Danube canal leaving her daughter, Else, with her uncle. Sergei wrote that he would have married "then and there", but he felt that had to observe Freud's rule that he should not make any life-changing decisions during the analysis (*ibid.*, p. 103). The Wolf-Man felt obliged to observe this rule despite the difficulties it gave him in his daily life, but it is not clear why his living with Therese was assumed not to be an important influence on his life, both then and later. Perhaps Freud's assumption was that his relationship with Sergei must take precedence over the relationship with Therese. Might it also have been Freud's defence against the homosexual elements in the transference?

Sergei's relationship with Therese, and its link to his relationship with his dead sister, Anna, throughout the analysis was perhaps as important to him in its significance for his emotional life at that time, as his relationship with his father. Freud seems to have been quite dismissive of Sergei's wish to make Therese an important focus in the analysis when he said in one session, "For twenty-four hours now I have not heard the sacred name of Therese!" (*ibid.*, p. 100). Was this another instance of the discordant agendas being followed by therapist and patient?

This is almost the whole of what he had to say about those four important years. The significance of Freud's attitude to Therese is emphasized in a letter that he wrote to Muriel Gardiner in 1970. She had asked him if he could evaluate his analysis with Freud and what it had done for him. He replied that it would be difficult for him to do this. Nevertheless he wrote,

> . . . when I first came to Professor Freud, the most important question for me was whether or not he would agree to my returning to Therese. Had Professor Freud, like the other doctors whom I had previously, said "No" I would certainly not have stayed with him. Professor Freud agreed to my returning to Therese—not at once, it is true, but nevertheless soon—I remained with him. This settling, in a positive sense, of the problem with which I was most concerned at the time naturally contributed a great deal to a rapid improvement of my state of mind. That was a very important factor, but it was really outside the sphere of my analysis with Freud. [*ibid.*, p. 103, fn.1]

This is a most interesting comment, implying as it does, that an important factor in the recovery from depression resulting from the death of his sister Anna was her replacement by Therese, but Sergei believed this to be unrelated to his analysis.

He continued by referring to the importance of the father-complex in the analysis, and relating it to the recent death of his own father. Freud had filled this void. He said that he was strengthened in his attachment to Freud when he was told that Freud had a great deal of personal understanding for him. He went on to claim that Freud never saw him in the really deep depression following his sister's death, which had led him to seek treatment from his previous psychiatrists. His emotional state had improved under the influence of Dr D (Dr Drosnes), who had accompanied him from Odessa to Vienna, and later introduced him to Freud. This contrasts with Freud's description at the beginning of his account that Sergei ". . . was entirely incapacitated and completely dependent on other people when he began his psycho-analytic treatment" (Freud, 1918b, p. 7). Freud's idea that Sergei had been helplessly dependent at the beginning of the analysis has been repeated uncritically by most commentators on Freud's paper, despite Sergei's denial and other evidence to the contrary. Might Freud have drawn rather wrong conclusions from the fact that Sergei was being accompanied on his journeys at that time? Sergei's account of what the two did together (he describes Dr D as a *maître de plaisir*) does not give a picture of himself in the condition that Freud claimed. Did Freud need to exaggerate Sergei's depression to add strength to his claims for his theory?

The Psychoanalytic Quarterly *letters*

The letters in *Psychoanalytic Quarterly*, the first to Freud in 1926, written while he was in an analysis with Ruth Mack Brunswick, confirmed that he told the Wolf Dream very early in the analysis, and it was just as reported by Freud in his paper. However, he disagreed that the animals in the tree were wolves. He was confident that they were Spitz dogs, with pointed ears and bushy tails. This realization seems to have come later, and his reference to them during the analysis as wolves may have been related to the wolf picture that his sister had frightened him with preceding the Wolf

Dream itself, and as a result it dominated his childhood fantasy. The solution, he agreed, came only at the end of the treatment. It seems to be implied that he had agreed both with the timing of Freud's interpretation of the Wolf Dream as well as its contents, but might he not be recalling his need to comply with Freud in order to retain the love he had been in danger of losing during his three year resistance, and might lose again in 1926? Freud in his letter, which Sergei had lost, had enquired whether had seen the opera *Pique Dame*, containing a scene involving the spontaneous opening of a window, before the had dreamt the Wolf Dream. Sergei confirmed again, in 1957, that he was sure he had not seen the opera before the dream. What this suggests is that some time during the period when he was writing his memoirs he was reminded about the Wolf Dream and Freud's interpretation, which makes his failure to refer to it in his memoirs even more surprising, since it had been regarded as so important. Perhaps, during the analysis it was not as important to Sergei as it was to Freud, but in his later transactions with the psychoanalytic community, it became important as a talisman for those interactions. He may have become trapped in Freud's didactic account, from which he was unable to struggle free, as his later conversations with Obholzer seem to have confirmed.

"Recollections of my childhood", and "Conversations with Obholzer"

Memories of Sergei's early life were recalled in these recollections, written when he was eighty-three. Gardiner (1973, p. 9), in her introduction to these memoirs, seems concerned to ensure that they did, in fact, support Freud's analysis. So, for example, she asserted that Sergei's memory of his illness from malaria in early childhood was during the same summer as the alleged occurrence of the primal scene, as if this somehow offered corroboration of Freud's construction of it. Freud wrote, "Probably for the very reason of this illness, he was in his parents' bedroom." Nothing in Sergei's recollection made Freud's supposition into a fact. He wrote, "I . . . have retained the memory of one attack. I dimly remember that it was in the summer and *I was lying in the garden*, and although I had no pain I felt extremely miserable, because of the high fever, I suppose" (*ibid.*, p. 19, my italics). He wrote no more about it. It may be that this rather vague recollection is more characteristic of the memory of an eighteen-month-old child than the one Freud had attributed to him.[1]

In the Obholzer conversations he rebutted Freud's interpretation of the Wolf Dream entirely and claimed that "It's very far-fetched" (Obholzer, 1982, p. 35). He also asserted that, in reality, viewing the primal scene as an infant would have been improbable

> . . . because in Russia, children sleep in their nanny's bedroom, not in their parents'. It is possible, of course, that there was an exception, how do I know? But I have never been able to remember anything of that sort . . . He (Freud) maintains I saw it, but who will guarantee it is so? *That it is not a fantasy of his?* . . . I cannot believe everything Freud said, after all.

> I have always thought that the memory would come. But it never did. [*Ibid.*, p. 36, my italics]

Freud supported his interpretations with copious details of the primal scene (Freud, 1918b, p. 37). It is as if the multiplicity of such details could somehow quell any doubts. Could it really be possible that, twenty years later, the Wolf-Man could convey those detailed recollections in his associations during his analysis, and then somehow forget all about them when writing his memoirs, even though they had been continually refreshed?

There is also a difference between Sergei and Freud about the implications of the influence of the English governess, Miss Oven. It was claimed by the family that Miss Oven was the cause of the dramatically changed behaviour of the infant Wolf-Man. He, in his memoirs, repeated the claim, as if he had never heard of Freud's refutation of it. He had always been a phlegmatic little boy, he wrote, until the governess arrived in the summer when he was 3½, (in a later addition, 1924, to his paper, Freud altered the time of the incident setting off Sergei's neurosis from 3½ to 3¼, so before the arrival of Miss Oven) and at the same time that his parents were going away for their usual summer tour. He was left at home with his sister, his Nanya and the governess. His maternal grandmother was left with the task of supervising the governess and his Nanya, which she failed to carry out adequately. From the beginning Miss

Oven and his Nanya were at loggerheads, mostly because the governess, who might have been alcoholic, initiated angry quarrels with his Nanya in his presence. He wrote,

> . . . angry quarrels broke out between Nanya and me on one side and Miss Oven on the other. Evidently Miss Oven kept teasing me, and knew how to arouse my fury, which must have given her some sort of sadistic satisfaction. [Gardiner, 1973, p. 20]

Freud dismissed this explanation on the grounds that, while he accepted the story of the transformation of the child's behaviour, it could not be a consequence of the governess's influence because ". . . the Englishwoman was sent away soon after the parent's return, without there being any consequent change in the child's unbearable behaviour" (Freud, 1918b, p. 19). His refutation is far from convincing, but his explanation was much more complex and depended on the application of his theories of sexual development, and his interpretation of the events as bearing the meanings he claimed.

The difficult behaviour, according to Freud, began with what he called the seduction of Sergei, when he was 3¼, by his sister, Anna, about which he, Freud, had absolutely no doubt. Its timing was crucial, but it was changed by Freud in 1924 so that it was not coincidental with the arrival of Miss Oven. How, in 1924, could Freud be more certain of this date than in the original that he had written soon after the termination of the analysis in August 1914? He had already asserted (*ibid.*, p. 14, fn.1) that it had been "possible later to determine almost all dates with certainty". How this might have been done is not clear, when, according to Freud, Sergei's knowledge of himself was considerable, but disconnected in terms of time and subject-matter. The earlier time supports Freud's construction and theory and was, of course, preferred, but there is nothing in the account of either Freud or his patient that established the time with the accuracy that Freud believed. Sergei, in Obholzer's transcription of his conversations with her, accepted the idea of seduction by his sister, but said nothing about its timing. He did, however, claim that his sister's rejection of him later in adolescence was the cause of subsequent problems about his choice of sexual partners, which continued into his eighties, and had never been cured by psychoanalysis (Gardiner, 1973, p. 20).

There are two things to be considered about Sergei's relationship with his sister. First, he was very rivalrous with her for their father's love, feeling that she had replaced him as the boy in the family so far as his father was concerned.

As an infant he had greatly admired his father and wished to be like him, but his love was not reciprocated because Anna had displaced him. Second, the story of the seduction related to two incidents—the showing of their bottoms on an occasion when they were in the lavatory together, and another occasion at about the same time when his sister had grasped his penis, giving rise to fears about castration, reinforced by his Nanya's threat when on another occasion he displayed his penis to her, as Freud's theory claims. Sergei makes no reference to either of these incidents, but it may be speculated that Anna's displacement of him with his father may have been as significant in his sexual development.

So, although the account of the unprecedented naughty behaviour of the child was the same, the ascription of the cause was quite different. Here again there is a conflict about the timing of the interaction between the two children, not only in relation to the seduction, but also in respect of Anna's teasing Sergei with a picture of a wolf. The timing of Anna's teasing him with the picture was not given, but Freud seems to have assumed that it was during, or before, the seduction (thus before the arrival of the English governess). Sergei, in his memoirs, related it to Miss Oven's sadistic teasing. He wrote, "Anna began to imitate Miss Oven and teased me, too" (Gardiner, 1973, p. 21). He continued by describing the actual event as he remembered it. Anna had promised to show him a picture of a pretty little girl. She covered it with a sheet of paper, when she uncovered it revealed a picture of a wolf standing on its hind legs, with its jaws open and about to devour Little Red Riding Hood. He began to scream and had a temper tantrum. "Probably", he wrote, "the cause of this outburst of rage was not so much my fear of the wolf as my disappointment and anger at Anna for teasing me" (*ibid.*, p. 21). So, in Sergei's account, it was clearly after the arrival of Miss Oven and not before. It was important for Freud's theory that the priority of the seduction and the castration complex should be firmly established so that the change in the patient's infantile behaviour could be disconnected from the arrival of the governess. Perhaps those incidents were of less significance to the patient himself, but it leaves a question about how much of Freud's reconstruction was conveyed to Sergei at the time of the analysis.

There seems to be some correspondence between the accounts of Freud and Sergei over the question of castration anxieties, and their consequences for the significance of the relationship between him and his father. Freud claimed that these anxieties stemmed from Sergei's alleged observation of the primal scene at the age of eighteen months, and his subsequent phantasy of being loved by his father in the same way that he had seen his father making love to his mother. Castration was both wished for and feared, but in both accounts it seemed as if father's love was more important to Sergei than the love of his mother. He described in his recollections of his childhood, before he was five years old, that he loved riding on his father's pony, sitting in front of him. He wrote no more about it but it might be regarded as some confirmation Freud's view that he had had an unconscious wish to be sexually used by his father, but it does not necessarily support the interpretation that it was a wish to take his mother's place in the assumed observation of the primal scene. In fact, as noted above, Sergei's father much preferred Anna, regarding her as if she were a boy. By contrast, it was said of Sergei that he should have been a girl. Did Sergei wish to be treated by his father like Anna, rather than his mother?

Freud had also written that the Wolf-Man's chronic constipation was a defence against his homosexual impulse towards the father, and that it had been cured when, in the famous phrase, "his bowel began, like a hysterically affected organ, to 'join the conversation' . . ." (Freud, 1918b, p. 76). The Wolf-Man, however, continued to suffer from chronic constipation to the end of his life (Obholzer, 1982, p. 47), and claimed that it had been caused by the prescription of drugs to cure his gonorrhoea, which had damaged his bowel, so there has to be some doubt about Freud's claim of a cure.

In his letter to Freud in 1926, he refers to memories related to castration provoked by a recent dream. One memory referred to his learning about operations performed on stallions, and another about ". . . my mother's story about a kins*man* born with six toes, of which one was chopped off immediately after his birth." (*Psychoanalytic Quarterly*, 1957, p. 450, my italics). Freud referred to the same incident in his account, but described the person to whom it had happened as a "female relation" (Freud, 1918b, p. 86), from which it was deduced that "Women, then, had no penis because it was taken away from them at birth" (*ibid.*). It is not clear from the account whether it was Freud or Sergei who had misremembered, and made this deduction. A careful reading of the whole paragraph in Freud's account suggests that the conclusion may have been Freud's supposition to confirm his theory. In his letter to Muriel Gardiner in 1957, Sergei expressed surprise at the extent that he had written about castration in the letter of 1926, and related it to the paranoid feelings he was experiencing during his analysis with Ruth Mack Brunswick at that time, rather than to childhood incidents as related by Freud.

Whatever the importance of the castration complex may have been, there can be little doubt that the Wolf-Man had a passive and compliant attitude towards men. This was illustrated by the strong influence that his male tutors had in his later childhood and adolescence, and by his continued reluctant compliance with two male analysts from the 1950s until almost the end of his life. They were evidently objects for the displacement of his wishful feelings about his father at a time when he believed that Anna had been the object of their father's interest and love. It is worth noting that, in the first instance, the male tutors had been engaged for his sister's tuition. Their presence and encouraging relationships with Sergei had a very profound effect on his behaviour. Freud was also the object of the same very powerful feelings. Might it not be that the discrepancies between these two accounts are a consequence of Sergei's compliance with Freud, so that he may have been experienced by Freud as assenting to those constructions in the analysis, when he may have simply been attempting to retain Freud's love? His transference to Freud, which never seems to have been worked through even at the end of his life, may have been the healing influence, such as it was, rather than the elaborate construction Feud made in his famous paper.

Ruth Mack Brunswick, in her analysis, claimed that the ambivalent father transference to Freud was a very significant aspect, which she had been able to resolve. She reported that in his unconscious phantasy Sergei had very angry, even murderous, wishes about Freud and herself. Sergei is reported as having said to Freud that after the end of his analysis in 1914 he had tried to wrench Freud out of himself, but he had been unsuccessful. During his writings about himself after Freud had died he seems to have been struggling with his ambivalence about father/Freud, and wishing to free himself. Magid believed that he had been left, after the forced termination, in a turmoil of fear of abandonment and desperate, frantic placation and compliance by Freud from which he never freed himself (Magid, 1993, p. 175). He may have been impeded in that by the continuing interest of the psychoanalytic community in him, and by the feeling that he was the most favoured son. Despite Ruth Mack Brunswick's claim that she had successfully dissolved his transference to Freud, in Sergei's conversations with Obholzer there was ample evidence of his continuing ambivalence about it.

The final material relevant to Sergei's story in his own words is contained in Karin Obholzer's publication of his conversations with her during the last years of his life (Obholzer, 1982). Obholzer reported that because of the Wolf-Man's debt of gratitude to his analysts, and the fact that he was financially dependent on the Freud Archive, she was not allowed to publish these conversations until after his death. Additionally, Eissler was against any publication on the grounds that only psychoanalysts were qualified to have any opinion on these matters (*ibid.*, p. 10); a somewhat arrogant dismissal of Sergei's own views and the public's capacity to understand those matters. In the transcripts of those conversations Sergei appears as an embittered man whose profound ambivalence about Freud, psychoanalysis, and the psychoanalytic world is plain. Some of the strength of that feeling is about his failure to have resolved his dependence on Freud and other psychoanalysts. He was especially critical of the idea of transference, and described it as dangerous, commenting that he had relied too much on others, and had lost in the end (*ibid.*, p. 46). None the less, whenever he felt himself to be in difficulties he sought out another psychoanalyst. In this he seems to have repeated a syndrome that was evident in his choice of tailors, dentists, doctors, and sexual partners, both during his marriage and after his wife's death.

Ruth Mack Brunswick had noted his repetitive behaviour of this sort with all those who provided service or treatment for him. Her account of him in her analysis comes closer to the personality disclosed in the transcripts of his conversations with Obholzer than that which appeared in Freud's story. She commented on the differences she found in him, in contrast to Freud's account of him

(Gardiner, 1973, p. 303). She described him as "being guilty of innumerable minor dishonesties", including accepting money under false pretences; and instead of being domineering with women was then completely under the control of his wife, even though he often resorted to prostitutes. This last characteristic as very evident in his conversations with Obholzer, where he frequently talked with her about his inability to terminate his relations with women whom he felt had exploited him for money, and their control of his relationships with them. He blamed his relationship with his sister, Anna, for his problems with women and complained that psychoanalysis should have been able to cure that, but that it had not and his life had been ruined as a result (Obholzer, 1982, p. 117).

The story of the Wolf-Man as told by himself, by Freud, by Mack Brunswick, and by Gardiner raise interesting questions about the nature of the concept of "cure" in psychoanalysis, about the implications of transference, which has played a more and more significant role as psychoanalysis has developed, and about the significance of the discordant agendas of the patient and the therapist, as displayed in Sergei's accounts of the analysis.

Note

1. Freud first claimed that the primal scene was an actual event; then that it was the result of adult imagination attributed to the early stage; and then that it was a phantasy.

CHAPTER SEVEN

HD (Hilda Doolittle)

Introduction

HD was a poet, born in 1886 in Pennsylvania to parents who were members of a Moravian community in which her maternal grandfather had been pastor. She was the only surviving daughter after her sister and half-sister had died in infancy, and the youngest child, alongside her four brothers (three half-brothers and one full brother). She felt that she was a misfit, and out of place in the family; and unable to feel acceptable to either parent. Friedman commented that, "Not a son and not the right kind of daughter for either parent, the child Hilda was caught in a bind of disapproval" (Friedman, 1981, p. 26). This may have been an important element in her bisexuality. From an early age she was interested in her dreams, fantasies, and a mystical access to the past. Her writings and poetry have been considered important in the study of the place of the female analysand in psychoanalysis, and of feminism, as well as being artistic productions in their own right. Some of her writing seems to have been a continuation, in another form, of the work of her analysis with Freud.

She had many lovers of both sexes after giving up her studies at Bryn Mawr. She married Richard Aldington and had a stillborn baby while he was away at the front in the First World War. Her eldest brother was killed in that war, and her father died soon afterwards. Her daughter, Perdita, whose father was Cecil Grey, was born in 1919. She formed an intense and long-lasting relationship with Winifred Ellerman (Bryher), sharing Bryher's husbands with her and allowing her and one of her husbands (Macpherson) to adopt Perdita when she was afraid that Aldington might kidnap her.

Throughout her life HD published poetry and novels that reflected her struggles with love, sexuality, birth and rebirth, and her preoccupation with communication with the dead, which were all part of the Moravian tradition of her mother's family. Her poems and other writing have been regarded as important contributions to the literature of feminism. She was aware of the various theories of homosexuality through her friendship with Havelock Ellis, and her analyses with Chadwick, Sachs, Freud, and Schmideberg, but her views about her own bisexuality were not limited by those analytic experiences.

Bryher was very supportive of her need for analysis and had introduced her to psychoanalytic thought during the 1920s. They carried on a daily correspondence about the sessions with Freud while they were in progress, as well as other matters (Friedman, 2002). Bryher additionally also wrote to Freud from time to time, since she was seeking to be allowed to train as a psychoanalyst. Bryher, intimately involved with HD's analysis with Freud, sometimes seemed to be as an alternative analyst for HD. The splitting of the transference in this way perhaps reflected her unresolved experience of being between her two parents. Bryher was also paying Freud's fees for his analysis of HD, whose analysis with Freud lasted for about three months in 1933, and at the end of 1934 for about five weeks.

Her experiences in those analyses were recounted in her *Tribute to Freud* (HD, 1985), which consists of two parts entitled "Writing on the wall" and "Advent". The book was described by Ernest Jones as ". . . surely the most delightful and precious appreciation of Freud's personality that is ever likely to be written." Bonnie Kime Scott (1995) has written that some of HD's work was concerned with an endeavour to escape from the influence of psychoanalysis and that she had revised "Freud's role as an analyst to something more like a medium" (*ibid*.). Two years after ending her analysis with Freud in 1934 she entered analysis with Walter Schmideberg until 1938. Friedman has written extensively about HD's work, life, and analysis (Friedman, 1981), and has published a volume of her letters written to Bryher and others while she was in analysis with Freud (Friedman, 2002).

HD's accounts of her analyses with Freud

HD published two accounts of her analyses. The first, written in 1944, was reminiscence and a reworking of the analysis with Freud ten years before. It was published during 1945–1946 (HD, 1970). Its title, *Writing on the Wall*, refers to an incident in her first analysis when she recalled hallucinating pictures appearing on the wall in a room where she was staying in Corfu. While preparing *Writing on the Wall* she had been unable to read the diary, from which the entries were later assembled for publication under the title of *Advent*. In 1948, she recovered her diary from Switzerland, where she had left it, in which she had recorded some material from each day's session, including her subsequent associations to it. These diary entries were concerned only with the sessions during March 1933. Freud asked her to stop writing them, although there were two brief entries for the two final sessions on the 14th and 15th June 1933. Susan Friedman claimed that the diary as published was not the original, which had been lost or destroyed (Friedman, 2002), presumably after it was recovered post-war. Both accounts were published together in America in 1956 and subsequently in the UK in 1970. There was a further account of her analysis with Freud, also written contemporaneously with it, contained in letters to Bryher (*ibid*.). Friedman thought of these various accounts as being like a palimpsest representing various levels of the analysis. She wrote that,

> Taken together, *Tribute to Freud*, *Advent* and HD's letters to Bryher represent a layered palimpsest of maternal transference in prose, one whose revelations and concealments reproduce the contradictions of women's public and private speech. [*Ibid*., p. 315]

In fact, the daily letters to Bryher were often mildly mocking of Freud. They also contained lots of gossipy material about the other events of the day and their friends, but they may have served as a counterpoint to the analysis and to the transference to Freud. Bryher was herself a part of the psychoanalytic community and well versed in the concepts and ideas of psychoanalysis. HD wrote later that Freud thoroughly approved of Bryher "who had been in the analysis all along" (*ibid.*, p. 50).

Much of what HD wrote during her life after the analysis has been considered to be both a continuation and revision of it, and her work contains many themes that had appeared in the analysis. They have been thought to be a counter to Freud's emphasis on the primacy of the masculine, and an assertion of the feminine values. They represent what I have called a discordant agenda. What is very characteristic of her writing, not only about her relationship with Freud, is the freely associative and poetic style that she used. Her thoughts seem to follow an unconsciously determined path and, in consequence, have a poetic significance in which multiple meanings are implicit in words and sentences leading to delightful and intriguing changes of imagery. An example occurs in her account of her session on the 6th March 1933. She wrote,

> I recall the Phoenix symbol of D H Lawrence and of how I had thought of the professor as an owl, hawk, or sphinx-moth. Are these substitutions for the scripture hen gathering her chicks? My daughter was born on the last day of March with *daffodils that come before the swallow dares* out of *The Winter's Tale*. Richard had brought me many daffodils, that English Lent-lily. [HD, 1970, p. 135]

The second sentence seems to have provoked a thought about her own "chick", which in its turn may have been prompted by the bird images in the first sentence. Moreover, the symbol of the phoenix, of rebirth, may link with the thoughts in the final sentence about Lent, Easter, and the resurrection. Underlying these associations may have been her unconscious preoccupations with birth, life, death, and rebirth, and the significance of the mother.

Advent, edited by HD in 1946, consists of notes written contemporaneously with the first analysis but covers only one third of it. Her letters to Bryher should be considered in conjunction with those notes, and together they form a coeval account of an analysis as it proceeded. As the quantity of material is so voluminous, for the purposes of this study, rather than track the analysis day by day, or week by week as has been done by Lohser and Newton (1996), it will be considered in terms of various aspects of her account, as far as possible in the terms she herself wrote.

Beginning

HD had for some time been considering the possibility of analysis with Freud to help deal with her writer's block. She had read some of his publications, was familiar with his ideas, and had been briefly analysed by Mary Chadwick and Sachs, who had recommended that she should seek analysis with Freud. Bryher urged HD to seek to be analysed by Freud, and arranged to pay Freud's fees for her. At the end of 1932, arrangements were made for HD to begin analysis with Freud on the 1st March 1933. Even before beginning, HD had, in fantasy, been forming a transference to him, as well as preparing herself for the sessions. From the end of February until mid-June 1933, HD lived in a small hotel in Vienna, enabling her to attend for five days a week. There were to be no demands on her time other than that required for her psychoanalytic hour. So she had time to write letters to Bryher daily, telling her about her sessions with Freud, and at least for most of the first month to compile a diary about her sessions, adding further associations later in the same day. In her first period of analysis, her life was almost exclusively concerned with it.

The story of her first session on 1st March is different in her diary entry than in her letter to Bryher on the same day, as well differing from the *Writing on the Wall*. In her letter she describes how frightened of Freud she was. She went on to refer to the presence of Freud's chow, Yofi, in the room, who had trotted towards her as she entered. In *Writing on the Wall* she wrote that Freud cautioned her that Yofi might bite her as she was a stranger. She was incensed by that, and was determined to show Freud that the dog would not treat her like a stranger; when she patted her Yofi did not bite. She wrote that she had been overwhelmed by Freud's consulting room with its antiquities. She did not want to lie on the couch, but she began to talk about her work with Mary Chadwick and Sachs. Freud immediately interpreted that she was disappointed in him. She denied it, feeling desperate. He reinforced the interpretation by saying that she was the first person who had looked at his pictures "preferring the shreds of antiquity to his living presence" (Friedman, 2002, p. 34). Then she yelled that his dog had liked her, and would not have liked her if he, Freud, had not. The session continued with her sobbing and trying to assure Freud that she was not disappointed in him, that in looking at antiquity she was really looking at him. She was terrified by his hammering on the couch cushion to emphasize his comments. Nevertheless, she felt that, by the end of the session, she had won by convincing him that she was not disappointed in him, although she still felt the session had been awful because of her sobbing, in a way that she hadn't with other analysts.

Freud's collection of antiquities made a profound impression on her and became the material for mythic associations in later sessions. He showed her a Vishnu figure and a small statue of Pallas Athene, which he said was perfect, but *"she had lost her spear"* (HD, 1970, p. 69). In this comment Freud was beginning to introduce his phallocentric concepts of castration and penis envy without making a direct interpretation. She did not respond. Later she discussed the incident without any reference to castration or penis envy (*ibid.*, p. 69), but the italicized words make it clear that she understood its implications. Her silence may have indicated her reservations about them. She described Freud as being like a curator in a museum, and later as the "sphinx moth, the death-head moth".

Although she continued to feel scared of him, by the end of the first week she was beginning to feel more settled, but, as Friedman says, there were signs of resistance already appearing. Perhaps ambivalence might describe it better and it was well conveyed by a comment she made in *Advent* as having "a center, security, aim. I am centralized or re-oriented here in this mysterious lion's den or Aladdin's cave of treasures" (*ibid.* p. 132). Her accompanying references to Lawrence's hostility to psychoanalysis and to Freud himself may have been unconsciously prompted by her darker feelings. Although, on the one hand, idealizing Freud, on the other, as the above comment suggests, she was inclined to be mildly mocking of him. "Anyone who gets within ten miles of Papa", she wrote in her letter to Bryher on 4th March 1933, "is a sort of mind God-in-the-making" (Friedman, 2002).

Transference and countertransference

HD began the analysis with a very powerful transference to Freud as the father. Her letters contain many examples of her idealizing associations. One appeared in her letter to Bryher, 15th March 1934, where she wrote that Freud was Jesus after the resurrection; he had passed the tomb. "He is the absolute inheritor of eastern mystery, and majic [sic] and is the absolute final healer." In another letter she again called him a latter-day Jesus who wished to rationalize the miracle. However, she oscillated between that and a suppressed or displaced negative transference. Her interaction with Bryher in her letters during the first of the two periods of her analysis seems to have been a displacement of some aspects of her transference, with elements of it only partially presented to Freud.

Freud responded with an idealizing countertransference regarding her as a talented student, and expressing admiration for her status as a poet. HD, too, believed she was a student of psychoanalysis, and hoped that she might be able to practise when her analysis ended. She felt embarrassed in one session when he told her that she had a rare kind of mind. She wrote to Bryher that, having been used to "man-brutality via Angleterre", it was more frightening to be told flatteries than to have a brick flung. He, rather seductively, also told her that through his work with her he had discovered a new idea that completed his theory of sexuality, namely, penis envy, but that he was not yet ready to write about it.[1] Friedman has pointed out that this claim was not true, since the concept had already appeared in some of Freud's previous writings. HD was uneasy about this development and wrote to Bryher on 3 May 1933 that they (she and Bryher) had to feed the light, but would find their niche in astrology.

More significantly, Freud identified her with his daughter, the beautiful Sophie, who had died of influenza in the post-war epidemic. She had given birth to the much-loved grandson, Heinele, who had also died while still an infant. The illness and death of Sophie had occurred at the same time as HD had been pregnant and suffering in the same influenza epidemic. In an early session Freud had shown her a photo of Sophie, which he kept in a locket on his watch chain. This particular aspect of the countertransference was complicated by the fact that his dog, Yofi, became pregnant and gave birth to two puppies during the first period of HD's analysis. Freud wished to give her one of the puppies, and it seemed symbolic of a wish to provide a replacement of the lost baby to the phantasied Sophie in HD.

Her negative transference seems to have been displaced on to her anxiety about the danger to Freud from the rising Nazi menace, with evidence of demonstrations on the street, and on one occasion by there having been chalk swastikas drawn along the pavement to Freud's door. She had been unable to mention that to him. Although they sometimes discussed the political situation, she was only rarely able to say anything about the events going on in the Viennese streets, which she found very alarming. Equally, her preoccupation with death was another factor that caused her some anxiety about its possible effect on Freud. His seventy-seventh birthday was celebrated during the first period of her analysis, and she was particularly conscious of his frailty and illness. It seemed that she feared he would be damaged by her. She recalled an occasion when her father had been injured in an accident when she was only ten years old. She wrote in *Advent*, "I have been frightened, I do not want to mention blood to the Professor. I opened the front door, ran out to welcome my father in the dark and found blood on his head, dripping . . .", and later she wrote, "How can I tell him of my constant pre-vision of disaster? It is better to have an unsuccessful or 'delayed' analysis than to bring my actual terror of the lurking menace into the open" (HD, 1970, pp. 138–139).

Some of HD's very early responses to Freud were closer to a replication of her relationship with her own father, of whom she was rather scared because of his remoteness, and whose scientific interests she could not understand. In *Tribute to Freud* she described how in some ways her father's study was like Freud's, with a similar stove and a collection of objects (although not antiques) on his table. He, too, had a couch on which he sometimes lay, as she was lying on Freud's couch. The transference as father was, however, displaced by a transference to Freud as mother. Freud interpreted that she had come to Vienna, her mother's honeymoon venue, in search of her mother. He also interpreted that her Greek travels in 1920 were a similar search for her mother.

This seems to have been the beginning of a very significant conflict between them about whether the relationship with mother was more important than with father in psychic reality. HD always wished to assert the primacy of the relationship with the mother. However, she found the idea of Freud as a mother figure unsatisfying. So did Freud. She recorded that he said, "... I do *not* like to be the mothering transference—it always surprises and shocks me a little. I feel so very masculine" (*ibid.*, p. 146, original italics). His concern about the maternal transference may have had some resonance with Klein's developing ideas about the good and bad breasts, and the significance of the mother in infantile development. At about this time, a rift with the London group of psychoanalysts was beginning. The relevance of the rift to HD's analysis may be demonstrated by the fact that Bryher, in March 1933, gave a significant sum of money to the Vienna group, rather than to the London group. HD recorded that Freud was very touched at the time, and wrote to Bryher to say how gratified he had been by the gift (letter to Bryher, 27 November 1934).

So, while it was important for Freud to maintain his stance that the primacy of the father, of the penis, and the normalcy of the male body were the ideas which mattered, contrasted with the castrated female body, HD reserved her position. She recorded several times, in various places, that Freud was not always right. In her poem, "The Master", written some time after her analysis with Freud had ended, she wrote,

> I was angry with the old man
> with his talk of man-strength,
> I was angry with his mystery, his mysteries
> I argued till day break ...
> ... woman is perfect. [1935]

This was what was being conveyed by her throughout the analysis, as she resisted Freud's theoretical stance, sometimes passively, sometimes actively. At the end of this first three-month period of her analysis she commented that Freud had to stick to his scientific guns, and that she had to stick to hers.

During the second period of the analysis, five weeks from the end of October 1934, she did not leak so much of it to Bryher in her daily letters. It was also clear that, although the experience was very intense, it did not occupy as much of her waking time as had the first period. It is, however, evident that her intense involvement with Freud did not alter her ambivalence about the interpretations he made to her. She wrote,

> ... the Professor was not always right. That is, he was always right in his judgments, but my form of rightness, my intuition sometimes functioned by the split-second (that makes all the difference in spiritual time computations) the quicker. I was swifter in some intuitive instances, and sometimes a small tendril of a root of the great common Tree of Knowledge went deeper into the subsoil. [HD, 1970, p. 98]

Earlier, in *Tribute to Freud*, she had written that there was an implicit argument in their very bones (*ibid.*, p. 13).

She made much more of her astrological interests and in an early letter to Bryher (5 November 1934) she wrote, "Papa, by the way, sneers at my astrology, but it makes me more SURE it is right. One wants both, I feel, to temper one with the other. But papa sneers so." She made comments of this kind several times and evidently regarded astrological signs and mythology as supplementary to, and in a sense a completion of, psychoanalysis. Added to this she thought of dreams as arising from a deep common strand of consciousness, rather reminiscent of Jung's idea of the collective unconscious, although she attributed this idea to Freud himself.

During this time Freud was interpreting her material in terms of his basic theory of the importance of sexuality in general and masculine sexuality in particular. Towards the end of the twenty-five sessions, he interpreted a dream she had told him as a manifestation of the primal scene, and that all her problems arose from that fantasy. There had also been other manifestations of what could be thought of as primal scene material before that. It seems likely that HD, while recording his interpretation, had some reservations about it, and understood her bisexuality, less in terms of identification with one or other of her parents in the primal scene fantasy, and more in the sense of the loss of both parents. She now knew that she had to be both woman and man.

Writing on the Wall

The hallucination of the images on the wall took place in a hotel in Corfu at the end of a sea voyage with Bryher in 1920, following HD's illness and the birth of her daughter. Friedman believed that some sexual intimacy may have occurred between HD and Bryher while they were in Corfu. HD said later, in a letter to Plank, that she had had a lovely relationship with Bryher, although it had not lasted long as Bryher had been utterly unresponsive. The evidence that the relationship with Bryher was particularly intense during this holiday may be inferred from the fact that Bryher shared the experience of the pictures on the wall by completing the final images, although she had not been able to see the first images.

The experience is described very fully in *Tribute to Freud* (*ibid.*, pp. 41–56), but only very sparsely in her letters to Bryher. In those letters she recorded only some of Freud's comments on the experience, but none of her own reactions to them. This is also true of her brief references to the experience in Corfu in her diary during the first month of the analysis. In *Tribute* she began with Freud's description of the hallucinations as a danger signal, although she did not understand, even after ten years, why he had thought of them in that way. The images were of the same clarity as an early dream of the Princess that she had reported to Freud in one of her early sessions. These images she believed were also like those of psychics and clairvoyants, and she seemed to describe them as being, at least superficially, outside the established province of psychoanalysis. She did record that Freud had interpreted that they were the expression of a desire for union with her mother. He had made a similar interpretation in general about her trip to Greece, associating it with its Hellenic name, Hellas, and with her mother's name, Helen. He also admired the complexity of the images, which he thought demonstrated a complexity of unconscious thought, as well as being a poem sequence that had not been written (letter of 19 March 1933).

As HD began to hallucinate, Bryher was present but could not see the images herself, although HD spoke about them to her. They began with a flat silhouette of a face of a soldier or an airman, who might have been anyone, but seemed familiar, suggesting a dead brother or a lost friend. This was followed by a goblet as large as the face, suggesting a mystic chalice. Then a design formulated itself in perspective in the shape of a tripod, like a spirit lamp they used to heat water (a *Spirit-lamp*). She thought of it as the tripod of classic Delphi, the venerated object of the cult of the sun-god, and a symbol of poetry and prophecy. The images, she thought, might be a sign, a warning or guiding sign, and became anxious. Parenthetically, she wondered in 1944 whether Freud had been right about their dangerous nature. She wrote that actually he had been, "though we sometimes translated our thoughts into different languages or mediums" (*ibid.*, p. 47).

After consulting Bryher, comparing her to the Delphic Oracle, she continued, writing that their hopes to visit Delphi had not been realized because of Greek unrest at that time. Had she had been able to walk along the sacred way she would have been made better from her illnesses. Delphi was the symbol of prophecy, prophetic utterance, occult or hidden knowledge. As Delphic utterances could be read in two ways, so could the images on the wall. They might be some unconscious communication from within, suppressed desires for forbidden signs and wonders, suppressed wishes to be a prophetess—to found a new religion. Or, perhaps, merely an extension of the artist's mind, a poem, or an over-stressed, high-powered idea, "a 'freak' thought that had got out of hand, gone too far, a 'dangerous symptom'" (*ibid.*, p. 51). Further images were like a ladder (Jacob's ladder), and figure of Niké, the winged victory, together with images like a military encampment, which she thought foretold a victory in the future, another war, after which she would be free.

She was then unable to continue, but she wrote that Bryher began herself to see another picture, without having seen any of the preceding ones. Bryher saw a sun disc containing the image of a man who was reaching out to the winged figure, and drawing her into the sun disc beside him. Until this last image, HD felt that she had to hold on for fear that she would miss the meaning of the whole if her concentration lapsed. She had to be immersed in it as if drowning, and would then emerge, not dead to life, but with a new set of values.

This was a very important experience, which had haunted HD ever since 1920, and she had hoped that Freud would somehow lay it to rest. In fact, she believed that he was the only one who could.

It is interesting that she made no mention of any interpretation that would have exposed its unconscious sources, beyond that of seeking a union and identification with her mother. The idea was certainly a possibility. Both Bryher and the Pythoness of Delphi were women with whom she wished to identify, perhaps a displacement for the identification with her mother. That she was able to recall the experience in such detail ten years later is not very surprising, but her understanding of it is in terms of classical mythology, and of prophecy. These are almost Jungian, rather than Freudian, ways of understanding the material, and it is noteworthy that she almost always understood her phantasies in that way, rather than in terms of Freudian sexual symbolism and development. The wished-for union with the mother was not in terms of a wish to own the penis and to take father's place with mother, nor even to take mother's place with father. Friedman claims that this was an unspoken feminine revolt against Freud's concept of masculine primacy, which enabled HD to find his analysis so invaluable (Friedman, 1981). She was able to discover and sustain the importance of her own femininity, and her bisexuality, because of Freud's emphasis on free association, allowing her to explore freely her own thoughts, and to accept or reject Freud's interpretations. Freud's own understanding of the infant's early sexuality as bisexual was a significant element in her capacity to resist his claims of the inevitable triumph of genital heterosexuality. So, in her recollection ten years later, the identification of the woman in classical and mythological terms remained the basis of how she understood the hallucination of the writing on the wall. The significance of her search for the mother was a matter about which she differed from Freud, and its importance to her was repeated throughout her analysis with him. She felt that it was the source of creativity and imagination, while Freud thought of it as the earliest stage of sexual development.

Dreams

Her account of Freud's concept of the significance of dreams and dreaming can be found in *Tribute to Freud*. She wrote that Freud

... had dared to say that the dream had its worth and value in translatable terms, not the dream merely of a Pharaoh or a Pharaoh's butler ... but the dream of everyone, everywhere. He had dared to say that the dream came from an unexplored depth in man's consciousness and this unexplored depth ran like a great stream or ocean underground, and the vast depths of that ocean was the same vast depth that today, as in Joseph's day, overflowing in man's small consciousness, produced inspiration, madness, creative idea, or the dregs of the dreariest symptoms of mental unrest and disease. He had dared to say that it was the same ocean of universal consciousness, and even if not stated in so many words, he had dared to imply that this consciousness proclaimed all men one; all nations and races met in the universal world of the dream; and he had dared to say that the dream-symbol could be interpreted: its language, its imagery were common to the whole race, not only of the living but of those ten thousand years dead. The picture-writing, the hieroglyph of the dream, was the common property of the whole race; in the dream, man, as at the beginning of time, spoke a universal language, and man, meeting in the universal understanding of the unconscious or the subconscious, would forgo barriers of time and space, and man understanding man, would save mankind. [HD, 1970, p. 71]

She continued in a similar vein for a further section in the book, but it is doubtful whether Freud himself would have recognized this description of his ideas. He had belatedly included in *The Interpretation of Dreams* a section on symbolism in dreams, but he did not make as large a claim for them as HD had. As with other passages in *Tribute to Freud*, this account seems to resemble Jung's thought. In this case, HD seems to have been almost echoing Jung's ideas of the collective unconscious and archetypes. Interestingly, in this excerpt she refers throughout to the "conscious" and "consciousness", rather than to the "unconscious" that was Freud's great discovery. During her two periods of analysis HD recorded thirty-one dreams in all. In only a few did she include Freud's interpretations of them. She occasionally said that Freud asked her to interpret her own dreams, but it may be that she had misunderstood that he was asking for her associations. Whichever it was, she usually recounted the dreams, sometimes continuing with her own associations, and sometimes mentioning a comment made by Freud. Three of her dreams seemed to have had special significance, and of one of them ("The Princess") she said had broken the back of the analysis. As that dream occurred towards the end of the second month of the first period, it may have been a little early to have made such a dramatic comment. They are discussed in the order that they occurred, beginning with one she called the dream of "The Princess".

"The Princess"

This early and very important dream was evoked by Freud's showing her his collection of antiques in another room. Since many of the items in the collection were Egyptian, they aroused reminiscences about her own visit to Egypt, as well as a dream about the story of the Princess's discovery of Moses in the basket. They disagreed about whether HD was the baby in the basket, or another, older child, Miriam, who was visible in the bulrushes in a biblical picture, called "Moses in the Bulrushes", in her childhood home. He interpreted that she wished to be Moses, a boy and a hero. But it may be that this important dream represented a more profound element concerned with the significance of the mother (the Princess in the dream) rather than the masculine identification offered by Freud. His reported interpretation may have been an attempt to apply to HD his concept of the primacy of the masculine, the significance of penis envy, and other elements of his phallocentric theory of sexual development. It may have also been related to ideas about his own identification with Moses that he had written about previously (Freud, 1914b), and that he was pursuing at that time, later published as *Moses and Monotheism* (1939a).

In *Tribute*, HD described the Princess dream as the most luminous and clearly defined of all the dreams in the analysis. Ten years later she was able to recall it in detail. The image of the Princess was most vivid, as well as the idea that the baby in the bulrushes would be found by the Princess. She was not sure whether Freud's interpretation of her wish to be the baby was right, but she wondered if she had a deeply unconscious wish to be the founder of a new religion, perhaps one in which the mother was an important figure (like Nut in Egyptian mythology, giving birth to the Sun God, Ra, every morning). Freud had himself identified with Moses, who, although not a founder of a new religion, was the dominating religious leader of the Israelites in the wilderness. HD sensed that in this wish to be a founder of a new religion, she may have had some unconscious rivalry with Freud. So the dream of the Princess may have announced the beginning of the rivalry with Freud over the question of male or female primacy. In the notes in *Advent,* made at the time, she wrote that she was not the baby in the basket, nor the founder of a new religion, "Obviously it was he, who was that light out of Egypt" (Friedman, 2002, p. 212). Additionally, she mentions in connection with this dream her sense of rivalry with a real princess, Princess Marie Bonaparte, whom Freud called "our Princess". She wrote, "But is it possible that I sensed another world, another Princess? Is it possible the I (leaping over every sort of intellectual impediment and obstacle) had not wished only, but *knew,* the Professor would be born again" (HD, 1970, p. 39, original italics). Perhaps this last sentence suggested that she felt that Freud might be a new Messiah, to be reborn after death, like Jesus.

Some of her associations about Marie Bonaparte, written ten years later, suggest that an interpretation of oedipal rivalry might also have been relevant. In fact, she had preceded those associations with some recollections of sitting with her father in his study holding a doll, calling it a triangle and a trinity following the recognized religious pattern (*ibid.*, p. 38). So, while this may be seen as an oedipal triangle, she had moved it on to another plane.

The beautiful dream (24–25 April)

This was followed by what she described as a beautiful dream. It involved Bryher, wearing smart clothes and earrings, taking her to visit a romantic young Prince who worked on a huge farm and lived in a dark old palace. Billows in a river loomed up, and small white steers, bulls and cows, emerged like wavelets. The Prince appeared and invited Bryher and HD indoors. (She interjected here that the bulls were not phallic, but their emergence from the river had poignant significance.) Others were present, and sat with the Prince, who was drawing with crayons.

> HD found herself in another room and saw herself naked in a sequence of mirrors. She saw that her front was like her back only smaller—and

the mons venus [sic] was like tiny buttocks—"majic [sic] mirrors". She wished to get away before the owner of the room awoke. She felt ecstatic about the discovery of herself—a Virgin in the "majic mirrors". Then she found herself in another room with heavy Victorian furnishings, and a church bazaar. Two Siamese cats were at large. She was frightened and wished that Bryher would come and buy one for her. She recalled that she had had two kittens which had torn her life to shreds.

She found herself outside the house where a gang of workmen were busy. They were dangerous men armed with pick-axes and spades. The head of the gang told her she could go through the tunnel in a train, and helped her on to one. She gave him a half-schilling, with which he was not pleased. She gave the guard a whole schilling—was it a tip or the fare and would he give her change if it was the latter? She felt mean. She got out and walked into a room near, or above the station, where Perdita, about two years old, was with HD's mother and aunt who were looking after her. Both were in black, and HD felt approved of. Perdita was in white. She left the house, and felt that she had broken, or quarrelled, with them over Perdita.

Then she was on a third train [she had not mentioned a second] whose guard seemed to approve of her. Papers were scattered on the seat, as on the tables at the café where she had coffee in reality. Would she have a "left" or "right" paper? The guard handed her a "white" or "right" paper and she felt pleased. At last she was at the place she had been trying to get to, and Bryher was there to meet her. Bryher asked Freud if he would dine with them in a fashionable, gay [in its old-fashioned sense] restaurant as it was his birthday. HD was surprised by that, but Freud accepted with alacrity. Mrs Freud was there, too, in a new hat, and HD was concerned about not having enough German to be able to talk to her.

She interpreted the dream for herself in astrological terms. Her vision in the mirrors, Freud interpreted, was the desire to be Venus, although she denied that and wished to be the Virgin. Virgo was the astrological house of her own birthday in September. She changed her mind the next day and agreed with Freud, although in astrological terms, because the room with the sleeping man and the naked woman was the astrological house of marriage. Freud said that they were both right. She went on to interpret other aspects of the dream astrologically without any reference to Freud's concepts of infantile sexuality, or to the oedipal theory. She felt there may have been a number of other combinations "yet with universal astrological symbolism" (Friedman, 2002, p. 212).

The prologue to the dream she associated to the cold distant father whose interest in astronomy frightened her. Other images in the dream "removued" (*sic*) the fear. The remaining mystery was recognized in the romantic interpretation of the star values. She claimed that Freud agreed with her interpretations, especially where they seemed to refer to himself as the Biblical dream interpreter, Joseph. "The oxen tremble" was the slogan or a great discovery, as the bulls trembled at the name of Freud, "the great discoverer of a new life, the prophet Joseph, the prince in the dream in disguise". The bulls may have been the milky way—mother bulls. HD interpreted that the bull-cows represented her desire to be impregnated by Sigmund Freud (the father–mother); the twin cats were Yofi's twins and she was the cat (in fact she signed all her letters with the name Kat, sometimes illustrated with a drawing of a cat).

In a postscript she referred to Egyptian symbolism with Bryher as the Moon and Freud as the Sun—mother-bull and father-cow. The trio was Bryher, Freud, and herself as the child. But she complained of having dreary feelings of pregnancy—a crisis in excelsis—and had linked up the simple facts of life with the stars. Finally, she interpreted the three trains as three men, Aldington, Grey (who had brought her through the tunnel to a new life), and Freud. At the end of her account of this dream she wrote that she had put Freud back with his wife in her new hat.

All of these images were, of course, susceptible to other interpretations, but it is clear that she did not fully subscribe to whatever Freud's interpretations may have been, except in respect of the wish to be impregnated by him, which may have been a consequence of Freud's own countertransference involving his feelings about his daughter, Sophie.

The primal scene

This dream occurred about two weeks before the end of her second period of analysis with Freud at the end of 1934. Although very brief, the analysis was very intense, as well as being more contained within the sessions. She had been fantasizing about oedipal material in the sessions preceding the dream. She wrote about it in her letter to Bryher on 19 November 1934. It was a terrible dream about Aldington, her husband, being in bed with Bryher. Aldington shot Bryher and then himself. She felt agonizing grief that Bryher had been killed. She interpreted it for herself that it was a dream about the primal scene. She wrote that the father–husband killed the mother by shooting her in bed. It also tapped into her war phobia, although she did not elaborate on this. Other associations followed about Freud as the father. She felt that she had linked it all up with the usual text book primal scene material. The death of the mother seemed to be related to fears about HD's own death because of her oedipal wishes to have a son with another man, which would have meant death. She later referred to the wish to have a golden Christ child "off the Christmas tree" but that meant the primal scene, and being killed by a man, the father. Through the use of religious symbolism she translated it into astrological representations, the wished for son became a sun-symbol, a gift of the father (God gives his son). Her father gives her, a Virgin aged seven, a son or SUN. There was no fight or rivalry with mother. She herself is a divine child born in Bethlehem. "I AM", she wrote, "born in Virgo though Freud discounts the astrological" (Friedman, 2002, p. 212). It is interesting that although this was recorded as primal scene material, Freud had not interpreted it in terms of fantasies about parental genital sexuality as he had for the Wolf-Man's dream.

In the penultimate week of her analysis, she referred again to this dream and seemed to be reporting Freud's interpretation that the dream explained everything in her life from masturbation to her mystical experiences in Cornwall and Corfu, to her anxiety about the possible kidnapping of her daughter, and to her war phobia. It is not evident that HD agreed with that, and she continued by saying that she had experienced the loss of both her parents so had identified with both in a bisexual way. She knew that she had to be both (as a result of the analysis?) and would work it out in writing. As was her custom she subverted Freud's thoughts with some of her own, and attributed them to the analysis.

Freud's unorthodoxy

It is evident throughout the various accounts that HD wrote of her interaction with Freud that he frequently behaved in a very unorthodox way. Although HD had not undergone any process of selection, Freud told her that he regarded her as a student, and that he preferred working with students than with patients. He talked with her about his own family, and notably about his daughter, Sophie. He told her how anxious he was about his grandchildren as the Nazi menace developed. He sometimes mentioned his other patients, and, for example, told her that he was very disappointed with Dr Wortis, whose analysis overlapped with HD's second period of analysis in 1934. He showed her some of his antiquities, and sometimes took her into another room to see some of them. What it may have meant to leave the couch, and the room, during a session was apparently never referred to by either Freud or HD. He told her that he did not value a gift given to him by some of his Indian students. He encouraged her to borrow some of his books. At the time of his seventy-seventh birthday celebrations he gave her some of the many flowers he had received as gifts. Many of these incidents might have been seen as enactments of Freud's counter-transference, although HD made no mention of any discussion of the various incidents in those terms, except perhaps in the incident of the offer of the gift of a puppy born to Freud's chow, during the first period of her analysis in 1933.

The place of Freud's chow, Yofi, seems to have been very significant. It was always in the consulting room and in the very first session Yofi played a significant role in the transference–countertransference interaction. HD made several references to Yofi in her accounts of her sessions and in her letters to Bryher. Yofi may have had some special significance for her in that she used animal nick-names for her friends and acquaintances. HD always signed herself as Kat, and heard from Macpherson that chows were thought to bite cats. She never told Freud about her nickname.

More importantly, when later Yofi was asleep and dreaming in the consulting room, making moaning noises as she did so, Freud explained that the dog was pregnant, and was having many strange dreams. She was startled by this news. Freud went on to tell her about Yofi's previous pregnancy, and that the pup had died about nine months later. Soon after this announcement Yofi gave birth to twins. A few days later HD wrote that she had dreamt that she had taken a bag of sweets from Freud to give to a child. Freud had interpreted that the bag of sweets was a uterus symbol, and that she was afraid of becoming pregnant by him. The following day he told her that he only wanted to keep one of the twins, and asked her if he could give her one of the puppies. She did not want to have the dog but could not think how she could refuse. She almost immediately began to feel as if she was pregnant, and this feeling seems to have persisted for several days. She realized that the issue of Yofi's pregnancy, and the offer of gift of a puppy, was something to do with Freud's identification of her with his daughter, Sophie, and a symbolic re-enactment of the events at the time of Sophie's death and the birth of Freud's grandson. The puppy may have symbolically represented Sophie's son, Heinele, who had tragically died at the age of four.

There were important issues for HD about pregnancy, birth, life, and death. She wrote in her letter to Bryher (27 April, 1933) that in a horrible dream, during the night before, the puppy equalled death, impregnation, and so on. Nothing of this appears to have been raised in the analysis. The problem of how to refuse the offer was the subject of many anxious exchanges between HD and Bryher for several weeks, and was eventually resolved when the unwanted male twin went to another person.

Friedman (2002) describes the offer of the puppy as an element in the gift exchange between Freud, HD, and Bryher. The reciprocity of that exchange was represented by the gift of money from Bryher and the offer of the puppy in return, and by the verbal exchange of gifts in the analysis with Freud. HD reciprocated with the epic dream of 24–25 April. Other dreams, in Friedman's view, represented a ritual circuit of emotional bondings and obligations symbolized by the "gifts". While on some deeply unconscious level that may have been true, nearer to the surface was the identification with the dead Sophie and Freud's grandson, and the fearful repetition for HD of her anxieties about her wartime and post-war experiences, evoked by the birth and offer of the puppy.

The place of Yofi in the consulting room and the analysis did not end there. At the beginning of the summer Freud and his family moved to their summer residence, and the analysis continued there. The conditions seemed more relaxed than in Vienna. Both Anna and Freud took their dogs with them, and Yofi continued to occupy her place in the consulting room, although without the puppies, who were kept in the garden. In one of HD's sessions, Anna's dog, Lun, invaded Freud's consulting room during the analysis. A dog-fight ensued. HD recorded that

> Yofi flew at Lun. Freud flung himself on the floor between them. I thought he would be torn to pieces, and Anna tore in screaming "papalien belovedest, thou shouldst not have done that." I rushed in Yofi's way and got Lun by the fur, and the maid intervened, and there was Freud sitting on the floor with all his money rolling in all directions under the still blooming orchids. Very funny. And tragic. … Shows just how terribly young he is—a born fighter, so frail. [Friedman, 2002, letter dated 18 May 1933]

Yofi and Lun were finally removed, but how the session continued is not recorded, and there appears to have been no reference to the incident in subsequent sessions. Or, at least, none was recorded in the subsequent letters to Bryher, which contain the only contemporaneous record of the analysis for this period.

It is possible to conclude that despite the unorthodox conduct of the analysis, perhaps even because of it, HD and Freud continued to hold each other in high and warm regard. HD's references to astrology were interwoven with references to classical Greek and Egyptian mythology and antiquities. These accorded with Freud's own interest in those matters, and with his references to his collection of Greek and Egyptian antiquities. So he may have been able to tolerate HD's discordant agenda, and her use of astrological material in her understanding of her dream symbols, even when he did not agree with her. All of that may have helped HD to feel quite safe with him, and to develop a capacity to disagree without fear of ridicule or rejection, sharing very deep thoughts and feelings, including her feelings about her fundamental bisexuality. He, too, was able to maintain his respect for her, as well as his total commitment in their sessions. So, despite the discordant agendas evident in this account, it was this mutual respect, coupled with the security of the boundaries of the sessions (with the exception of the invasion by Anna's dog), rather than their recorded content that enabled HD to gain from the analysis and to continue to work on its the material in her subsequent published work.

Note

1. Friedman discussed this in *Psyche Reborn* (1981) and questions whether this claim was true because Freud had written many times about female sexuality and the idea of penis envy was at least implicit in those texts.

CHAPTER EIGHT

Dr Joseph Wortis

Introduction

At the time of his analysis Wortis was married, and his wife was with him while he studied in London and Vienna with Havelock Ellis and other eminent psychologists and psychiatrists, as well as with Freud. Before his marriage he may have had some sexual encounters with other young women, to which he made some passing references in his account of his work with Freud. Very little about his childhood and family life is mentioned in the record of his analysis. After leaving Vienna, he practised as a psychiatrist and neurologist in America and published about seventy articles in scientific journals, but it is evident that his practice was uninfluenced by Freud's theories or by his experience of analysis with Freud. His most important contribution to psychiatry was the introduction in America of shock treatment for schizophrenia.

He wrote that his book about his experience with Freud excluded personal material because the book was not about him, but about Freud and his theories (Wortis, 1954), although his account can hardly be regarded as a serious critique of them. On grounds of privacy, and the protection of others, he excluded much personal material, but so far as can be told he was also very economical about it in the analysis itself. The analysis was described as didactic by both Wortis and Freud, although Freud at one point said that it was no different from an ordinary analysis. During its course Wortis regularly wrote an account immediately after each session, on 4 × 6 inch record cards, in a nearby coffee house. Although it may be relevant to consider how far notes of this kind are veridical accounts of what occurred, particularly where they record Freud's own words, they may be little different from those provisional case notes made by therapists following a session. These notes were published in 1954, twenty years later than the events they described. It is not known how much they had been edited in the process of publication. As HD had done, Wortis published a further note about his views of Freud's theories and practice with his memoirs. Unlike those of HD, these comments were much more critical than the contemporaneous material.

The analysis

Wortis had a particular interest in homosexuality and this was one of the reasons that he sought an analysis with Freud. It was not consciously because of any personal concern about homosexuality, but so that he could learn something about it, for professional reasons, from Freud's theories of sexuality. It may have been that there were unconscious anxieties about his own homosexuality but these did not emerge in the analysis, although he had frequently argued with Freud about his theories concerning homosexuality, and whether or not it was harmful. Wortis used Freud's idea that homosexuality was a universal part of individual sexual development to argue that it was only repressed because of social antipathy, rather than because of any inherently undesirable characteristics. Freud regarded homosexuality as one of the phases in the development towards full heterosexuality, so it meant that homosexuals were developmentally arrested or had regressed. Sexuality could only be healthy when it was expressed genitally between men and women. But so far as Wortis's notes go, Freud did not directly interpret the anxiety about homosexuality.

The sessions took place daily from early in October 1934 until the end of January 1935. Since Wortis was fluent in German, the analysis was conducted in that language, but his notes were written in English. He was evidently ill at ease from the beginning and was anxious that he might become concerned with unpleasant retrospective thoughts leading nowhere. It quickly became evident that he had reservations about free association, and argued with Freud about whether it was really possible. The stream of associations would, he thought, be influenced by Freud's presence as well as by the kind of material he knew Freud would be expecting to hear. Although Freud had disagreed with him, Lohser and Newton (1996) point out that Freud himself had made the same observation in "An autobiographical study" (Freud, 1925d). Wortis mentioned that Freud's chow sat at the foot of the couch, but he did not make as much of this as HD had, apart from commenting on one occasion that Yofi had sat licking her genitals. He sent Freud a greetings card at New Year 1934 containing his drawing of himself, lying on the couch, with Freud sitting behind, and Yofi sitting at the foot of the couch, but he could not mention the dog in his associations. In an early session, when Wortis was obliquely expressing some anxiety about dependency, Freud interpreted that there had to be an element of dependency in all relationships "even with a dog" (Wortis, 1954, p. 23).

Frequently Wortis would defend himself against the revelation of painful feelings and experiences by denial. He apparently also denied the significance of psychic factors by claiming that neurosis was a maladaptation between the individual and the environment, and that it could be cured by external changes. He claimed not to have any neuroses himself, at any rate not at that moment, although he believed he had cured himself in the past when he had taken up his first hospital post. Despite that, he was concerned lest the analysis might bring to light some latent schizophrenic tendencies that he feared he might have inherited, while denying that they were significant.

He dealt with this anxiety by trying to turn the discussion into an examination of Freud's theories. Freud interpreted, rather sharply, that Wortis had a way of leaving the solid ground of fact for generalities unintelligible to Freud, and to lose himself in abstractions of which he (Wortis) had no knowledge (*ibid.*, p. 30). In

Wortis's account, Freud frequently adopted a rather caustic tone in his responses to him, and in return he complained of Freud's criticisms of him. Wortis's defensiveness evidently irritated Freud, and he rapidly became disenchanted with Wortis as a patient. HD reported that Freud had told her during her second set of sessions which overlapped with Wortis, that he (Freud) was disappointed in him. That disappointment and irritation was very evident in many of the sessions.

This was even more evident when issues about homosexuality were raised. Wortis denied that he was in any way personally concerned about homosexuality, and regarded it as simply a choice of sexual expression that could be made, quite rationally, without harm to the individual, perhaps using a strong intellectual defence to ward off his anxiety about homosexual wishes. Although Freud seems to have made no interpretations about that defence, Wortis, in fact, adopted a powerful argument in favour of the expression of homosexual behaviour, claiming that it was no less natural than heterosexuality, using Freud's theoretical papers asserting that a homosexual phase in infancy was universal. Wortis argued that there was no ground for its repression if that was the case, nor for any kind of social or criminal sanctions, which were a consequence of irrational prejudices. It might have been expected that Freud would have attempted to explore Wortis's defences against his unconscious anxieties, whether or not his intellectual arguments were sound in themselves. If Wortis's record was correct, it produced from Freud an increasingly didactic response about the necessity for the repression of homosexuality, claiming that all social structures depended on the sublimation of homosexuality. Wortis wrote (*ibid.*, p. 100) that Freud believed that, "Our entire government, our bureaucracies, our official life, all operate on the basis of homosexual impulses, which are of course unconscious and not manifest . . .". If this were not so then havoc would break out, Army discipline could not be maintained; moreover, homosexuality had been found to be universally undesirable, even in Classical Grecian times. Even more surprising was Freud's claim that if homosexuals were allowed to be teachers they would prefer certain pupils for emotional reasons "and the best students would not get scholarships" (*ibid.*, p. 124). Freud also claimed, without citing any evidence, that most English schoolboys had homosexual experiences, but got over them. Homosexuality in adults, Freud had asserted, was an example of pathologically arrested development, but it could only be cured if the patient wished to change, but its repression was essential. It should be noted that this is a much more precise claim than that sublimation of impulse is generally socially desirable.

In the course of this discussion Freud launched into an attack on sexual mores in America. Wortis recorded him as saying that men in America did not know how to make love because they had no premarital experience. In contrast, European men took the lead, and that was how it should be. Wortis timidly asked if it would not be best if both partners were equal? That was a practical impossibility; the superiority of men was the lesser of two evils, said Freud. The American woman was an anticultural phenomenon (*ibid.*, p. 99). Unsurprisingly, Wortis wrote that he had left that session feeling confused.

From Wortis's account it seems as if Freud became increasingly critical of him as the analysis proceeded, and that he particularly disliked being involved in arguments about his concepts and theories. Wortis felt that he was being unjustly criticized by Freud if he tried to raise what he felt were conventionally appropriate scientific questions about Freud's theories and methods. At an early stage, Freud interpreted that Wortis's interest in abstract questions was because he was not interested in himself.

The issue of resistance had been considered earlier in the analysis, and it had been regarded by Freud as an essential element in the process. Freud had commented that neurosis might appear in analysis if it was rooted in the personality, but then it could be cured. It was clear that Wortis had been anxious about the possibility that he might be unconsciously neurotic, and he frequently sought reassurance from Freud that he was normal and healthy. Freud's comment led Wortis to confess that he was afraid of his unconscious. Freud's response to that confession was to threaten to conclude the analysis immediately, if that was how Wortis felt (*ibid.*, p. 58). A few sessions later, when Wortis was again wondering if the analysis was not progressing, Freud agreed suggesting that they should continue for a further two weeks, and then stop if there was no improvement. Without any further discussion of the issue the analysis continued until its arranged termination date two months later.

At the end of the third month, with one further month to go, Freud became extremely angry with Wortis, who claimed that he would have to learn to analyse himself. According to Wortis, Freud burst out that he had no right to do that, he knew nothing about it and was a "bloody beginner" (*ibid.*, p. 128); Freud would disclaim responsibility for him if anybody asked about him. In response, Wortis associated to a dream in which he was running from one bus line (the Freud Line) to another bus line (the Adler Line). He did not report any interpretation to this dream, but associated it to having attended a party given by Adler's daughter, which had prompted the thought that Freud's views about homosexuality and social structure were really Adlerian. Freud responded by again outlining his views about homosexuality, psychoanalysis, and social arrangements.

Occasionally the issue of homosexuality occurred in a dream. One early dream was of a kitten licking one of Wortis's fingers. Wortis associated to his having caught his finger in the bed that night, and earned a rebuke from Freud for confusing the day's residue with the unconscious meaning of the dream. On the following day Freud interpreted that the dream represented some feminine elements, but was evidently not using any associations to reach this conclusion, and instead relied on his own version of the symbolic meaning of the kitten symbol. Small animals *always* meant females, Freud claimed. On another occasion Wortis dreamed that he had joined in a discussion about homosexuality. Freud commented that he guessed that it was engaging Wortis's attention. Wortis then tried to turn it into a discussion about sublimation. Did active homosexuals sublimate less? And why were dreams only wish fulfilments? Freud responded that dreams were different *essentially*, and not only qualitively, from waking thought (but that contradicted what he had said on the previous day when he had claimed that dreams were simply a continuation of waking thought). Wortis was hardy ever able to disclose any of his own anxieties about homosexuality, either through his dreams when homosexual themes occurred, or on any of the occasions when he talked to Freud about it in an abstract, theoretical way. On only one occasion was he able to disclose some anxiety about his homosexuality, when he dreamt that Schilder, with whom he worked, had been insane two years before. Freud asked if

Schilder's homosexuality showed and Wortis agreed that it did. Wortis himself was anxious that if he became psychotic he might be homosexual. He did not record anything further on this occasion, so that the anxiety seems to have been left hanging.

Throughout the analysis Wortis regularly reported his dreams, between fifty and sixty of them, but few of them seem to have aroused Freud's interest; or, at least, Wortis recorded Freud's interpretations on only very few occasions. Often he did not record his own associations either. The first report of a dream occurred in the record of the eighth session, after Wortis had raised the general issue of dreams and dreaming. Freud indicated that dream analysis was a basic element in the psychoanalytic process. The dream was that Wortis had embraced Freud's servant girl, and that Freud had been scandalized. He recorded no associations, and Freud had simply replied that "That dream is not of much importance, but we shall see" (*ibid.*, p. 35). There was no further reference to it in subsequent sessions. In view of Freud's insistence on the importance of dreams in psychoanalysis, this response seems surprising. It does not accord with Freud's view of the importance of even trivial associations as having relevance in the exploration of unconscious meanings, whose significance might lie hidden beneath apparently insignificant material.

A second dream was mentioned in the following session and was about Havelock Ellis and his wife, Françoise. In the dream Wortis was talking to Ellis and his wife. While he was doing so, he noticed that a large number of foreign-looking men and their wives were coming through the door, and into the kitchen. He thought, how would so many people get into the small house? It would burst. His only association was to his belief that Françoise was sexually interested in him. Freud's interpretation was that while some of Wortis's interpretations were correct (although Wortis did not mention any), others were hidden because of his prejudices. The dream was an anxiety dream related to a hypochondriacal idea, although Freud did not say what that idea might have been. In the following session, Freud interpreted that the servants entering the house might refer to Wortis's brothers and sisters entering the womb. Equally, the thought of Ellis's wife having a sexual interest in him was oedipal. Wortis regarded that as all rather farfetched.

In a series of sessions early in the process it is possible to see something of the struggle going on between the patient and the psychoanalyst through successive dream reports. Wortis began by reporting a dream that was directly critical of Freud and psycho-analysis. He had dreamt that he was attending a lecture in psychi-atry given by Professor Meyer, who wore bourgeois side-whiskers and looked older than he was. In his associations he equated Meyer with Freud, whose psychology, Wortis said, was bourgeois. Freud indignantly refuted this by saying that science could not be bour-geois because it was only concerned with universally true facts. It is noteworthy that both Freud and Wortis ignored two other dreams referred to in this session, which might have been more productive in terms of Wortis's own psychology. (They were, first, of walking with his father in the cold; and second, of his landlady, who had murdered her Negro woman servant.) In the following session, one of a number of dreams involved Wortis's hospital work and his giving a poor patient a sum of money, either 65 groschen or 3 schillings 65 groschen. Freud took up the reference to figures and said that numbers were always significant. In this example, they might mean the days of the year. Wortis responded to the word "year", and thought that it meant that he was concerned with how many years his present work might last, and how long it would it would take to cure the neurosis he had thought he had. But he noted that he did not think that those associations had anything to do with the dream.

In the next session, Wortis reported that he had dreamt that his landlord, who resembled Freud, had told him that he must leave as he had been wandering the house at night like a criminal. Associating to a remark of Freud's that it did not matter if the patient was a saint or a criminal, he felt that Freud thought he was more a criminal than a saint, although he might be industrious and talented. He thought that Freud was not very interested in him, and that he (Freud) sometimes forgot things. He went on to enquire of Freud whether he thought that the cause of homosexuality might be found by neuro-anatomy, and this was related to lectures he was having with Professor Marburg. By way of conciliation, Wortis said that he was very pleased with his analysis, and his early problem had cleared up. Freud expressed some reservations about that, and interpreted that a previous dream of walking with his father, and another of talking to a London policeman, might have had homosexual implications. The session ended with both expressing some satisfaction about the analysis. Freud thought Wortis was cooperating more and not being so critical (*ibid.*, p. 69). Briefly, they shared a feeling that they were working more productively.

The accord was rather short-lived, and in a session where Wortis was enquiring about the difference between a didactic and an ordinary analysis, Freud interpreted that Wortis was asking where they were getting in his analysis. He further interpreted that they were not getting very far, and that Wortis was a "so-called" normal person, but that he was too contented with himself. In a following session, Freud and Wortis agreed that little or no progress was being made and that perhaps the analysis should end in a couple of weeks. Wortis tried to insist that he had characterological problems, but Freud made no comment until the following session. He then interpreted that while Wortis was consciously self-critical, unconsciously he was proud, complacent, and resistant to analysis despite his respect for Freud. Wortis reported that he left that session feeling depressed and discouraged.

A dream in the twenty-ninth session, which involved Wortis's wife operating a fish-chopping machine, was interpreted by Freud as meaning that Wortis felt that he was being put through the works in the analysis. He went on to interpret the symbolism of the fish as a well-known penis symbol, but apparently had not interpreted anything about castration fears. Since Wortis did not record any of his associations, if, indeed, he had made any, Freud seemed simply to have relied on his own understanding of the symbolism, derived from folklore, philosophy, and dreams, to reach this conclusion. Wortis evidently criticized Freud's interpretation. Freud rejected his criticism, and told him that he was too young to have ideas about it (*ibid.*, p. 83). While thanking Freud for this explanation, Wortis recorded that he left the session in distress as he did not believe in the theory.

Perhaps because Wortis was sceptical about free association and was not good at producing associations to his dreams, Freud may have felt he had no alternative but to make use of the meaning of symbols to help Wortis to get in touch with his unconscious thoughts. This appeared to make the interpretations rather prescriptive, not arising from the patient's personal unconscious in a way that might have made them more integrated with the material, and less like an abstract exercise. So, for example, Wortis reported a dream of sitting with his wife in the gallery of a theatre, watching a man in military costume doing tricks with a sword. During the performance, looking down, he feared he would fall, and called out to his wife for help. Freud disagreed with the thought that the dream meant that Wortis feared that there might be a war. He went on to interpret that sitting in the theatre meant watching coitus and feeling frightened, as children were frightened by witnessing the primal scene; a drawn sword meant sex; and falling was a symbol of femininity and birth, with which he thought that Wortis identified, and was disturbed by it. He added that dreams occur more among men than women, and more among heterosexual men than others. Wortis asked if that could be demonstrated statistically, but Freud's response was not recorded. Somewhat cryptically, Wortis wrote that he had never seen coitus (*ibid.*, p. 85).

Many dreams, or the interpretations of them made by Wortis, were dismissed by Freud as being too thin, or not in accordance with Freud's theories. Wortis's interpretation of a dream of being shot in the street by a detective as meaning "that I am being threatened and told unpleasant things in analysis, but I don't care and go my own way" (*ibid.*, p. 95) irritated Freud. He said that this attitude made further analysis impossible, but nevertheless continued for the remaining thirty sessions without any greater success in coping with Wortis's persistent negative transference. Freud apparently treated this as recalcitrance, and on one occasion advised Wortis to learn not to argue back; that he should accept things he was told, consider, and digest them. Those problems, he interpreted, were a consequence of Wortis's narcissism and unwillingness to face unpleasant facts (*ibid.*, p. 115). Wortis, in fact, agreed with Freud about his narcissism, wishing that analysis would help him to deal with it. Freud's criticisms of him did nothing to assist him to come to terms with it, but often made him tell Freud how much he respected him personally, perhaps, in he hope that Freud would reciprocate.

On one occasion he told Freud that he was our greatest psychologist. Throughout the analysis Wortis craved for Freud's love, but persistently aroused Freud's ire by arguing about his theories, asking for the kind of scientific proof that Freud was unable to provide. Neither Wortis nor Freud seemed able to turn from the rather sterile conflict in which they had become embroiled to an exploration of the personal meaning of this interaction; the foundation of the clinical process.

An illuminating example of the way in which a promising start somehow failed to lead into the deeper unconscious meaning of dream material occurred on 20 December 1934 (*ibid.*, pp. 113–114). Wortis, noting that Freud was in a "very good mood indeed", reported a dream of being on a skiing trip with his wife. Freud asked, "Are you planning to go skiing for the holidays?" This encouraged Wortis to say more about the dream, and in particular that the snow on a distant peak gave way and slipped. He thought that the dream meant that there was a contrast between danger and peace; danger in the distance and peace with his wife. He added a further interpretation that it meant "perhaps fancifully, annoyance with the analysis but inner peace and love anyway". Freud, he recorded, accepted his interpretation on the basis of his associations. Wortis then went on to say that the interpretation corresponded to his feelings about Freud, who did not treat him nicely, although that, perhaps, was his own fault. He should not judge Freud by his behaviour towards him; he might be quite different with others. Wortis respected him highly as a scientist. He thought Freud had approved of what he was saying. Freud then made it clear to him that he was not interested in criticizing or changing him, but in teaching him and removing impediments standing in the way of instruction. The session continued in this vein without reaching any illuminating insights. The difficulty with didactic analyses, Freud said, was that there were no symptoms to provide for convincing demonstrations.

The session having begun well, in Wortis's view, ended in some discontent about his narcissism, which he would be very glad to give up, he claimed. "That would be altogether desirable", Freud replied, rather tartly. Perhaps in this session what I have called discordant agendas were most evident. Wortis's agenda was to understand Freud's theories. Freud's agenda was to teach about psychoanalysis through experience of the process and not by examining the theories in an academic way.

The sessions during the last month of the analysis (January 1935) seem to have been anticipating the ending, with Wortis raising general issues rather than focusing on his own psychological issues. The sessions were devoted more and more to abstract discussions about their differences over the normalcy of homosexuality, about the nature of Jewishness, about the antagonism that he perceived between different schools of psychoanalysis, about the value of organic methods of treatment for psychological disorders, and sometimes to challenging Freud's psychoanalytical ideas, suggesting that they might be related to Freud's own psychopathology. More of Wortis's dreams seem to have had a manifest heterosexual content than in those he reported early in analysis. It seemed that he might be withdrawing from his preoccupation with homosexuality. Wortis said that he did not intend to work with sexual problems, or with homosexuality, in the future. He told Freud that Mrs Wortis was pregnant, to which Freud responded by saying that it was high time, but apparently made no attempt to explore Wortis's unconscious reactions to the event. In their manifest content, however, Wortis's dreams frequently contained references to sexual intercourse with others than his wife. Perhaps there was not time to explore their meaning, and Wortis himself made no connection between his wife's pregnancy and the wish for sex with other, non-pregnant, women.

The analysis petered out rather than ended. In the last few sessions Wortis expressed his concern that he had not benefited as much from psychoanalysis as he could have done. In a dream of saying good-bye to Freud in a friendly, informal manner, he felt like a bad schoolboy. His guilty feelings came from the sense of not having done well in analysis. Freud asked why he thought that, but Wortis did not record his own reply. As a parting gift, instead of a photograph that Wortis had asked for, Freud gave him an autographed copy of one of his books.

Wortis, like HD, wrote an additional note about his experiences with Freud at the time of the publication of his original record. Unlike HD, Wortis's additions were far from a paean of praise of Freud's influence upon him and his life. It was in fact a reasoned critique of the assumptions on which psychoanalytic theory rested, and a rejection of Freud's technique. He was firmly against the location of problems of neurosis and psychosis in the individual in isolation from the social and familial world. In that he appeared to be adopting the views of the object relations theorists, but he equally rejected those views on the grounds that they, too, had adopted the basic biologism of the classical theory in locating the object relationships internally. He also claimed that psychoanalysis had a strong class basis, and that its patients were drawn largely from the well-to-do middle and upper classes, who could afford to pay for frequent and long-term treatments. The poor, and blue-collar workers, were not to be found in the patient group of psycho-analysis, and their mental problems were more likely to be related to the impoverished social conditions in which they lived, rather than to the esoteric formulations espoused by psychoanalysis. Freud had dissented from this by referring to the opening of a clinic, and the fact that qualified psychoanalysts were obliged to take one or two patients without fee. Wortis also asserted that, if anything, psychoanalysis could at best be only a preliminary to treatment. Freud had expressed a similar view in claiming that psychoanalysis could only give insight, and the work of therapy had to be the task of the patients by themselves (Freud, 1905d). He had told the Wolf-Man that analysis was like buying ticket for a journey, which the patient had to undertake himself. The experi-ence of HD also bears this out, in that the writer's block she suf-fered at the time of her analysis was not relieved until several years after she ceased treatment with Freud, although she had, of course, continued analysis with Schmideberg during the late 1930s. The writing of her *Tribute to Freud*, many years after her analysis had ended, suggested that her continued fantasied interaction with him had enabled her to work at her problems even after he had died. Wortis did not continue the journey, perhaps because he had not bought the ticket and had been unable to give up his discordant agenda of intellectual enquiry about homosexuality.

CHAPTER NINE

Catherine Rush Cabot

Introduction

Catherine Cabot's life and very long analysis are described in a book edited and narrated by her daughter, Jane (Reid, 2001). Catherine, later known as Katy, was born in November 1894 to a family whose ancestors had emigrated to America in 1683. Her parents, who met in Hawaii in 1893, had married in January 1894. Katy spent the first six years of her life with her mother and her paternal grandmother in Philadelphia, while her father, a distinguished naval officer and recipient of the Congressional Medal of Honor, was away at sea except for a brief period of a few months ashore at the US Navy War College. For the next four years Katy lived in Paris with her mother, attending school there. For the following two years they lived in Boston, while her father was again on shore duty. In America Katy attended school, where she made lifelong friendships but also had some very unpleasant experiences with other children, which, *her* daughter wrote, ". . . tainted her view of America" (*ibid.*, p. 20).

Throughout her adolescence Katy was mostly in boarding schools in France, Germany, and Italy, while her mother joined her father in his foreign postings. In vacations Katy often stayed with school friends and their families. Although she became fluent in four languages, the frequent moves from one country to another, in two continents, "made it impossible for her to put down roots anywhere" (*ibid.*, p. 24). As Jung discovered later, she remained ungrounded.

Aged eighteen in 1913, Katy rejoined her parents in New York, where her father, having been decorated for bravery in a local action in the West Indies, was commanding the Brooklyn Navy Yard. For the winter months of 1914, Katy and her mother went to Bermuda instead of Paris. While there, Katy suffered from a depression for the first time, and then met a British naval officer, whom, she later said, she might have married had he not been killed on the last day of the First World War. Her father remained in command at the Navy Yard until 1919, although he had been due to retire three years earlier. Although Katy was able to enjoy the social life that her father's position provided, she had another, more serious, depressive breakdown with claustrophobia, and was treated briefly in a clinic. Katy's daughter, Jane, believed that this breakdown occurred because of her restricted life with her parents, with no objective other than to marry and settle down. She had had no thoughts about a career, so had not gone on to higher education; as a result her energy had turned inward.

Katy had already met her future husband, James Jackson Cabot, in 1917, but they were not engaged until he returned from war service in 1919. They married later in the same year, after she had recovered from the influenza epidemic of that time. Her husband then joined his father's firm in a low-paid managerial role.

Because of a shortage of money, Katy was unable to travel abroad to relieve her discomfort with American provincial life in Charleston, Virginia. Her daughter believed that it was this that doomed the marriage, although her parents never divorced. Jane wrote, "With no trip in view, the young couple found excitement in Boston in another direction. They decided to have operations" (*ibid.*, p. 33). With some difficulty, Katy became pregnant three years into the marriage, and Jane was born on 1 July 1923. Katy became pregnant again when Jane was four, but miscarried, later telling her daughter that, as he was a boy, she had been glad not to have had him. She had no further pregnancies.

After a short European tour with her husband and daughter, she began to spend the hot summer months at White Sulphur Springs, where she could play golf and dance. The winter months were passed in Baltimore or Washington. Her husband was often left with Jane, and visited Katy at weekends. When Katy took Jane with her, she engaged a nurse to look after her. She travelled more widely from 1927, sometimes with and sometimes without her husband and daughter. Katy and her husband made their last trip together to Hawaii at the end of 1929. Jane, aged six stayed behind with her paternal grandparents, and was discovered to have a heart disease. To convalesce, Katy took her to San Remo to stay near her parents, now living in Italy. Katy used Jane's illness as an excuse to stay in Italy and abroad for as long as she could. For much of 1929 Jane was in various hospitals having different treatments, ending up in a hospital in Zürich, where Katy, made contact with Jung, and began analysis with Toni Wolff. She also made tours to other countries after this, leaving Jane with a nurse.

While Katy was touring in Spain in 1930, she received a message that James, her husband, had been paralysed after a riding accident; developing a brain abscess as a result of the accident, he died in the same year. Katy had returned to the USA with Jane, now seven years old, to be with her husband during his terminal illness. Although short of money before her husband's estate was settled, Katy returned to Europe after the funeral, wanting to get away from the Cabot family. While living in Switzerland, but not in Zürich, she continued her intermittent analysis with Jung and Toni Wolff. When her husband's estate was settled in 1931, she received one third of it, and Jane inherited two thirds. The income Katy received from her share was insufficient for her needs, so she had to look for work. She gained an advertising contract, which paid her a large sum, using some of it to tour while leaving Jane in a boarding school.

After the death of her husband, Katy began other relationships. The most long-lasting was with Major Tommy de Trafford, an English officer living abroad and separated from his wife, a former barmaid. There were problems in this relationship with de Trafford, partly because of his wife, whom he never divorced, but also because of his diminished sexuality. Much of their life together involved social activities and touring abroad. For propriety's sake they did not live together until after the war started in 1939, when they lived together for reasons of economy. De Trafford died rather suddenly in 1942, leaving half his estate to Katy and half to his estranged wife.

All this time Katy was in analysis with Jung and Toni Wolff, but her sessions were often interrupted for long periods by her tours abroad. Even during the war years, when she elected to stay in Switzerland rather than return to the USA, she made trips to other towns in Switzerland, meeting friends and playing golf, interrupting her analysis as a result. She continued to exhibit the restlessness that had always been a feature of her life. Her daughter commented that her mother had lived in two continents but was at home in neither.

In 1943 the twenty-year-old Jane married a British officer, Pat Reid, who had escaped from Colditz, and was serving as assistant Military Attaché at the British Legation. Their first child, a son, was born in the following year. Jane went on to have three more children and broke with the family tradition, established by her grandmother and mother, of having only one child. Katy continued her round of social events, interspersed with sessions with Jung. Soon after the death of de Trafford she formed brief relationships with other men. In 1945 she began analysis with Dr Meier while resuming her interrupted analysis with Jung, as well as her social contacts with Toni Wolff. By this time Katy was being regarded as a trained psychologist and, according to Bair (2004), was practising with patients, although Katy made no mention of this in the accounts of her sessions and nor did her daughter in the Biography.

Katy resumed her journeying as soon as war was over and foreign travel became possible again, punctuating her analysis with Jung, often for weeks or months at a time. It is not clear how much of her time was spent with Dr Meier during this period. In 1947, Katy's mother died. Katy was then alone in Switzerland, as Jane and her husband had been posted to the British embassy in Turkey. The following year she took her parents' ashes to be buried in the Arlington Cemetery in Washington. A ship named for her father had been launched in 1945, and Katy kept in touch with all its captains until she died. In 1949 she "fell madly in love" (Reid, 2001 p. 559) with Vincenzo Visconti-Prasca, an Italian count, a former senior officer in the Italian army, who had fallen on hard times. He was known as Cencio, and was working as a fisherman with his own boat. When Katy first met him, he was separated from his wife. To pursue this relationship Katy began to live more in Italy than in Switzerland, losing contact with Jung and her Swiss friends. As divorce had been abolished in Italy soon after the war, Cencio could not easily get free from his marriage. Katy pressed him to seek an annulment, which he began in such a desultory way that it was never obtained. Twelve years after their first meeting, Cencio's wife died unexpectedly. Katy and Cencio married in April 1963 and she became a Contessa. Later she converted to Catholicism from a Protestantism she had never practised so that she could be buried with her husband in the family tomb. She died in 1976.

The analysis

Katy, just before she died in hospital, gave her daughter a brown paper parcel. Jane, having no idea what it was did not open it at once. When she did she found her mother's diary of her contacts with Jung written over many years. There were also many letters from Jung himself, from Toni Wolff, and Emma Jung, together with others from friends in the psychological community in Switzerland. The early section had been handwritten, and the later years were typed. When preparing the manuscript of the book for publication, Jane discovered that her mother had taken shorthand notes of her sessions while they were in progress. This may account for an impression that Jung was responding to questions with lengthy replies in many of the sessions, making them more like tutorials than analytic therapy. Perhaps Katy's note-taking prompted Jung to behave in that way in response, although Jung's use of his technique of amplification sometimes meant that the amplification was done by himself instead of the patient, perhaps giving an example for them to follow. The diary was not published immediately, but in 2001, when it would not breach any privacy since all the major participants were dead. Then the verbatim material of the sessions was contained within Katy's biography, with comments about them by Jane, who added details of her own life with her mother concurrently with the analysis.

The account is surprising, not only in respect of Jung's conduct of the analysis, but because at the same time Katy was having

sessions with Toni Wolff, which were not recorded, but were sometimes discussed in Katy's sessions with Jung. Bair, in her biography
of Jung, wrote that this experimental practice was becoming conventional and that Jung would refer his patients to a therapist of the
opposite sex, often in a quasi-supervisory way, while continuing to
work with them himself (Bair, 2004, p. 377). Additionally, Katy was
attending the Psychological Club, first as an interested individual,
and later as an elected member. Occasionally she met Emma Jung,
sought her advice, and from time to time had sessions with her.
Correspondence was exchanged with Toni Wolff, Emma Jung, and
Jung himself during the intervals in the analysis, and when she was
away abroad on her frequent trips. Jung and his family also enjoyed
many social occasions with Katy, her daughter Jane, Toni, and
sometimes including Katy's men friends. Jane commented that her
mother could not keep regular sessions with either Jung or Toni
because of her urge to fly off and not to be tied down (Reid, 2001,
p. 70). Perhaps it was defensive against her claustrophobic fears.

Although it is not clear whether all the sessions with Jung were
recorded after she began her diary in 1933, but assuming that they
were, they tended to bunch together. Their timing seems somehow
to have replicated her punctuated relationships as a child with her
mother. Her acting out in this way with Jung and Toni may have
had greater significance in the process of therapy than may have
been recognized at the time. It is feasible that Katy was behaving
like her mother, who often went off abruptly, leaving her to the care
of others. In effect, Katy was abandoning Jung and Toni as she had
been abandoned herself. Although apparently unremarked by
either of them, they were unconsciously made to be her child self
struggling with the absence of her parents. Perhaps, in reversing the
roles, she was able to master the childhood trauma.

It is not clear what the nature of Katy's contract was with either
Jung or Toni. On one occasion she complained to Jung that Toni
ought to be paying *her* twenty francs for the session. (She paid Jung
and Toni twenty francs each per session.) Her contacts with Jung
often seem to have been rather ad hoc, and on one occasion she
arrived at his house unannounced while on a journey to Bad Ragaz
(Reid, 2001, p. 44). When gaps between the sessions occurred it
seems that no fixed arrangements were made to recommence at a
later date. In one of the war years, when she was seeing Jung rather

more frequently, she wrote to him in January, having seen him only a few weeks before, that she had heard that he was beginning to see patients again in the following week and asking if he could fit her in (*ibid.*, p. 319). It is evident that no arrangements to continue after his Christmas holiday had been made in the previous session.

After September 1939, when war had been declared, the number of sessions increased, and those final months of 1939, together with the following two years, were the most intense and frequent of all her analytic sessions with Jung. Even then there were often long breaks, especially in the middle of the years. Thereafter, the sessions tailed off considerably, with only two in 1942, none recorded in 1943 and 1944, five in 1945 spread over the year, and in 1946 and 1947 only one in each year. After eleven years there was a final meeting in 1958. In all the intervals there was correspondence between Katy, Jung, Emma Jung, Toni Wolff, and some of the members of the Psychological Club.

All this may seem very unorthodox to the modern therapist, and Katy's daughter, Jane, who herself became a Jungian analyst later, commented that modern practice had become more professional. Unorthodox it may have been, even though the unorthodox may have been becoming orthodox at this time, but perhaps there was some unconscious wisdom in the process. It was as if the structure, composed of Jung, Toni Wolff, Emma Jung, together with the Psychological Club, provided a container for this very uncontained woman, who appears to have replicated in her treatment the circumstances of her infancy and childhood while gaining some understanding in her analytic sessions of the unconscious sources of her distress. During a session in November 1940, ten years after her first session with him, Katy told Jung that he had given her a good "bringing-up" (*ibid.*, p. 299), which suggests that the process of repeating it in different circumstances may have been beneficial. Jane commented that at that time the Jungian community was small, with Jung in the role of the village elder with his analysands. She wrote,

> In those circumstances it was unavoidable that personalities were discussed in analysis. What looks like idle gossip was a necessary part of the therapy. Discussions of personalities between therapist and patient may seem inappropriate today, but in the pre-war days

of analysis they were the usual thing and may well have been helpful. [*Ibid.*, p. 75]

Furthermore, it is very evident from these sessions with Jung, and from what may be glimpsed of the work with Toni Wolff in Katy's discussions about them with Jung, that the object of this therapy may have been very different from the other therapies in this book. For example, Jung was concerned with identifying Katy's psychological profile in terms of his psychological concepts: with the conscious–unconscious split-off aspects of the personality, and the compensating interaction of one with the other; and giving advice about how to deal with those issues. This seems to accord with Jung's view "that the first stage of the therapy was to leave no doubt of [the analysand's] personality and function" (Bair, 2004, p. 376). The professional issues arising from this unorthodox treatment may be worthy of further discussion in the final part of this book.

The sessions have been recorded very lengthily, and it will be possible to consider only some of the themes of the process as a whole. The very earliest sessions, beginning in 1929, were not recorded at all and were mostly with Toni Wolff, only occasionally with Jung. Katy wrote to a friend in March 1930 to tell her that she was in analysis with Jung and that it was hard work, but justified by its results. So, although there were simultaneous sessions with Jung and Toni Wolf, Katy evidently thought that it was her work with Jung that mattered. She wrote to Jung in December 1933, telling him that, although she had only seen him three times in the autumn term, she was beginning to understand what he was trying to say to her.

It was your last Seminar combined with my last hour that brought to me all that you have been trying to tell me. I was deeply touched by some of the things you said in the last Seminar, and the heart that was behind, or *in* the things you said to us that day made me realize what I was lacking. [Reid, 2001, p. 181]

Katy's relationship with Jung and Toni Wolff

Katy did not record any of her sessions with Toni, and it is not known whether they were as irregular as those with Jung. When

Katy was away from Küsnacht she saw neither of them. Although she had positive feelings about Toni, and on one occasion dreamt that she was identified with the eighteen-year-old Toni, she often complained to Jung about her relationship with her. The first reference to the work with her occurred when she told Jung of her great admiration for him and her corresponding dislike of Toni. On that occasion Jung tried to help her heal the rift with Toni. But by the end of 1933, Katy told him she hated Toni, who had said that she would not see Katy again. She had then invited Toni to dinner, and found her very cold. Jung said that she had certainly released Katy's feelings. By contrast, some time later Katy told Jung how people praised him and Toni as a magnificent team of psychologists. They laughed uproariously at Jung's response that they (he and Toni) were a good pair of horses to pull people uphill. She now thought much better of Toni without saying why her opinion had changed. Jung responded rather ambiguously to that development. In a later session, Katy referred to her jealousy of Toni's relationship with Barbara Hannah, who was another member of the Psychological Club. Katy also resented Toni's advice to marry de Trafford.

Toni's comments about de Trafford often conflicted with those of Jung. Toni had told her that she, Katy, was ahead of de Trafford and her view was that if he were to be analysed, he would prove to be empty. Toni had also written to Katy about the reason for de Trafford's reaction to the suicide of the wife of a friend. She wrote that, ". . . it happens that people just dead, draw after them another person into death, or try to . . ." (*ibid.*, p. 194). Jung, however, seemed to take a different view, and thought that Katy might be responsible for de Trafford's bad moods. He worked at the problems of her relationship with de Trafford using concepts about the unconscious interaction between couples.

At times it was also clear that Katy was feeling closer to both Jung and Toni. Toni was hosting. Katy's forty-fifth birthday celebration and had written to her about it, saying that both she and Jung would be there. Jung had said on another occasion, when Katy had refused an invitation from Toni because she had nowhere to stay, that she could have stayed at his house, since he had many guest rooms. But this sense of Jung and Toni being together for Katy was rare. More often they were at cross-purposes. In one session at the end of November 1939, Katy had asked Jung why Toni was so hard, rough, and gruff at times. He gave her a lengthy character analysis of Toni, perhaps rather inappropriately, since Katy was still having analytical sessions with her. Katy asked Jung whether he could analyse Toni and cure this aspect of her. He said that he could not because Toni was not ready for it to be tackled yet, and embellished his opinion with further thoughts about Toni's psychopathology. Katy thought she would, in future, disregard this aspect of Toni and think only of her good sides. The year's work ended with advice from Jung to the effect that she should keep an open mind about herself and to consider everything as if it might have some reference to herself, particularly in her relationships with others, instead of being just an objective matter.

Despite a dream in 1940 involving a more intimate and friendly relationship between Katy and Toni, at the end of the year Katy was complaining to Jung about Toni's being too demanding and clinging. Jung again described Toni's psychology in detail, and the way he understood Toni, but he made no mention of the nature of his own more intimate sexual relationship with her. He advised, "Never mind what mood she is in. Disregard it—for it's all vapor" (*ibid.*, p. 309). There is no record of what Toni or Katy made of this and other similar comments, or of how Katy dealt with the amount of personal information Jung was giving her about Toni, or of what might have been made of the splitting between the positive and negative transference and the projection of those transferences into Jung and Toni, respectively. In some respects, this split reflected the relationship that Katy had with each of her parents: her father, the distant but charismatic naval hero, and her mother, neglectful and unloving. Nevertheless, in spite of this splitting in the analysis, Jung and Toni remained attached in reality, and were there waiting and available when Katy returned from her many journeys and absences.

In a later session, when Katy was again complaining to Jung about Toni, the evidence of the split between the positive and negative transference was once more very plain. But Jung did not interpret that split, neither did he explore its possible sources, nor comment on the acting out of the situation with her parents. Instead, he told Katy that he had asked Toni about their incompatibility, and that Toni was impenetrable and could not see herself.

This was followed up in another session with comments to Katy about Toni's psychological condition and advice that Katy should end her analysis with her, because they both had the same "Lump". Katy wrote to Toni to say that she wanted to end the analysis with her, but in fact continued with it, telling Jung that the feeling between them was better, although Toni remained deficient in terms of feeling. That accord did not last long, partly because Toni had written to Katy chiding her for failing to attend an important meeting at the Psychological Club, of which Katy was now an elected member. After that, Katy told Jung that she would not wish to know Toni as a friend because it would mean getting behind in the dirt and becoming her charwoman (*ibid.*, p. 354). He responded by saying that the surface Toni was the best, and Katy should accept that as the real Toni, with all her faults. To establish a relationship with another, one should not wish for more than there is. Katy should also accept *herself* as she was, with all her own faults, if she was to be able to understand others. He added that he was not able, and did not wish, to discover the real Toni behind the presentation. However, Katy then invited them all, Jung, Emma Jung, Toni, and others to a meatless dinner. (A meatless day was a Swiss innovation in May 1941, to assist with wartime rationing.)

The problem about the missed Psychological Club meeting and Toni's response to it continued to rankle. Jung sided with Katy, telling her that Toni and another member of the Psychological Club should not have written to her so sternly. He said that Toni had a hell of a mother complex and Katy should stand up to her. Katy responded to that by telling him of her difficulties with her own mother. He agreed that her mother was awful.

As the difficulties about Katy's relationship with Toni continued, Jung advised her to write to Toni about her impertinence at the meatless meal. She did so, and Jung told her that he had seen her letter and Toni's reply, and had told Toni that she should not write in that way. He agreed with Katy's description of Toni as a small, frail, pathetic creature (*ibid.*, p. 362). In the penultimate session of 1942, there was a further exchange about Toni. Katy wanted to discuss her reading of *Psychological Types* with Toni, and keep it on an intellectual level, whereas Toni wished to think about it in personal terms. Jung advised her to stick to her point, and keep to the "impersonal stuff" (*ibid.*, p. 400). He made a very disparaging comment about Toni's dislike of studying, depending on her brilliant brain instead, and compared her adversely to his wife. On another occasion, when Katy complained about the way Toni always interpreted Katy's personal world, he again advised her to try and stick to the impersonal, as she did with him.

It was very clear, as her dreams and other interactions with him showed, that Katy idealized Jung and that no negative transferences were allowed to intrude. They were all split off and projected on to Toni and other members of the Psychological Club. Jung appears to have colluded with that. This triangular relationship between them seems to have been of great significance, although what Toni's thoughts about it were is not known. As has already been suggested, it may be that the interaction within the triangle was a transference from her experience with her own parents, but it does not appear that it was interpreted by either Jung or Toni.

During the later years of the analysis Katy began to refer to Jung as Onkel (Uncle), to which Jung made no objection when she used it in their sessions. This mode of address was accompanied by a protective feeling towards him, and concern about others who imposed themselves on him. This concern may have been related to her parents' absences, feeling unconsciously resentful that they were responding to the claims of others on them, rather than to her own. Jung made no reference to that, however, simply agreeing that others did impose themselves upon him, and did not really appreciate him. She asked Jung, when he said he was ahead of his time, how he felt about not being able to leave a successor to continue his work. He replied that his books and papers would serve to pass on his ideas to succeeding generations and that he had no need of an heir.

The "Lump"

One recurring matter was Katy's problem with the "Lump". It seemed to be a profound and dynamic unconscious condition, whose source and substance she could not describe. It was first mentioned in the earliest recorded session in May 1932, when she wrote that she was beginning to see Jung more often to help deal with it. She used the term to describe her basic psychological condition, which was causing her to have panics. Perhaps the term "complex" might also have been applied to it. She once referred to its getting loose and rolling around, like an inherited, unassimilated piece, playing imp-like tricks and ruining things. Jung interpreted its contents in different ways at different times. Importantly, he thought it contained her unconscious wish for, and claustrophobic fear of, containment, the counterpart of her conscious wish to be free and unconstrained. It might also have been seen as an inter-action between claustrophobic and agoraphobic fears. He related it to her frequent conscious fear of riding in a funicular, where her unconscious fear of containment was tempting her to jump out of such an enclosed space. In one session, Jung referred to her anxiety in the funicular as resulting from her parents' neglect of her, evok-ing an ambivalent wish for containment, but he believed it was leading her to express its opposite consciously in her many travels (*ibid.*, p. 121). That feared descent in the funicular, he interpreted, was symbolic of her descent into the collective unconscious where she would lose her personality and be indistinguishable from any of the others who would be there (*ibid.*, p. 362). She was also enclosed in the human body, from which she could only be freed in death, which accounted for her ambivalent fear of dying, mentioned once in a dream. Jung, somewhat enigmatically, twice wondered what the "Lump" might do to her when she died.

Jung also told her that the "Lump" contained many aspects of her shadow side, some of which she did not know about, as well as her sexuality. He urged that she *must get the shadow out* (*ibid.*, p. 91), and that the way she could do that was to write her fantasies down so that she could know herself without self-consciousness. Other unconscious aspects of her psyche also seemed to be contained in the "Lump", and included negative aspects of her animus. Jung commented that the birth of the animus in the analysis was often preceded by feelings (anxious disturbances) like that which, for her, had continued until her son had been born. The son was identified with herself as a bad shadow. (This comment seems rather opaque, as Katy had in reality not borne a son, but had miscarried. Per-haps symbolically, the emergence of the animus, in the analysis and in this session, was the psychological birth of the son who had not been born in reality.) Now it would be all right, and the bale-ful shadow had lifted from Katy, allowing her to glimpse the unconscious contents of the animus contained within the shadow. She might also be able to get into the "Lump', if she were not so self-conscious, by diving down to the basic facts, instead of keeping herself above them.

In one session, towards the end of her wartime sessions, she had a fantasy that the "Lump" had gone into Jung's office. He had opened it up, letting out the Fairy Queen, from whom Katy had been excluded at birth, so she had been imprisoned in the "Lump". Interpreting for herself she said that it meant that she had had qualities that her parents' rearing had sent into a grey lump, never to come to life until opened by Jung. The fantasy ended with the two of them beholding the Son of Man and God the Father in a starlit sky. Jung told her of a Greek text he had found in which the lump had been described as containing the spirit of God, which had to be liberated as the Soul of the World. She must allow others to draw her out so she could realize inner things. Her fantasy of the "Lump" was an intuition about her soul, and it would not roll anymore when her soul had been liberated and no longer needed to be protected by that "Lump" (*ibid.*, p. 349).

The "Lump" was also related to her anxieties about her feelings of inferiority and wish for social prestige. To this I now turn.

Conflictful feelings about social contact and social position

Katy's daughter considered her mother as a snob, always wanting to mix with those who had a social position. Perhaps, not surprisingly, this was accompanied by a feeling of inferiority that was often repressed, forming yet another aspect of her "Lump". It also extended to her membership of the Psychological Club where she often felt she was held in contempt by some of the leading members. According to Bair (2004, p. 385), her analysis was mostly concerned with how she could adapt to the fractious personalities competing for Jung's attention. He, early in the recorded sessions, took this conflict up with her. She had dreamed that she had a swollen right thumb, and a man suggested cutting it open with a yard-long knife, and disinfecting it.

Jung did not ask for her associations, but with reference to a Roman practice of cutting off the right thumbs of enemy soldiers to prevent them being able to fight with their swords again, he inter-preted that, as the right hand denoted wisdom and she had been living unwisely, she wanted him to cut the abscess to relieve the infection caused by her wrong living with a social crowd in St Moritz. He advised her to avoid those social contacts, and referred to his own way of dealing with those temptations. It is not clear what Katy made of that, and the session ended with Jung's further advice that she should live among decent people, and not with the St Moritz crowd.

Jung's interpretation of her Juanita fantasy (Reid, 2001, p. 100) was also significant in understanding the conflict between her feel-ings of inferiority and her wish to find an important place in society. It concerned Juanita, who lived gaily, married, and then returned to gaiety, finally entering a convent, saying good-bye to gaiety and her husband. Jung interpreted this by referring to Katy's childhood with her parents, making herself deaf to their language (this related to an earlier session where he had interpreted a problem about her inability to feel through her ears being caused by her father's bad language), preventing it from reaching her heart since it would have made her too unhappy. Her defences against her parents had grown over the years, like a rhinoceros hide, and had resulted in an internal split. One part of the split had become ascetic and had been repressed, and the other part, conforming to her parents, had panics. He thought that her returning year after year to Zürich meant that she was looking for the ascetic way of life. She said that the reason she returned repeatedly was because she had found a gold mine that she could never give up. Jung thought that her neurosis did not warrant such continual adhesion to him. This seems rather a surprising comment in view of the sporadic nature of their sessions, and that there had just been a year's interruption in their work together. Continuing to explain, he said that because of her defences she had forced herself into a way of life completely foreign to her desires, in that her desire for asceticism, which had been repressed in childhood, was now seeking to achieve conscious expression. She wrote that she had only vaguely felt it before, but now it had been made conscious she was left feeling shattered and afraid (*ibid.*, p. 101). This interpretation was followed in subsequent sessions by references to the interaction between opposites in the psyche not requiring the choice of one instead of the other but some kind of synthesis, but her animus was preventing the development of that synthesis (Jung described it as a joke of her animus), and disabling her from "hearing" (as in the feeling through the ears). Putting it colloquially, she did not have to choose between the café and the convent; a choice with which her father had presented her. Jane commented caustically, if realistically, that ". . . my mother would see her situation pretty clearly for a while but then fall back into her old ways of thinking and behaving The café society she thought she had outgrown would attract her again" (*ibid.*, p. 103).

In an *ad hoc* session, she told Jung she was feeling un-natural, which he related to feelings of inferiority. She should not try to act naturally because this would only reinforce the feeling of being un-natural. Her sense of inferiority also had something to do with national characteristics, and Jung made a variety of comments, based on national stereotypes. So, for example, for Americans their feeling of un-naturalness sprang from a sense of primitiveness, but Katy had some European style because of her upbringing. Jung frequently made use of stereotypes of this kind to explain wartime events, as well as using them to account for individual behaviour. So, when Katy on one occasion referred to her animal instincts, Jung commented that Americans kept far away from their instincts, but Katy should combat that by keeping track of her dreams of instinctive beings. He also thought that Katy was too involved with society, in its general sense, and that this was a manifestation of her internal hollowness, and of being ungrounded. Jung worked with Katy on her problems with members of the Psychological Club in the same way. Problems between the members were often related to their national characteristics as Jung understood them. So Katy's jealousy of Barbara Hannah was related to the difference between Barbara's English upper and middle class mores and Katy's American origins, drawn from stereotypes about both. He often interpreted her bad relationship with others in the Psychological Club as being a consequence of the projection of her own bad feelings on to them. She should learn to recognize those bad feelings as part of herself. In one session, Katy felt that she had had a very painful time when Jung enumerated her many shortcomings, which he believed had been repressed into her "Lump", and were then projected into others with whom she then had a bad relationship. Summing them up, he said that if she found everyone terrible then there was something wrong with *her* (*ibid*., p. 377). This had been a consistent theme throughout the analysis, but presented with much greater force in that session.

In another session, Katy's "social" complex was discussed in connection with a dream.

> I had a hole in my arm out of which poured caviar. I went into a chemist and the chemist said that she could not take care of a thing like that, and I must call a doctor. In the meantime, I fainted and said, "So this is dying" (*ibid*., p. 335).

Jung interpreted that the caviar coming out of the wound meant that there was something vital to her social complex. Somewhere she must have qualities to fit into society, but that her social side was not satisfied. The caviar was a symbol for the conversation of a person of quality. As it was coming through her arm and not elsewhere, it meant that it was a disease. She told Jung that, because of her lack of education, she could not converse very well. She needed to study more, and was reading *Psychological Types.* Jung interpreted that Katy's feelings of inferiority were related to her American identity, and conflicted with her wish to get on in society. She understood that conflict by reference to the Taoist concept of the Ying and Yang and the need for balance. Her social complex had countervailing aspects that had been repressed into the contents of the "Lump", making her behave in an artificial way. The resolution of the problem was to live naturally and simply, although how she was to achieve that while under such powerful unconscious pressure was not made clear.

The need for balance between the unconscious and conscious was a frequent interpretation in relation not only to her social complex, but also to other aspects of her psyche. Her unconscious contained aspects of herself, which were the obverse of what she was consciously experiencing, and were often projected into others, when she might be able to recognize them as belonging to herself. Her "Lump" could also be understood as her container for some of these unrecognized parts of herself, including the shadow. Further explorations of her social complex continued in this style until the end of the recorded sessions in 1942. Whether or not the analytical work had helped Katy with her social complex, she received the social recognition she sought when she married her Italian Visconti after his wife died, becoming a Contessa. When she died she was buried in his family tomb, having become a Catholic with that objective in mind.

De Trafford

Katy met de Trafford after the death of her first husband, Jane's father. He was one of several men she felt attracted to and discussed with Jung. She eventually settled with him until his death in 1942, although they never married because he could never bring himself to divorce his first wife. Although, for the sake of propriety, they did not live together until after 1939 when war had been declared, they had a mild sexual relationship that Katy complained about as not being sufficiently gratifying to her. Jung interpreted this in two ways. First, by saying that her sexuality had been repressed in her relationship with de Trafford, permitting her to rejuvenate and embellish her life. It is not quite clear how he reached this conclusion, since Katy was complaining about her absence of sexual rejuvenation. Moreover, it conflicted with other interpretations that she may have internalized something of de Trafford's diminished sexuality. Second, he interpreted this unconscious exchange as a consequence of the inevitable change in male and female sexuality with age. Men, he claimed, become more like women as they age. As their anima emerged they became less interested in sex so long as they did not resist it. Conversely, women become more like men as their animus developed, but if they allowed their spirituality to develop with it they would not become so disagreeable. The male animus diminishes with age and the anima becomes stronger; the converse happens with women. Jung did not explain why this should be. It was an observation.

Subsequently, Jung interpreted de Trafford's unconscious, diluted suicidal feelings, indicated by his wish to narcotize himself through very heavy smoking. Katy responded by telling Jung of her wish to stab one of de Trafford's friends. Jung said that the friend was probably suicidal and went on to say, "When you are dealing with a person whose unconscious wants him to make an end of his life, you have a tendency to want to kill him" (*ibid.*, p. 189). Katy's conscious fantasy was an expression of a wish to help him on his way, but Jung did not say if this also applied to de Trafford, whose diluted, unconscious wish to die he had just interpreted. He did say that de Trafford could be helped through Katy's own analysis, and in the next session reinforced Toni's advice about marrying de Trafford. However, the problem was not about Katy's wish to marry de Trafford, but his inability to seek a divorce from his wife.

The de Trafford theme was continued when Jung interpreted her dream of being in a house with a murderous young man as meaning that something dangerous was afoot, with murderous consequences. Katy responded by telling him of her wish to kill de Trafford when he was in a bad mood. In this it seemed that de Trafford was expressing some of Katy's projected bad feelings rather than just his own. Jung made some interesting interpretations about the threesome consisting of Katy, de Trafford, and his wife, who, in fact, lived in New York with a lover. Jung thought that De Trafford had internalized his wife's bad anima, which wanted to destroy his relationship with Katy, and this called forth murderousness in her, and that de Trafford could not look the truth about his marriage in the face (*ibid.*, p. 220).

In one of her sessions, Katy reported de Trafford's dream of being weighed down with weights brought to him by a man in classical robes who asked him if a hand grenade was heavy enough. Jung interpreted this by reference to the British unpreparedness for war compared with the Germans and Italians. He went further, saying that de Trafford had the same attitude to personal problems as the whole British nation. Katy did not record her response to this interpretation.

Dreams

Jung usually interpreted dreams without reference to Katy's associations, tending to use his own associations and classical references to understand their meaning. The following examples are characteristic of the way Jung worked with his patient's dreams.

She called one "The Great Dream". It involved meeting Jung on the Parthenon and asking him how she could equal his spiritual development. In the dream he had told her she must lie down in a pool and die for a thousand years. She did so, and had many painful experiences eventually becoming unconscious. One thousand years later she found herself lying on a sunny beach with a peaceful background, with the Parthenon on a hill.

In his response, Jung told her the classical meaning of several of the elements of the dream. She then asked him how she could develop spiritually. He replied that she must die and be reborn, going back one thousand years; becoming a child in the mother's womb where she would have no persona; living and being moved by the unconscious. The spirit would then seize her, lifting her up in great pain and then return her to earth again (*ibid.*, p. 130). Some time after this dream Katy was unwell, and had to spend several weeks in bed. Jane thought that her mother's prolonged illness at this time might have been a response to Jung's interpretation of the Parthenon dream and the need to be reborn after one thousand years.

There were some sequential dreams involving classical statuary and Katy reported his interpretation as follows:

> ... [in] the foregoing dream of statues, Greek and then granite statues appear. These are people made into stone. The fashionable, my worldly aspect. And then I make the descent into the unconscious and meet the woman of granite—the woman who has been changed into stone. If I am made of granite I am unchangeable—a sort of mother. I come out in the form of my own child. I am rejuvenated with the psychology of a young girl in curious contrast to the dead person of granite. Through the descent, it is as if I had been transformed into the granite, I am now hard society; inside infantile and in a hard shell like a crab! Now my *inside* must become like granite and *outside* like a child. If someone sticks a dagger into me the dagger won't enter because of the inside granite; the dagger will break itself against the granite. [*Ibid.*, p. 316]

This account seems somewhat incoherent and may not have been completely understood by Katy. Her daughter commented that her mother had been quite pleased with this image of herself being soft outside and like granite internally.

In 1940 she told Jung of three important dreams. The first involved being at a social occasion where there were many famous people present, as well as herself and de Trafford. Jung and his wife were also there but had to leave because their dog had died and had to be buried in their garden. Jung asked her if she would like to see the dead dog, but she declined, wishing to remember him as he was alive. At the end of the party she left to have dinner and found Toni already there, and she squeezed Toni's knee in an intimate way.

Jung interpreted Katy's dream without asking for her associations. He commented that they shared a feeling about the dog in the dream, which was indicated because she had told him about it, but not the others. Squeezing Toni's knee was also an expression of intimacy, and of being on better terms with her. The dream was a compensation for a conventional feeling of distance and uncertainty. Its main gist was to fortify the feeling of rapport, liberating her from her unconscious, and giving her a certainty, and a foothold (*ibid.*, pp. 275–276).

The second dream was told in a session in July and followed some discussion about the Psychological Club members; about change in de Trafford since his return from London; and the progress of the war.

The dream concerned payment of Jung's bill, which he had presented without any accompanying personal note. She had then gone to a ball where she was reading a profound book by Jung, but her teacher told her she would prefer her to be reading a grammar book. She then had some letters to give to soldiers at the charity ball, and one for her was from Jung, enclosing an account for some ham, and included some very profound thoughts. She told Jung that she was glad to have had something of his soul. He had come to the ball for the soldiers, and his soldiers had stopped him in Küsnacht on their way to heaven. She said that it was no wonder they saw so little of him these days when such things were occurring at his house. How could he tolerate them [the patients and others?

Jung pointed upwards, and she saw his soldiers, dressed in eighteenth century white silk shirts and velvet knee breeches going past as on a cloud. She thought that Jung could not save our souls unless they wished to be saved.

Interpreting without her associations, Jung said that the dream was in three parts: first, the Teacher who wished her to learn something simpler first; second, their personal relationship with fun besides analysis; and third, seeing him as someone playing an important role in contemporary spiritual problems. Katy felt that she was unconsciously sharing in the extension of Jung's ideas, and that she was trying to fit him into a larger frame to be able to widen her own horizon. He said he felt that he meant far too little in the present, although he did belong to the world and to the great psychical and religious currents of their time (*ibid.*, 286–289).

The third dream, although more than five months later, after a break until the beginning of November, was rather similar and involved Jung sitting in the clouds in the place of the Lord, with many people around him. It was like Raphael's Last Judgment, with Jung on the throne of the Lord. Many people were going up to speak to him, as Katy was, but could only shake his hand. She felt terrible that she could not speak to him. She went to the back and said to someone that she hated having to leave Jung forever. The other person understood.

Jung interpreted that she should not make it her exclusive goal to have hours with him, and that there were others she should try to be useful to in other ways. As she had received from him so she could give to others, and she could spread consciousness, but not necessarily professionally. This seems a rather surprising interpretation, as Katy had never been exclusively involved with Jung and had always had sessions with Toni. She still suffered from panics in the funicular, which he told her meant that she still had something to realize. She felt that she was ready to bud like a bush, but was not so sweet. She needed warmth for the buds to open, which she could not get from Toni, who had too many icicles.

Ending

Although the ending was more by chance than design, there seems to have been something about Jung's complex interpretations during the sessions in 1941 and 1942 which may have presaged a termination. However that may have been, Katy did not see Jung again for analysis for nearly three years, until January 1945, although a comment at their first meeting in that year suggests that she may have met Jung but had been unable to record anything, because of her grieving for de Trafford, who had died in 1942. There were, however, many letters from Emma Jung and other members of the Psychological Club in the interim. There were also some social meetings; for example, when Jung and his wife attended the wedding reception for Jane. While it is not clear whether there were any further sessions with Jung until 1945, her first recorded session with him in that year coincided with her beginning analysis with another analyst, Dr C. A. Meier, the first president of the Jung Institute.

The sessions in 1945 seemed even more like tutorials than before: they were concerned with Jung's explaining to her some of his ideas but with little of much apparent immediate relevance to herself. He did describe her as a psychologist, which may account for the explanatory nature of these sessions. In the single session in 1946, they briefly discussed her relationship with another man. Jung told her that the nature of her relationships was related to her inferior function, which was one with the collective, and also related to her social function. The current man friend represented both of these characteristics. The analysis petered out rather than coming to a formal end. Because the work with Jung was being conducted in conjunction with an analysis with Toni Wolff, none of which was recorded, the therapeutic nature of that work remains enigmatic. It is evident that Katy did benefit in some ways from these concurrent analyses, but it is impossible to assess how Katy dealt with the disharmony she engendered between them. Was it simply a re-enactment of her relationships with her mother and father, which was apparently never interpreted by either analyst? What is to be made of Jung's reiterated view that Katy should try to avoid the personal stuff with Toni and to try and confine her to impersonal stuff? What is analysis if it is not about the patient's "personal stuff"? It may be that Jung was referring to the ideas of the collective unconscious and the archetypes, to which he may have given greater emphasis than Toni. These concepts often seemed to be a more significant aspect of Jung's work with Katy than the more personal issues about her relationships with her various men partners. A great deal of the therapeutic effect of this analysis may not have arisen wholly from the *interpretation* of the content of Katy's unconscious, but from an unconscious re-enactment in the therapy of her childhood trauma, with Katy in the role of the frequently absent parents and Jung/Toni as her projected self reparatively surviving the absences. Her unconscious agenda may have been discordant with Jung's and Toni's agendas (as they seemed to have been with each other), but that discordance did not appear to affect the outcome.

CHAPTER TEN

Discussion

Freud

T hese three analyses of his patients took place at two very different points in Freud's life, but the patients' accounts of them have some interesting similarities. All describe Freud's vehemence in the sessions about matters on which he had strong feelings, to the extent of hammering on the couch to emphasize his opinions. In all of them he apparently led the patients to believe that they had particular significance for him. All three were treated as students, although only Wortis was formally taken on for a didactic analysis. Both the Wolf-Man and HD had felt flattered by this, and each felt especially privileged by Freud's praise of them. In the case of the Wolf-Man the position of the favourite son was both loved and hated by him. The resistances of both the Wolf-Man and HD seem to have been attempts to ward off Freud's powerful wish to impose his theoretical concepts on them. Each had a different agenda from Freud, but HD was more able to sustain hers without either open conflict with him or complete compliance. Wortis was unable to take advantage of that special position of being a student, although clinging to his wish for a didactic experience. His intense ambivalent wish for Freud's love impeded the formation of a positive transference within which he might have been able to diminish his defensiveness about his unconscious homosexual anxieties. But he may not have been seeking to be analysed in a personal sense, but to learn more theoretically about Freud's concepts. The term *didactic* may have had different meanings for each of them. As a result, his maintenance of his conscious resistance was counterproductive for him, and, unlike HD, he gained nothing from his work with Freud.

All describe various occasions when they seem to have been offered information about Freud's personal and family life. There were also occasions when Freud introduced extraneous matters such as discussions about politics (communism and fascism) in the sessions with Wortis. On other occasions with all three he discussed various personalities in the psychoanalytic world, and other contemporaries of his. Some of this seems to have been on the basis of gossip, and HD remarked that Freud enjoyed a gossip with her. He seemed to be far from the impersonal, neutral psychoanalyst of the theory. In fact, for all of them his personality and charisma were important factors in the interaction between them.

Most of all Freud was concerned to discover the fundamentals of his theory in all of them. This was most marked in respect of the Wolf-Man, in whom he purported to find his most basic concepts. It is clear that these were matters of interpretation rather than fact, so that in later life the Wolf-Man rejected them, and complained that he had failed to find the memories that Freud had attributed to him. It was evident that for all three of them Freud, through his interpretations, was imposing his ideas about the contents of their respective unconscious minds upon them. They all in various ways rejected them, although two, subject to the power of Freud's presence, made some semblance of acceptance, to a greater or lesser degree. The Wolf-Man seemed under the greatest pressure to accept, and the importance of Freud's famous paper provided him with an identity that he adopted, and with which the psychoanalytic community colluded for the rest of his life. His protests, as described in Obholzer's book, about this and the overpowering positive transference he felt that Freud had nurtured, were prevented from being published by Eissler until after the Wolf-Man's death. Additionally, for the first three years of his analysis he had a different agenda from Freud, concerning his relationships with Anna and Therese.

HD went along with Freud's interpretations, while silently recording her dissent in her letters to Bryher, and offering her own alternative and supplementary interpretations. For both the Wolf-Man and HD, it is possible to see a discordant agenda enacted as resistance. The Wolf-Man sustained his resistance and agenda until Freud's threat to terminate the analysis led to his capitulation and compliance. For HD, the discordant agenda was very much more subtle, and did not lead to overt resistance but to a silent mainte-nance of her mystical interpretations in the therapy and expressed in her letters to Bryher, accompanied by apparent compliance with Freud.

Wortis was much more outright in his rejection of the interpre-tations and the theories on which they were based, although he wished that he had been able to respond more positively. He often incurred Freud's wrath and rejection in response. Although he craved Freud's love, it may be that its homosexual implications led him to ward Freud off.

Lohser and Newton (1996) draw attention to the absence of transference and countertransference interpretations in the accounts by HD and Wortis, and explain this by commenting that this tech-nique was a later addition to the theory of therapy. They assert that Freud was much more interested in making the unconscious conscious, which he often accomplished through modifying the technique of free association by a rather more directive process. They do not note, however, that Freud's interventions of that sort might invalidate the subsequent associations. He was, in fact, suggesting the material he was seeking. Wortis thought, cons-ciously, that he was supposed to produce associations of the kind Freud was expecting, and that they were not really free because of that expectation. Despite that, it was evident that, in all three, the issue of a very powerful transference was highly significant.

What was even clearer was that Freud, apparently quite uncon-sciously, acted out the countertransference. In the case of the Wolf-Man he not only flattered him about his understanding of psychoanalytic ideas, but talked of him as being superior to others who were *bona fide* students. He made him feel very special by shar-ing with him anecdotes about his own children and family, as well as writing the important paper about him. That he occupied a special position for Freud may have been emphasized by the gifts of money when he had lost his remaining fortune after the First World War, and was seeking work in Vienna. The continuation of these gifts after his analysis with Freud had terminated, and into the period of his analysis with Ruth Mack Brunswick, and by the Freud Archive later, after the Second World War, may have added to the Wolf-Man's feeling that he was the favoured son, even though towards the end of his life he wished he had not been so bound to Freud and the psychoanalytic community. He spoke of having tried to wrench Freud from his mind after he had ended the first period of analysis in 1914. It might have been better for him if the positive transference had been dissolved rather than reinforced.

In respect of HD, the acting out of the countertransference was even clearer. Very early in her analysis it was evident that she had unconsciously taken the place of his beloved daughter, Sophie, who had died in the post-First World War influenza epidemic, from which HD had also suffered. The acting out went even further in the events surrounding the pregnancy and the birth of Yofi's puppies. HD was dimly aware that something about Sophie's pregnancy and death was being re-enacted by Freud in his wish for her to have one of the puppies, echoing the birth of Sophie's son, who had survived when she had died. She responded by feeling very oppressed, and by producing symptoms of pregnancy. She agonized with Bryher about how to refuse the gift without offending Freud, finding it difficult to introduce her wish to refuse the offer into the analysis. None of this was analysed by Freud, who seemed to have been unaware of what was happening between them. This failure to be aware of such a strong countertransference repeated the same problem that he had had in his analysis of Dora, who, he believed, had wanted to fall in love with him (Freud, 1905e). For HD, despite her subdued, unacknowledged conflict with him, he evidently provided a sufficiently safe container for the conflict to be held.

For Wortis, the acting out was of the negative countertransference. He was subject to inconsistent treatment by Freud, who often criticized him very sharply for his failure to work properly in analysis, and to give up his criticisms of the process and the theories. As a result Wortis felt rejected, and an object of Freud's attack. He was left bewildered and bemused when he felt that Freud was not acknowledging that rejection, and behaving as if he could not understand why Wortis should feel hurt by what he was saying. The implication was that it was only for Wortis's own good, and, as Freud often remarked, his comments were not meant personally; although in such an intensely personal interaction they could hardly have been understood in any other way. In the final session, when Wortis was attempting to express his guilt for not having been able to do well in analysis, feeling as if he had been a bad schoolboy, Freud replied enigmatically, "What makes you think that?" It was as if the difficulties in the analysis had not really existed, and that Freud had never expressed very strongly negative and rejecting feelings about Wortis. In fact, the container provided for him by Freud was very paradoxical, as his concluding comment suggests. So, Wortis could never have felt safe with his challenges to Freud. Neither could he be enabled to adapt to Freud's agenda, nor be helped to understand where his resistance, and possibly his homosexual impulses, may have originated.

Of the three of Freud's analyses discussed here, only one seems to have had an unequivocally satisfactory outcome—that of HD. Even for her that outcome was long delayed, coming only in the Second World War when HD was living in London during the Blitz, and as a result had been able to come to terms with the war phobia that had been one of the reasons she had entered analysis with Freud. This was coupled with the lifting of her writer's block, which had been another reason for seeking analysis. It would be difficult to say whether, in view of her further analysis with Schmideberg, that these outcomes were entirely the result of her work with Freud. HD was, however, sure that Freud's influence had been determining. She continued to work over the experience, perhaps reinforced by her analysis with Schmideberg. Her writing of *Tribute* in 1944 provides abundant evidence of her feeling of indebtedness to Freud, despite their covert differences. It may also be evidence for his view that the outcome of analysis comes after its termination when patients make the journey for which the analysis had equipped them.

It has been believed that Freud's analysis of the Wolf-Man had been very effective. Freud claimed that he had discovered the basis of the Wolf-Man's childhood neurosis, that he had relieved him of his completely dependent condition on others, that he had cured him of his chronic constipation, and had resolved the his preoccupation with lower-class women. Even leaving all that on one side, the psychoanalytic community believed that Freud had enabled the Wolf-Man to adjust successfully to his very changed circumstances in his life in Austria after he had lost his fortune, and had to seek a job that he held until his retirement, although this sounds like *post hoc, propter hoc.* All of those claims were denied by the Wolf-Man. He was never able to remember anything about the famous primal scene, alleged to have been the source of his neurosis. (I have discussed above why his inability to remember it may not have been the result of further repression.) He did not agree that he had ever been dependent on others in the way Freud described. He reasserted that the difficulties with Miss Oven, her influence on his sister, Anna, and the conflict with his nurse were the reasons for his neurosis. He denied that Freud had cured him of his constipation, which had persisted to the end of his life. Obholzer's conversations with him revealed a very disgruntled man, preoccupied with his relationships with the women who dominated his life after his wife's death. He remained angry about the transference that Freud had evoked, which he felt had never been resolved, and had been transferred to the psychoanalytic community as a whole.

The analysis of Wortis hardly seems to deserve that designation. He seems not to have derived any benefit from it. His anxiety about his lack of fundamental self-esteem, displayed in his sense of rejection by Freud, whose love he craved, may have been generated by his unconscious homosexual fears. That anxiety may have led him to ward Freud off, and to argue with him on theoretical and scientific grounds, so that Freud could not find a way of reaching his core neurosis. Freud's dislike of Wortis was very evident during the course of this work. It may have impeded the formation of the working alliance essential to the success of any analysis. Wortis's resistance to psychoanalysis hardened after the analysis had finished. The final comments in his account rejected psychoanalysis as unscientific and therapeutically ineffective, except as a preliminary to orthodox psychiatric treatments.

Jung

Jung went much farther than Freud in allowing his patients access to his private life. He joined them in social events, and mixed freely with them in the Psychological Club, as could be seen in his analysis of Catherine Rush Cabot, whose story, published posthumously, seems to be unique among Jung's patients. The story of another patient, Christiana Morgan, was told briefly in her biography (Douglas, 1993). I have not used it separately because there are only fragments of it, and some of the important points about it are made by the biographer and not by the subject. I will, however, make reference to it in exploring some of the issues arising from Catherine Cabot's analysis.

It is very evident how different Jung's work was from Freud's. Although both were interested in what was unconsciously influencing the patient, their disagreement about what the unconscious might contain was quite profound. Jung had believed at the outset of their collaboration that he had empirically demonstrated that Freud's concepts were true. After his break with Freud and the international psychoanalytic community, Jung began to develop his distinctive ideas about the psyche and its unconscious aspects. These seemed to have originated in his own vivid, marginally psychotic fantasies as a child, his experience with psychotic patients in the Burghölzli hospital, and finally in his experiences of fantasy and imagination in the period following the break with Freud. In fact, as Freud had done, he created his theories about the psyche from his own inner experiences and fantasies. He refined from it a number of concepts about the psyche in general, but with emphasis on the importance of reaching a psychotic layer of experience containing important primeval, eternal and communal elements. To these he gave the names of the collective unconscious and the archetypes.

Some of these can be seen in Catherine Cabot's account of her analysis, where the striking differences from Freud's approach can be seen. For example, Jung related her panic in the funicular to the conflict between her conscious and unconscious wishes in a way that was very different from Freud's use of the idea of repression of instinctual drives. Jung's concept was of the compensation in the unconscious for conscious wishes and perhaps *vice versa*. Hence, her desire to jump out of the imprisoning funicular cabin was compensatory for the equally frightening wish to be held and contained that she had not experienced with her parents, and particularly not from her mother's care. Her claustrophobic anxieties were contrasted with her agoraphobic fears, and each compensated for the other.

Although Freud did not completely adopt the image of the impersonal, anonymous therapist characteristic of analysts of more recent times, Jung rejected the idea of anonymity. Both his theory and his technique were markedly different from Freud's. He was much more present personally for Katy than Freud was for his patients, and joined with her and Toni Wolff on many personal social occasions, such as private lunches and family celebrations. If Toni Wolff had wished to practice anonymity, Jung prevented that by his intimate revelations to Katy about Toni's psychopathology and his opinions of her. Additionally, he mixed freely with patients and other Jungian therapists at the Psychological Club, where he gave lectures, presentations, and joined in discussions. There seems to have been a sense that the collective, in its non-technical meaning, was a significant but perhaps unrecognized part of the treatment, as Katy claimed in respect of one of his lectures.

The interaction between transference and countertransference played little or no part in the verbal transactions in the analysis. Jung's comments on his co-therapist, Toni Wolff, may have been a kind of re-enactment in the countertransference of the way in which Catherine experienced her parents. Her father was the charismatic war hero, as Jung was the charismatic father figure in the Küsnacht world; her mother was the hated, difficult parent who had abandoned her to the care of strangers, and who became embodied in Catherine's interaction with Wolff. In that interaction Jung took her side against Wolff, giving information about his co-therapist that might have been counter-therapeutic. Curiously, it was not. The re-enactment in the therapy of Catherine's experience of her parents, coupled with her own frequent abandonment of the quasi-parental pair, which I believe reversed her own abandonment as a child and adolescent, making the substitute parental couple into the abandoned object, may have contributed to the healing experience rather than to have detracted from it. In the terms of the possibly two discordant agendas of therapist and patient, which I have discussed as creating difficulties in the analysis, it may be that Jung's much less rigid practice enabled Katy's unconscious wish to deal with the psychic problems created in her familial relationships to be worked at unconsciously, while Jung followed his own agenda of analysing her "lump" and other manifestations in the psychological terms he was developing. It may be said to have been successful, not only in relation to Katy herself, but also in facilitating her daughter, Jane, to break the nascent family tradition of only having one child to be left frequently in the care of strangers.

Christiana Morgan was a very important patient for Jung who could produce intensely mythical and mystical fantasies and images in way which helped to confirm for him his ideas about the structure and content of the psyche, at a deep psychotic level. She has not written an account of her analysis with him, but there are references to it in Douglas (1993) that have some significance for my argument about discordant agendas. They also bear out Henderson's contention (Henderson, 1975, p. 115) that Jung could not be put into any frame. His analysis of Morgan bore little resemblance to his work with Catherine. With Morgan he was much more concerned with her deep unconscious archetypal fantasies, which he interpreted largely in terms of his own concept that women's role was to act as an *inspiratrice* for men (Douglas, 1993, p. 150). This led to the discordant agendas between analyst and patient, with Morgan attempting to assert her fundamental feminine power against Jung's traditional prejudices about women. Douglas wrote that Jung's difficulties in this respect were both personal and cultural; men in general did not expect this erotic power from women and could deal with it only by love-making or rape (*ibid.*, p. 164). The analysis never recovered from this basic conflict. It bears some similarity to the discordant agenda in HD's experience with Freud, but that conflict was much gentler, and she was able to sustain her independent femininity without making the conflict overt.

In general, although all these analyses took place during the early development of Freudian and Jungian practice, they may contribute to the discussion of boundaries, and the analytic frame, which began in the latter half of the twentieth century. They suggest that the benefit from analysis, in the widest sense, may be derived from different variations in the approach to boundary keeping and the therapeutic frame.

PART III

PATIENTS IN TRAINING AS PSYCHOANALYSTS OR PSYCHOTHERAPISTS

CHAPTER ELEVEN

Prelude

A number of patients in training have written about their experiences. Blanton and Kardiner, both analysed by Freud, and Dr Little, have each written important book-length accounts of their analyses. Kardiner, analysed by Freud in 1921–1922, wrote an interesting account of his analysis, although it is not evident whether he was relying on contemporaneous notes or simply on his memory. He supplemented the story with some subsequent reflections in 1977. Blanton (1971) wrote notes of some of his sessions during the first period of his analysis, often with long gaps between the diary entries. He wrote rather fuller notes of the three brief occasions during the 1930s when he returned to Freud while he was in Europe during the summers of 1935, 1937, and 1938. His notes of the first, and longer, period of his analysis are somewhat sketchy, and resemble those made by Wortis, although they are not so full. Dr Little relied on her memory rather than notes made at the time, giving general impressions of each of her three analyses. Her account of her work with Winnicott is much the most graphic and detailed of them. She did not record individual sessions for any of the analyses.

The fourth member of this group, Jeffrey Masson, did not describe all the sessions with his training analyst, Dr Schiffer, in Toronto. He kept some notes at the time and used these to supplement his memory. The history of his analysis is summarized in the second chapter of his book, *Final Analysis* (Masson, 1990), with further comments in subsequent chapters, as he described other aspects of his training.

Qualifying as a psychoanalyst after seven years, and eventually taking up a very senior position in the Freud Archive, Masson was very critical of the process of psychoanalytical training, its institutional arrangements, and professional practice embodied in its institutions. He wrote critically of Freud's abandonment of his Seduction Theory (Masson, 1992), and its replacement with a theory emphasizing the phantasy of the sexual events about which patients complained, rather than their reality. The rejection of his criticisms by the psychoanalytic establishment led eventually to Masson's leaving psychoanalysis altogether, feeling thoroughly disillusioned with what he had experienced. The immense conflict between himself and Dr Schiffer, arising from Schiffer's considerable narcissism rather than from any other source, was very evident.

Others have written more briefly about their training psychoanalyses. Guntrip described his two analyses with Fairbairn and Winnicott in a paper (Guntrip, 1975) raising interesting questions about the therapeutic nature of psychoanalysis. John Hill discussed the differences between his three Kleinian analysts in his experiences with them. He was quite disillusioned by the first two (Hill, 1993). Arthur Couch wrote a paper devoted to a critique of modern analytic practice (Couch, 1995), and referring to his analysis with Anna Freud, giving sympathetic vignettes of her technique.

All of these therapists raise in an interesting way the impact of differences between their analysts, where they had had more than one, and the implications of those differences for the nature of therapy and psychoanalysis. In some of them it is possible to see that, even if the outcome was benign, that there was, in fact, a discordant agenda between the analyst and analysand. In Masson's case the agendas were not simply discordant but counter-therapeutic. The narcissism of the analyst, as described by Masson, was so great as to make any effective therapy impossible.

It is often claimed in psychoanalytic circles that the uninitiated cannot really understand the processes of therapy. So patients, or others, writing about the practice of psychoanalysis will be influenced, it is claimed, not only by their ignorance of the theories, but also by their own unconscious biases and resistances. An important element in the stories in this section is that, unlike those of patients not in training, these writers could not be accused of being unsophisticated, or of being unaware of their unconscious resistances. Because of their participation in formal training and induction into the mysteries of psychoanalysis, they were not naïve. So, if they are critical of the process, their criticisms cannot so easily be dismissed as those made by other patients not in formal training. It will be recalled that two of the patients (HD and Wortis) in the previous section were regarded by Freud as being in training. However, this was never formalized, and they were not involved in a lecture programme, or in supervised practice, so their experiences may be seen as different from these accounts.

Blanton published nothing about his more formal study when he returned to New York to continue training with Brill. Although he was in training with both Freud and Brill, and later became a training analyst, he was less sophisticated than the others discussed here. He had, however, read Freud's work closely, and in this, he may have resembled the Wolf-Man, who had also made himself familiar with Freud's writings. Knowledge of Freud's works is not usually sufficient to avoid the accusation of naïveté, but, with the possible exception of Wortis, all of those who have written about their analyses had gained some understanding of their unconscious processes in therapy. So, even without the addition of formal training, critics, having undergone analysis, might be expected to understand something of their unconscious resistances, while those considered in this section might be able to make powerful and legitimate criticisms, if they were so inclined. Masson's example, however, demonstrated how difficult it is to have such criticisms accepted.

CHAPTER TWELVE

A. Kardiner

Introduction

Kardiner was the son of a Russian Jewish immigrant family, born in New York in 1891. He had an elder sister born in Russia eight years earlier. His rivalry with her in childhood was suppressed until late adolescence. The family lived in poverty in New York, and were in emotional as well as economic distress both before and after his mother died when he was three years old. Kardiner's own distress about his mother's death was a significant matter in his analysis with Freud. His father remarried later, and Kardiner took to his stepmother at once, although her explicit sexual seductiveness made him anxious. He respected his father, although he was a stern disciplinarian. In childhood, he had difficulty with his Jewishness, both at school and in the neighbourhood where they lived. His academic progress at school was handicapped by that, and by his need not to compete with his less able sister. He was gifted as a musician, playing the violin before he went to school, and could entertain his family and friends with his songs. Despite early educational failures in late adolescence, he passed exams and began training for medicine. This was given up when he was having an unhappy love relationship with the librarian of his university. He eventually returned to his medical studies, and became interested in psychological medicine. Consulting Frink, his neurology teacher, he entered analysis with him. After Frink died four years later, he was accepted for analysis by Freud, becoming a qualified psychoanalyst practising in New York. Later in life, he married and had a daughter.

Frink

Kardiner wrote very little about his analysis with Frink. He knew nothing about psychoanalysis when he began, fearing that he was in some unidentifiable danger, The danger was revealed when, remembering a childhood ballad called *Sweet Alice, Ben Bolt*, he mistakenly substituted his father's name for Alice who, in the ballad, was dead. Frink made, for Kardiner, the devastating interpretation that he wished his father to die. Kardiner felt he was strongly dependent on his father, and could have not had such a wish. He asked why Frink thought that, and he replied, "It was that you envied him the possession of your step-mother" (Kardiner, 1977, p. 10). He left the session in a state of anxiety, without having challenged Frink, and not understanding the nature of unconscious memories. As the anxiety did not diminish, he felt he would have to get out of the analysis.

While in that state of anxiety, he had two dreams. The first involved being in a cellar containing lots of old, broken furniture in disarray. Overhanging one side of the cellar there was a balcony with three Italians standing on it, who were urinating over him. He woke feeling humiliated and depressed. In the morning, he went to his work in the hospital, where he saw a man who had lost his memory, and he thought that he might also lose his memory. In anxiety, he took the afternoon off. Returning to his room, he slept and dreamt of being in bed having intercourse with his stepmother. In that dream, he felt there was something unusual; he was ripping something up as he penetrated her. He told Freud that Frink had been unable to help him understand those dreams. That ended his account of his analysis with Frink. After four years, Frink died while Kardiner was still in analysis.

Freud

It was evident to Kardiner that Freud did not make much effort to isolate his family life from his analysands. In Freud's waiting room there was a family photo album lying on a table, although Kardiner could not identify many of the people pictured in it. Arriving, or leaving, he often saw Freud's wife, Martha, on the stairs with a basket filled with food purchases. When Kardiner first met Freud for a preliminary interview before beginning his analysis, Freud asked him what he had "got out" of his analysis with Frink. Kardiner replied, "Nothing." Freud said he wished to correct him; he had got a little neurosis from his analysis with Frink. By contrast, Kardiner wrote that he looked on his analysis with Freud as one of the peak experiences of his life (*ibid.*, p. 28).

His early sessions with Freud were concerned with recounting his life story. In the first session, Freud listened without interrupting, but before its end, he asked Kardiner if he had prepared the material for the first hour. When Kardiner wondered why he was asking, Freud replied that it was because it was a perfect presentation. Kardiner left feeling elated and impressed, looking forward eagerly to his next hour. In it, he recounted more of his recollections of his childhood, his relations with his stepmother and her seductiveness with him, and his fear she might have other children. He recalled his father's abusive relationship with his mother, provoked by her refusal of intercourse because she was already ill and feared further pregnancies. At that time, his father was very harassed and irritable because the economic depression made it difficult to provide for the family. Freud thought that Kardiner had probably identified with his mother, although he had no recollections of her, or of what she looked like, except for seeing her shrouded face in her coffin. Recollections of her seemed to have vanished after the arrival of his stepmother.

He continued his reminiscences of his life, and of his sad relationship with K, the university librarian, with whom he had fallen in love and wished to marry. After several months of intermittent courtship, she had rejected him in a most hurtful way. Freud interpreted that K's treatment of him had precipitated a repetition of his reaction to his mother's death, confirming his feelings of worthlessness, abandonment, and depression. Freud, however, reassured him that he would never be defeated by his depression.

Kardiner later told Freud the dream of three Italians urinating on him, and his dream of intercourse with his stepmother, dreamt during his analysis with Frink. Freud asked for his associations. He associated to one of his father's apocryphal stories about Jesus, whom he described as a bastard, a trickster, and a flimflammer (*ibid.*, p. 53). The story continued with Jesus stealing a holy talisman, stitching it into his leg to enable him to fly about, demonstrating his supernatural powers. The High Priest performed the same trick, and was able to fly higher than Jesus, pissing on him from above, humiliating and exposing him, and robbing him of his magical powers. He also associated to the Italians, believed to be murderers and quick with the stiletto, who lived in the same neighbourhood in his childhood. Freud made a complex interpretation. The three feared Italians represented one big Italian, who was his father, by whom he had felt humiliated and belittled. The story of the amnesiac patient (see under "Frink" above) was a projection into the future of his past fears. He feared not what was going to happen, but what had happened. If Frink knew of his murderous intentions towards his father, he feared that he would withdraw his love, and his father's humiliations of him would return in the transference with Frink. Freud interpreted the second dream as an assertion of Kardiner's masculinity, and associated with the life and death struggle with his father. Freud said there was nothing unconscious about his feelings for his stepmother; they were a manifestation of the Oedipus complex.

Freud went on to interpret Kardiner's fears of Frink as reopening and re-enacting his repressed fears of abandonment, and his inability to be assertive with his father. Those anxieties had been transferred to Frink, who might humiliate him if Kardiner exposed his competitiveness with him. The dream of intercourse with his stepmother was an attempt to deal with those anxieties in a more assertive way. Kardiner felt that Freud, unlike Frink, had been able to focus the analysis on his relationship with his father, as well as recognizing the provocative behaviour of his stepmother, which had stimulated his assertiveness, and his guilt about his father. However, these interpretations left Kardiner feeling agitated, disturbed, and bewildered.

That night Kardiner dreamt he was standing on an embankment, watching some men digging in a trench. He kept begging them to stop, because they would not find anything of value, only an old rag. When they did, and he told them that he had been right, there was nothing there. He associated to a story about the loss of a valuable necklace, which was lying in the gutter. An old man came along and picked something up from the gutter, while failing to see the necklace. He was arrested, protesting his innocence; he had only picked up a piece of string. That dream was followed by a fragment of another about an enormous, unmoving, and indifferent cat of which he was not afraid.

Freud felt that these dreams confirmed something very important. The first dream meant that Kardiner did not want Freud to continue to explore his relationship with his father. He did not want the relationship with his father formed after his stepmother arrived to be replaced by the original relationship with his angry, neglectful father. When Kardiner asked why he had not wanted the later relationship disturbed in the analysis, Freud said that the change made it possible to live with his father, to forget the angry father, and remain submissive and obedient so as not to arouse the dragon. Kardiner, at the time, felt able to accept this interpretation. Many years later, however, he felt that Freud, the discoverer of the transference, had made a mistake. He had failed to recognize that it was Freud that Kardiner feared now. His interpretation had made the analysis a reconstruction of the past, instead of an examination of the present. He felt that he had made a pact with Freud not to display his aggression, remaining compliant to secure Freud's protection, sealing off an important aspect of his character, and ensuring his entry to the psychoanalytic profession. Freud had the power to sanction, or prevent, that process. At this point Kardiner's agenda, to become an analyst, was discordant both with his own wish to be analysed by Freud, and with Freud's construction of Kardiner's relationship with his father.

Freud interpreted the dream about the cat as being about Kardiner's stepmother. He had some silent associations about his stepmother, and said that he would always be grateful that she had been a stabilizing force in his life. Freud disagreed. Although providing a structured environment, she had been sexually overstimulating, adding to his guilt about his father. As a defence, Kardiner had fled into unconscious homosexuality, enabling him to identify with his helpless natural mother, rather than with his angry, aggressive father. Kardiner found this interpretation puzzling. His wish to identify with the female was based on a belief that the female had an easier life than the stressed male, the wish to identify with her was to escape the hardships of the male role; it had not interfered with his erotic drive. He asked Freud to explain the reference to homosexuality. Freud said that his identification with mother involved giving up his identification and rivalry with his father, guaranteeing father's continued protection. This seems to have been rather a surprising response, as it might have been expected that Freud would have interpreted the wish to become father's sexual partner in place of mother, as he had interpreted a similar homosexual wish with the Wolf-Man. Asked what he could do about it, Freud replied that Kardiner should come to terms with it.

Kardiner discovered later that the issue of unconscious homosexuality was a part of all analyses, as it continued to be in his own. It was a further example of his discordance from Freud's agenda to interpret Kardiner's associations in the light of his theory. However, the interpretation of his identification with the female led to a startling discovery. He dreamt about a mask, and awoke feeling apprehensive. He told Freud that what had frightened him about the mask was its immobility; it neither smiled nor laughed, and lacked any expression. This was followed by other dreams in which he was looking at himself in a mirror, with an immobile reflection. If he smiled or frowned, the reflection was unchanged. Freud commented that probably the first mask he had seen was his dead mother's face. This thought was frightening, but he realized from his associations that he might actually have discovered his dead mother when he had been alone in the house with her. He remembered a superstition that the soul of the dead person would enter the person who was with her when she took her last breath. (He was later to discover from his sister that, in fact, he had been alone with his mother when she died (Kardiner, 1977, p. 11).) Freud interpreted that the mask represented the mother's face; all masks or wax figures evoked the old terror of death. Kardiner did not record his reaction to this discovery, although it seemed to be genuine recovery of a profound, repressed, disturbing memory.

The analysis ended, after six months, with a discussion about working through, and the responsibility of the patient to deal in his own time with the unconscious material that had been uncovered. Kardiner had thought that the analyst had some responsibility for that, but wrote that Freud believed that the discovery of the Oedipus complex and unconscious homosexuality, together with their origins, was all that was needed. This emphasis on Oedipus and homosexuality as the important aspects of this analysis, rather than on the discovery of the repressed memory of his mother's dead face, seems surprising, but it is evidence of Freud's wish to seek conformity to his ideas of sexual epigenisis as the basis of unconscious fantasies and neurosis. The patient should apply those insights to his current life himself after the formal analysis had ended. This was similar to the comment that had been reported by the Wolf-Man.

Kardiner had failed to notice in Freud's original letter that their contract had been for six months. When Freud announced the termination at the beginning of March 1921, Kardiner felt that it was premature, and he was aggrieved about it. He wrote nothing about the process of ending, except that in the last month, the analysis drifted, and the meaning of two dreams he reported during that time was not discovered. His impression was that the analysis was left unfinished. He asked for, and received, an autographed photograph of Freud in the final session. Freud had wished him well, hoping he would eventually make a good marriage.

Kardiner also wrote some general impressions of Freud's analytical technique. He had asked Freud how he rated himself as an analyst. Freud had replied that he did not have much interest in therapeutic problems, he was too impatient, he was more interested in theoretical problems, and found that he was paying more interest to his current ideas rather than listening to the patient, and, finally, he became tired of working with a patient over the long term (*ibid.*, p. 54). Freud's agenda was, therefore, discordant with Kardiner's agenda.

While Freud was a brilliant interpreter of dreams, he made no use of the libido theory, or of anal eroticism, even though Freud believed that unconscious homosexuality was an important part of the analytical process, together with the Oedipus complex. Freud worried about the fate of psychoanalysis, particularly when it was being described as a Jewish science. A good deal of the time in

Kardiner's sessions was taken up with gossip about colleagues and rivals. Jung, however, was never mentioned. Freud also talked about his own family, and asked Kardiner, who was leaving Germany via the port of Hamburg, if he would visit his son-in-law and grandchildren who lived there, but he did not do so. Kardiner wrote that he was very fond of Freud, who was charming, witty, and erudite, but it was difficult to reconcile the man in the consulting room with the giant outside it; Freud's image in the consulting room did not accord with the man who had written the books.

While Kardiner was in Vienna, the Stracheys and Rickman were also there, being analysed by Freud. They had heard that Freud often talked to Kardiner in his sessions. Strachey and Rickman had been curious to know whether those reports of Freud's discursiveness were true, so they invited him to tea. Kardiner told them that Freud talked all the time in his sessions (although not, as he recorded, in his early sessions), and was quite garrulous. Strachey and Rickman told him that, in their sessions, Freud never said a word; and that, sometimes with Rickman, he even fell asleep. Kardiner concluded that Freud's silence must have given rise to the English school, where the analyst says nothing apart from "Good morning" and "Goodbye".

Afterword

In addition to his account of his analysis with Freud, Kardiner also wrote about how he felt about the analysis in 1977. He began by recording his admiration for Freud's brilliance, speed, and accuracy. His greatness as an analyst depended on his ability to make his interpretations in simple, everyday language. Kardiner identified the interpretation of the dream of the three Italians as the pivotal point in the analysis, opening up the defensive amnesia of his early life, its humiliations and distresses, as well as freeing him from the resistance to analysis developed in his work with Frink. He described Freud's analysis of his phobia about masks as a masterpiece, lifting the repression of his memory of having seen his mother lying dead. Nevertheless, he felt that Freud's interpretation of his identification with his natural mother as part of his unconscious homosexuality, and as a resolution of the Oedipus complex, had been erroneous. It had been a consequence of Freud's theoretical position about a homosexuality phase being universal among men. Kardiner thought that his dream of intercourse with his stepmother demonstrated that his "drive towards the woman was totally uninhibited" (*ibid.* pp. 61–62). There can, of course, be more that one opinion about that, and the sexual feelings about his stepmother might also have been seen as defensive against his homosexual wish. Without access to more material, there can be no resolution of the problem in this context.

Kardiner repeated the criticism he made at the time of Freud's failure to take up the issue in the transference, and to deal with Kardiner's placatory feelings towards him as a repetition, in the present, of those same feelings about his father. This repression of his assertiveness in the face of a powerful other reasserted itself later in life. In what he described as a review analysis, he had consulted Hans Sachs, who had confirmed Freud's original interpretation of unconscious homosexuality. Again, Kardiner found that repeated interpretation unacceptable, but could not challenge Sachs. He had to work it out for himself, and in his own self-analysis found that he had to discard this hypothesis to be able to establish a freedom from the blind spot Freud and his followers had created. Evidently, Sachs, like Freud, had an agenda that was discordant with his patient's, i.e., to confirm the theories rather than to see whether they fitted.

Finally, he wondered about Freud's having said nothing about Kardiner's bachelor status, simply hoping that Kardiner would one day have the luck to meet somebody he could marry. Kardiner recorded that, many years later when he was feeling mildly depressed, he had met a woman whom he married, and had a daughter with her. He congratulated himself on having been fortunate in his marriage, despite his disastrous early life.

To conclude, he wrote a brief critique of psychoanalysis in 1977, particularly in its institutional arrangements. To some extent he anticipated the criticism of it made by Masson, Kirsner, and Kernberg (*ibid.*, pp. 68–69), and complained about the dogmatic control exercised by those he called the Keepers of the Orthodoxy. He thought that Freud's basic ideas needed to be supplemented by studies of the way that individuals adapt to their environment, using the psychological mechanisms that Freud had originally identified. He felt that the necessary scientific information could not be gained from the study of individual patients on the couch, which should be replaced by field studies of human development.

CHAPTER THIRTEEN

Smiley Blanton

Introduction

B orn in 1882, Blanton did not begin psychoanalysis until
he was forty-seven. He grew up in Tennessee, which his
wife described as the Old South (Blanton, 1971, p. 8). He
was an only child in a rigid, bourgeois Presbyterian family. His
mother died while he was still young, and shortly afterwards
his father married her sister. He grew up in a household containing
his parents, uncle, grandparents, and two black servants. He was
the centre of attention, but his maternal grandmother, whom he
idealized, was aggressively controlling and critical of him, setting
him high standards to reach. However, he felt that he had been
spoilt. He had little in common with his father. At school, he had
few friends and did not get on with his teachers. His Sunday reading consisted largely of the Bible and Shakespeare (*ibid.*, p. 7).
Although in his adult life he professed to be without religion, he
meant that he did not believe in institutionalized religion. He
nevertheless had deeply religious feelings, reflected in his attempts
to form an alliance between religious experience and psychoanalysis.

He was not a good student, and, with difficulty, graduated from Vanderbilt University, Nashville. After his undergraduate studies, he was accepted in the graduate English course at Harvard, studying, and acting in, several of Shakespeare's plays. He went on to drama school where he developed an interest in stuttering and speech defects, leading to medical studies and psychiatry, graduating at Cornell in 1914. He married in 1910, but had no children. The couple were both analysed, and Margaret, his wife, met Freud on two occasions during Blanton's analysis. They worked together professionally on matters of common interest. She wrote movingly about their relationship with each other in a biographical note at the end of the published edition of his diary.

He served in the US Army Medical Corps during the First World War and between 1916 and 1928 held various psychiatric posts. He then went to Vienna to study psychoanalysis with Freud, intending to become a psychoanalyst himself. Returning to America, he continued his training with Brill. He visited Vienna and London at intervals between 1935 and 1938 for further brief analytic contacts with Freud. After his analysis, he devoted the remainder of his life to the integration of psychiatry and religion, while continuing practising psychoanalysis privately. He wrote on psychiatry and religion and, with his wife, co-authored works on speech pathology. He died in 1966.

The analysis

1 September 1929–23 April 1930

The first period began on 1 September 1929 and continued, with two very short breaks, until 23 April 1930. There was a further period of two weeks in August 1935, and another twelve sessions in August 1937. The final period was in September 1938, consisting of six sessions, terminated by Freud's need for further treatment for his cancer (*ibid.*, p. 113). Blanton intermittently wrote a diary of his work with Freud. Edited by his wife from a transcription of his hand-written notes, it was published posthumously in 1971 as *A Diary of My Analysis with Sigmund Freud*. Because there are many gaps and truncated accounts of the sessions, Mrs Blanton described the diary as containing selected highlights and noteworthy incidents in the analytic hours. Her husband had intended that it should serve as a basis for an unwritten monograph on Freud's methods. These notes are, therefore, a somewhat disappointing account of his analysis. He evidently formed a strong positive transference to Freud and, as the record shows, returned to him as often as he could for further brief periods of analysis. Lohser and Newton (1996, p. 119) describe this, rather dismissively, as being like a Christian pilgrim searching for a miracle cure.

Blanton arrived at his first session feeling very anxious. He had accidentally cut his finger and was suffering from colitis, which he knew afflicted him when he was emotionally disturbed. Additionally, he was about twenty minutes late because his taxi driver did not know the way. He half-sat/half-lay on the couch in Freud's consulting room. Freud enquired what he knew about psychoanalysis, and Blanton replied that the patient should lie on the couch, with the analyst seated at the head, that he should speak freely about whatever came into his mind, and relax completely. At Freud's invitation, he relaxed. Assuring Freud he was happy to be seeing him rather than Adler or Jung, he gave a brief account of his history, reporting that he felt insecure about his life in general. Freud was interested, rather than being coldly detached as Blanton had anticipated. He ended the session himself, in mid-sentence, when he heard the clock strike the hour. Freud said he was sorry that the hour had been so short. As he left, Blanton enquired about Freud's holiday. Freud said he would be leaving in fifteen days to go to Berlin for a for a month before his holiday, and that Blanton could accompany him to Berlin, or wait until he returned to Vienna. He chose to go to Berlin with Freud.

Most of the sessions, until Freud left for Berlin, were recorded, with a gap between the tenth and sixteenth sessions. Blanton, although beginning to feel more accustomed to the situation, was resistant and anxious for much of this time. Freud instructed him not to prepare what he intended to say. In the second session, as he was giving an account of his life and training, Freud interrupted to ask if he had any children. Blanton only had a pet dog. Freud commented that the feeling for dogs was the same as for children, except there was no ambivalence or hostility with dogs; Blanton disagreed (Blanton, 1971, p. 24). The session ended before Blanton was ready, and he left feeling depressed and disappointed without understanding why. He thought that he might fear plunging into his real difficulties and frailties. As Blanton spoke no German, the analysis was being conducted in English. At the beginning, communication was also impeded by Freud's prosthesis, so they had difficulty in understanding each other. In time they became more accustomed to each other's speech.

Blanton felt he was making financial sacrifices for his analysis and feared that Freud might not appreciate that. He expressed some displaced hostility to Freud by talking about doctors who did not give adequate return for their fees. He evidently thought that he was not referring to Freud, and gave an example. There may have also been some repressed anxiety that he was not paying Freud enough. Without making a direct interpretation, Freud said, perhaps ironically, that Blanton hoped he would be repaid for the financial sacrifices he had made to come to him. He advised that Blanton must be patient and they would get to deeper layers, and that he, Freud, would be less silent and give more of himself (*ibid.*, p. 28).

The same anxiety and resistance characterized the following sessions. When Freud interpreted a dream as indicating an unconscious, unfavourable feeling about him and the analysis, Blanton was surprised that, even unconsciously, he might have such thoughts. Then he associated to the thought that he might be afraid that he could be cheated, and not get what he had come for. Freud accepted that anxiety, and later tried to encourage him by saying that it took time to develop the right attitude and overcome resistance, but Blanton would, with help (*ibid.*, p. 34). In another session, they talked about the influence of Adler and Jung on psychoanalysis in America. Freud was dismissive of the progress of psychoanalytic ideas in America in the short term; Blanton thought that they would spread widely in the next ten years. Blanton may have reassured Freud that he was fully committed to psychoanalysis and Freud's practice, and optimistic about its prestige in America, while repressing his disbelief and resistance. Freud's responses may have concealed his concern that this particular American might not make much progress in the short term.

Blanton wrote no further notes until immediately before he and Freud left for Berlin, recording that Freud talked for most of the time, "or at least half of it" (*ibid.*, p. 32). After Blanton reported a dream, Freud gave him a rule that the analyst should never try to discover its exact meaning, but should help the patient to overcome his resistances. When Blanton was reluctant to mention some of his associations, Freud repeated his rule that he should give free rein to the unconscious, without making any moral judgments; the depth of the unconscious could only be reached in that way. The diary was then interrupted until early November. In a footnote, Mrs Blanton wrote that while she was in Berlin with her husband, she had met Freud by appointment and was deeply impressed by him.

Thereafter, the diary notes become very spasmodic with only one entry for the rest of 1929, then a few each month until April, and a final one in June 1930. In November, Freud, asking him if he was not fed up with discussing only dreams in his analysis, said he should say what was in his conscious mind. Blanton then gave two more short dreams, saying that they were full of meaning, but without recording what it was. Dreams did not need to be a mile long to be valuable, Freud said. Psychoanalysis was hard to go through, Blanton replied. Freud then gave him a lecture about the difficulty for those practising analysis to be in analysis themselves, since they lacked naïveté. He went on to describe the differences between the conscious and the unconscious mind.

Mrs Blanton, in a footnote, referred to a difference between Freud and her husband about the authorship of Shakespeare's plays. Blanton, in the light of his knowledge of Shakespeare, was convinced that "the man born in Stratford" had written them. Freud had been convinced that he had not, and gave Blanton a book arguing the case for another author. Blanton wrote later that he had been very upset, and could not have confidence in Freud's judg-ment, or continue the analysis, if Freud believed Shakespeare had not written the plays (*ibid.*, p. 37, fn.). Blanton asked his wife to read the book. It set out the case for Edward de Vere. He was depressed by the discussion with Freud, but Mrs Blanton believed she recog-nized that as resistance, and persuaded her husband to read it. He was not convinced, but realized that it was a serious work. On their return to America, Blanton continued the argument by sending books on the subject to Freud, who always wrote to thank him.

Blanton wrote two consecutive diary entries in January 1930. In the first, he flattered Freud, telling him that he was rereading *The*

Interpretation of Dreams, and was very impressed by it. He compared Freud to Descartes and his principle, *Cogito ergo sum.* It seemed as dramatic as that. Freud had not intended to be so dogmatic, saying that it had not felt very dramatic at the time. Blanton did not record any interpretation of his need to flatter Freud. The following day, Blanton told Freud that he was afraid of being too superficial in his summer lectures about mental hygiene. Freud advised him to keep to the facts.

To demonstrate, he presented him with an argument against Adler's views about organ inferiority. Children did not feel inferior because they had inferior organs, Freud claimed, but because they were not loved. If organ inferiority was involved, the parents' attitude towards the inferior organ caused it, but it was mostly their mothers' responsibility that children were not loved in the early phases. He did allow that when girls saw that their brothers were more loved by their mothers, they might conclude that the crucial factor was the possession of a penis, but he did not conclude that this might be an instance of organ inferiority in girls.

The next diary entries were in the middle of February 1930. Blanton told Freud that he had to save from his meagre teacher's salary to buy a copy of Freud's works. Freud gave him a copy of his *Collected Papers* in four volumes at the next session. After that gift, Blanton recorded one of several dreams. It was a dream of the war when soldiers were defending a railway station. A frisky dog was hauling a box full of cartridges between pillars holding up the roof. His associations were to his own war experience of the Germans bombing Nancy station, then of packing boxes that he had made to move books some years ago. He equated Freud's books to ammunition, and the defence of the station to the defence of psychoanalysis against attackers. The station pillars were the pillars of society who would not have accepted Freud's works so easily if they had understood their revolutionary character. His associations to other dreams around the same time also led to his thoughts about Freud's books, but he wrote that he was unable to get anything from these dreams. Freud interpreted,

> For the past few days your dreams have been growing more and more obscure. This can only have one meaning: There is a change in the transference. It is probably due to the present of the books.

You will see from this what difficulties gifts in analysis always make. [*Ibid.*, p. 42]

It is not clear whether Freud had intended his gift to be an object lesson. Blanton wrote no more about it. In the next recorded session, Freud gave Blanton another book, by a Dr Roback, about the place of Jews in literature, art, and the sciences. Freud said that he did not think much of it, nor did Blanton. Neither commented on the meaning of making a degraded gift to Blanton

A few days later Blanton was about four minutes late after allowing himself to be detained by his partner (not his wife) at a dancing class. Blanton felt flustered, and wished to account for his lateness as being due to a difference between his and Freud's watch. Freud said that his watch was usually right, and asked if he had been at the dancing school. Blanton then said that he had left with ten minutes to spare to get to his session but could not get a taxi. Blanton wrote that he then began his analysis, as if this exchange about the time and the reason for his lateness and flustered state had no relevance to it. Freud later wondered if Blanton had accepted some of the criticisms of psychoanalysis and the theory of errors and slips in a paper by Roback. If it was relevant to Blanton's late arrival and an attempt to avoid giving the reason for his lateness Freud made no link with it. He simply dismissed the paper as being full of inaccuracies, and without interest.

In the next reported session, Blanton claimed that Freud had talked for most of the time about Blanton's dream of a Methodist preacher, and a stupidly designed church the preacher had built. The dream included references to two steps to the front door so arranged that they could become stools for children or adults; red and gold decorations on the walls; a ceiling veil with clouds painted on it and lights resembling the sun and the moon; golden oak furniture; a rear tank for immersion, with a small cast-iron bath tub too small for immersion, broken at one end. Blanton's associations were that the church was analysis and the dream was a criticism of it. Too much was made of the anal aspects of life, especially of the child. The decorations were put in to add richness to the religion of analysis, which was only suited to the very intelligent, for it would be very arid for the average person (*ibid.*, p. 46). The dream of the stupidly built church suggested that Blanton wished to disparage Freud's theories, and express his unconscious negative transference.

Freud congratulated him on his being able to associate, but disagreed with some of his interpretations. Decorations might mean something else. The veil and lights meant that heaven had been taken away by analysis. The broken tank meant circumcision; a Jew had built the house and was showing him round. All of that may have had some reference to a discussion in previous session of the question of Jewish and Christian psychoanalysis. The session ended with considering whether the choice of profession could depend on sublimation. Freud illustrated the possibility by claiming that most psychiatrists need to reassure themselves about their normality, and they gained that reassurance because they felt that they were more normal than their patients. Blanton was a psychiatrist.

Blanton only wrote about five sessions in March. The first was a wonderful hour he had talking to Freud about his *Collected Papers*, and his *Three Essays on the Theory of Sexuality* (1905d), but not about himself. Freud had gone on to give advice about technique, which could be learned only from personal teaching and experience. Two dreams in the next session were interpreted by Freud as meaning that Blanton had repudiated psychoanalysis when it was not being carried out to rule, and that he had doubts about being able to present psychoanalysis in the best light. Blanton might be too optimistic about getting analysis accepted as it always aroused resistance, citing Jung as an example, who thought he had overcome resistance in America by modifying analysis.

The three remaining sessions written up in this month were concerned with aspects of Freud's theories of sexual development. He told Blanton that there had been some modification in his views about the development of the more complex sexuality in girls, than in boys. Mrs Blanton's studies had provided confirmation of the fact that neonatal boys experienced erections, Blanton said. The discussion of one of Blanton's dreams, in the last session in March, concerned the way that boys compensate for enforced passivity by immediately becoming active. Freud, rather didactically, claimed that when women have affairs they were unable to continue with analysis, since they became so involved in them that they were then lost to analysis. Men, who were emotionally less deeply involved in affairs, could continue their analyses. Were American women more like men in that respect, Freud asked?

Freud's need of emergency treatment terminated this analysis, and he recorded only three sessions in April 1930. In them, Blanton seems to have diverted Freud from making interpretations to discussions of theory and technique. Even a dream about Blanton's dog swallowing a porcupine so that Blanton had to operate on him to get it out, was not related to his concerns about Freud's pending operation, or to Blanton's feelings about Freud's dog being in the consulting room. Before the final sessions, Blanton had been to Budapest, where he had met Ferenczi, and had missed some of his appointments. In them, he began a theoretical discussion about some critiques he had read of Freud's *Civilization and Its Discontents* (1930a, which Freud dismissed. Blanton then raised the question of negative transferences, which he claimed not to have himself. Freud commented that Blanton had had mental reservations about psychoanalysis.

Despite that, Blanton believed that Freud had assented to his continuing to study in New York, and to his being able to practise at the end of a year.

3–17 August, 1935

Five years later, when visiting Europe, Blanton arranged to have twelve more sessions, paying for them in advance. As before, he was anxious about whether the payment was sufficient, and he impressed Freud with the sacrifices he was making even to pay the same fees as five years ago. He told Freud that he had been much happier in the five years since his analysis. Freud asked him if he had been helped personally by the analysis. Blanton replied that it was the most personally helpful thing that had ever happened to him (Blanton, 1971, p. 54).

It was clear that Blanton was seeking to use Freud as a consultant for his work with patients in New York, and to take the opportunity to talk about theory and technique. He wrote that he would speak about himself subjectively, but did not record anything of that nature in his first diary entry. The following session continued in the same vein, with some discussion about Ferenczi and his methods, as well as more questions about technique. He asked

Freud about his children. Freud told him that his three sons all had left Germany because no Jew could expect to get justice there. The only subjective matter recorded concerned a dream, not described. Freud had interpreted that Blanton was disappointed, wishing to leave before his time to become a member of Freud's family.

Freud wanted to avoid being used as a consultant, but Blanton continued to divert the discussion from himself to impersonal matters, or his patients. As the sessions progressed, Freud seems to have given up the attempt to analyse and to accept Blanton's discordant agenda. A dream about Queen Victoria concerned Blanton's identification of Freud with the queen and his own grandmother, but over two sessions the work with this dream was diverted again into a discussion of Blanton's patients.

The two final sessions in this series were the same mixture of Blanton's seeking advice about his patients, of general discussion about issues relating to Freud himself, and of rather brief analyses of dreams. Blanton's ambivalence about Freud was never far below the surface. The negative was contained in some rather oblique thoughts about Jewishness, compensated for by an over-idealization of Freud himself, and of Jewishness. Jews had become hated, but Freud and Einstein, both Jewish, were the two greatest minds in the world. More than that, two of nine members of the US Supreme Court were Jews. Three of Blanton's dreams seemed to have represented passive, childish wishes for Freud's love, and he wrote that Freud agreed, saying that Blanton should continue with his self-analysis of his dreams He thought Freud had assented to his belief that he was the not neurotic, nor had any fundamental defect which would prevent him from successfully practising as a psychoanalyst. He left hoping to return the following summer, although Freud felt he could not promise to wait for him.

1–13 August 1937

Although Freud was on holiday at Grinzing, an arrangement was made for Blanton to see him for further sessions, including an invitation to Mrs Blanton to call on him. The Blantons had made a detour to Vienna on their way to Lourdes to study the cures that were believed to have occurred there. These were discussed in the first hour. Freud expressed disbelief in them, except in the case of functional disorders. Blanton set up the agenda for these sessions by saying that he had no special reason for coming to see Freud except for the general help Freud could give him, and the joy the hours gave him. However, at the end of the hour, he raised something that obviously had been bothering him. The mother of one of Blanton's patients had written to Freud to ask if Blanton was a good person for the treatment of stuttering, and Freud had assented. She had gone on to ask if Blanton was a good analyst, and Freud had shaken his head (*ibid.*, p. 56). It is not clear how she could have seen a headshake if this exchange had been by correspondence. Blanton wrote that, if that event had happened, Freud had been wrong; Freud said that it had never happened. So, whether or not this exchange had taken place in writing, Blanton, in fact, may have had some doubts about Freud's opinion of his psychoanalytic credentials. Did he perhaps wonder if Freud's pessimistic views about psychoanalysis in the USA could also have included himself? His concern in each period to assure himself that Freud approved of him as a psychoanalyst may suggest that he needed to ward off his own self-doubts. The meeting ended with a further exchange about Lourdes and about the timing of his future sessions.

After this preliminary meeting, the first full analytic hour was on 2 August, but very little of note occurred within it. Blanton asked if Freud could recommend a dermatologist to deal with some itchiness he was suffering. There followed some confusion about the times of future appointments and of Mrs Blanton's meeting with Freud. Blanton then raised a technical question about dreams as wish fulfilments, and their appearance in analysis. The following day the time of the hour was changed. After a reference to a suitable dermatologist, Blanton wrote, "I then began my hour." It is interesting that Blanton excluded some things as not being part of the analysis, although they occurred within the time-boundary of the session. Mrs Blanton was more perceptive, and asked whether she should go to Paris for two weeks while her husband was having his analytic hours, so that her presence did not interfere with the transference. Neither Blanton nor Freud thought it would, so she stayed.

In the next three sessions, Blanton recorded little or nothing about his personal phantasies, nor any analytical interpretation that Freud might have made. His ambivalence about Freud was again evident when he told an apocryphal tale of Freud having fallen asleep in an analytic hour with a patient, which Freud denied. The positive aspect of the ambivalence was unconsciously expressed when he came to the next session bearing a copy of *The Inter-pretation of Dreams*, telling Freud that it was his bible, rereading it every year (rather like his rereading of the Bible in his youth). He again used Freud as a supervisor, discussing some of his cases and seeking guidance on theoretical concepts relevant to them. Mrs Blanton spent twenty minutes of one of the hours with Freud. Her account of that meeting is much more illuminating and alive than anything Blanton wrote about his sessions. What he felt about losing nearly half a session while his wife talked with Freud was not mentioned, but he told Freud that she had appreciated the opportunity of seeing him.

In one session, Freud offered him an opportunity to say some-thing about what he described as undiscovered matters, but Blanton simply deflected the discussion into some conceptual issues about dreams, as if they had nothing to do with himself. The remaining sessions, even the final one, as reported, continued in the same vein. In the final session, Freud's dog was present, and Blanton commented that the dog had come to see him. Freud agreed. Then Blanton wrote, "I began by expressing the sadness I felt at having to go. Then I asked a couple of technical questions" (*ibid.*, p. 64). So, even at this point, Blanton was unable to think about the meaning of his sadness, or of the defence against it.

The session ended with his wish to return again next year.

30 August–7 September 1938

Since Blanton had last seen him a year ago, Freud had been able to escape from the Nazis to come to London. Freud was in poor health and it was not certain that he would be able to see Blanton. In the event, the sessions had to be terminated prematurely because of Freud's ill-health. However, Blanton wrote of their first meeting that Freud "seemed as full of energy, as eager and as keen as I had ever seen him." That seems to have been a very considerable denial of Freud's actual condition. Most of the session was concerned with enquiries about Freud's being settled in London, about inter-national affairs, and an attempt by Blanton to get Freud's help with a patient that they had discussed the previous year. The only personal note concerned a dream that Blanton had been unable to "analyse" properly. Freud thought it dealt with repression.

The following sessions were very discursive, mixing thoughts about Blanton's dreams (not described in the diary) with discussions about the international situation, and Blanton's visit to Lourdes. Freud commented on Blanton's resistance, and he responded by telling Freud a concealed wish that he hoped to set up a psychoanalytic group in Nashville when he retired. He wanted Freud's view about that, and whether he would support his application to the New York Institute to become a training analyst. Freud felt he could not have any influence with the New York Institute, as they seemed to be on the verge of declaring independence from the International Association. He did, however, agree that Blanton was competent to be a training analyst.

The remaining sessions were much affected by Freud's state of health and impending operation. The impression given by Blanton's diary notes is that they were concerned with general gossip about American psychoanalysis, interspersed with technical advice about theoretical issues. Perhaps Blanton's reluctance to enter into issues of a deeply personal and unconscious nature colluded with Freud's depleted capacity resulting from the debilitating nature of his illness. In the final session, when he had referred to having had three dreams, he asked Freud if dreams in the same night were connected. This was an odd question from one who had read and reread *The Interpretation of Dreams*, in which Freud refers specifically to this matter (*ibid.*, p. 76). Blanton then interpreted one of the dreams as meaning that Freud's operation would go well, which Freud described as a wish fulfilment. Then the following exchange occurred, "One of my dreams had to do with the fear of homosexual attack on me." "That", said Freud, "is the cause of the greatest resistance and fear in men" (*ibid.*, pp. 83–84). The generalized response perhaps indicated a reluctance to interpret the transference. That might not be surprising in the final analytic session that Freud believed would be the last time that he would meet Blanton.

In this final session, Mrs Blanton had spent the first ten minutes with Freud and her account of her conversation with him is again much more illuminating about both herself and Freud than anything that her husband had written. As usual, there was nothing about the meaning for Blanton of this warm relationship between his wife and Freud. With Freud's admission to hospital, the analysis ended rather abruptly.

Because the diary is incomplete, with the account of many sessions unrecorded, it is quite difficult to assess this analysis. What happened in the unrecorded hours might have been highly significant and different from those that Blanton wrote up. If these diary entries were supposed to be the highlights of the analysis, it may be wondered what the less exciting, unrecorded meetings were like. What seems to be missing from Blanton's account of his analysis is anything about his personal history, and his situation in what must have been a very untypical household. To say the least, there might have been something significant about the death of his mother, followed by her replacement by her sister, that would have been analytically germane. Nor is there any mention of his marriage, although his wife was present in some of his sessions. What seems evident in all these sessions is that Blanton had a discordant agenda through which his powerful, denied resistance to Freud was expressed.

Mrs Blanton wrote some footnotes, which seem very perceptive. She also wrote very movingly about their relationship in her "Biographical notes and comments" (*ibid.*, p. 88) at the end of Blanton's book. She wrote of the rift in their marriage resulting from the analysis

> . . . Professor Freud became his beloved father figure, and his grandmother and I, who had been identified with his grandmother, were dethroned. His necessity to accept everything that I said as gospel truth was dispelled, and he became very negative. Of course it is probable that changes in me that I cannot see were factors also. But I do know that thereafter my role became entirely different. [*Ibid.*, p. 98]

She went on to describe how the marriage nearly broke down because of these changes. They parted for while until her husband persuaded her to return. She wrote that after they were both analysed, ". . . another Smiley developed and doubtless another me". What is evident, although absent from Blanton's account, is that their analyses had radically changed the nature of their relationship, which became companionate rather than passionate. Freud was not interested in their relationship, despite the occasions when he had met Mrs Blanton during some of her husband's analytic hours.

The image of Freud that emerges from this account is congruent with the one conveyed in the narratives of his other patients. First, he had a powerful, charismatic personality, which led to intense transferences, although, apart from Mrs Blanton's biographical material, it is difficult to discern it in Blanton's diary entries. There his response to his transference to Freud was, by turns, sycophantic and resistant. Freud's interpretations seemed often to be didactic, and derived from the symbolism without having been related to Blanton's associations, in so far as he recorded them. Similarly, as in the other accounts, Freud often engaged in gossip about others in the analytic and scientific world, as well as about himself and his family. With Blanton, as with others, there seems to have been no analysis of what this information may have meant in the therapy. In fact, it is hard to see from this diary how many of the transactions described could be considered analytic in any recognizable sense. Nevertheless, when asked by Freud how the analysis had helped him personally, Blanton had replied that as far as personal understanding went, it had been the most helpful thing that had ever happened to him (*ibid.*, p. 98). Were it not for his wife's biographical notes at the end of the diary, it would be quite difficult to believe that.

CHAPTER FOURTEEN

Dr Margaret I. Little

Introduction

G rotstein, in his Introduction to Margaret Little's account of her analyses with three different analysts, wrote that she was "apparently the victim of frightened and unattuned parents" (Little, 1990). Her earliest memories were of "being in the way" and "a trouble" when she, her mother, and her older sister Ruth all had whooping cough. Her mother and Ruth were in bed together, she was in a cot by herself and began coughing and vomiting. When her father came home he was quite unsympathetic to her plight, angrily asking her mother why she could not "*stop* that child being sick" (*ibid.*, p. 27).

She was the second of five children, two of whom were boy twins born ten years after Margaret. Her younger sister died at the age of twenty-eight. All the other children had their difficulties. As a sickly child, with an undiagnosed hiatus hernia and a coeliac condition, she felt she was an irritant and a threat to the supremacy of her older sister. Her symptoms were dismissed as being imagined, or psychogenic, which she should have been able to control (*ibid.*). Until the age of ten, Margaret was compelled to rest every afternoon in a darkened room without toys or books. She felt so ashamed that she had to gnaw a candle to get small fragments that she could chew.

Her relationship with her mother, who made her feel crazy, was particularly complicated (*ibid.*, p. 51). She agreed with Winnicott's description of her mother as being chaotic. Her mother was also dominating, controlling, and a compulsive meddler, even controlling the games that her children could play. Margaret had been unable to detach herself from her mother, despite her warm and self-sacrificing father's stability and reliability (*ibid.*, p. 35). She and her family seem to have had a problem about mourning, and in childhood, she was unable to grieve for the death of a close friend; and the family were unable to mourn the death of her grandmother, or of her father.

Margaret Little managed to cover up her "abnormality", despite these very dysfunctional family relationships. She attended school, passed exams, won a scholarship, and qualified in medicine. She became a general practitioner, and eventually a qualified psychoanalyst. She wrote movingly about her experiences as a medical student during the First World War, of her time as a general practitioner, and particularly about her experiences of death in patients and relatives as well as her own physical illnesses and the insight she had gained from them. She married late in life, and wrote of her husband's death from cancer.

The analyses

Dr Little's account of her three analyses was published twice, first as a paper in *Free Associations* called "Winnicott working in areas where psychotic anxieties predominate: a personal record", and again in 1990 as a book, with some additional material, entitled *Psychotic Anxieties and Containment: A Personal Record of an Analysis with Winnicott*. Some of her other professional papers are concerned with the issues of neurotic and psychotic transferences and countertransferences that were central to her experiences in her analyses with Ella Sharpe and Winnicott. Professionally she situated herself in the Independent tradition.

She began her account with the developments and differences introduced Freud's classical formulations by the object relations theorists in general, and Winnicott in particular. She hoped that her story might be a way of providing some essential case material to illustrate his technique. She emphasized that her accounts of her analyses were her personal experiences of the different analysts who had treated her. She also expressed her anxiety about writing in this personal way, and that she might worry those who adhered closely to classical theory and practice (*ibid.*, p. 40).

Dr X

The breakdown of her close friend and live-in housekeeper made Dr Little realize that she, too, needed treatment. She began treatment with a Jungian analyst she called Dr X. She wrote only briefly about her treatment between 1936 and 1938, but it had helped her to break free from this very dependent and clinging friend; however, Dr X had failed to notice the depth of her disturbance (Little, 1981, p. 237). He also encouraged her to train as a psychotherapist at the Tavistock Clinic. At the end of the treatment, he assured her that she needed no more analysis, only synthesis, but nevertheless introduced her to Ella Freeman Sharpe.

Ella Freeman Sharpe

From Dr X's introduction in 1939, she had a preliminary session with Ella Sharpe in 1940. She wrote that feeling terrified, she *"ran from the house in panic"* (Little, 1990, p. 36). A year later, she became emotionally involved with one of her patients, and since Dr X was not available, she returned to Ella Sharpe in 1940. She again felt terrified and lay rigid on the couch, but nevertheless began analysis with her. Sharpe's classical approach, interpreting in terms of infantile sexuality and oedipal wishes, was not relevant to her problems of identity and fear of annihilation. Dr Little asserted that this was not a transference neurosis, but part of a psychotic transference based upon actual infantile experiences and the classical approach was irrelevant. As a result, her work with Sharpe was a constant struggle, and she felt unable to get across that her real problems were about existence and identity, predating any infantile sexual phantasies. In the transference, Sharpe became identical with her mother since she could not provide a place where it was safe to *be,* but only one where it was safe to be *sexual or hostile (ibid.,* 20). She did not feel safe with, or accept, interpretations of her dreams as phantasies of violent intercourse with her father and destructive wishes towards her mother. Even though her critical feelings about Sharpe were very intense, after six weeks Dr Little expressed a wish to train as a psychoanalyst. She was encouraged to apply and was accepted. So her analysis became a training analysis, but she was conscious of the discordant agendas between them. She continued to struggle with the irremediable transference to Sharpe of her crazy mother.

Ella Sharpe, she wrote, always encouraged her in her training, praising her work. In the continued struggle between them in the analysis, Dr Little was unable to convince her analyst that what she was saying about her parents was not phantasy, but a reality. The crazy, disorderly mother in the analysis became herself, reintrojected from the transference to Sharpe. Her recognition of her own and her mother's psychosis was dismissed as phantasy, so Dr Little felt that she was back in her confused infantile estate, re-enacted in the present interaction between herself and Sharpe. She was prohibited from knowing anything beyond the classical interpretations, extended into the real relationship of patient and psychoanalyst. From her medical knowledge and observation, she knew that Sharpe was suffering from a serious heart condition, but the psychoanalytic rule forbade her from mentioning it.

Even with that chronic conflict, the analysis was deemed to have been a satisfactory training experience. As she was scheduled to read her paper for full membership, her father was unexpectedly taken ill and died. A week after his funeral she was to read-in, and asked if it could be postponed. She recorded that ". . . Miss Sharpe insisted that I should read it" *(ibid.,* p. 26). She felt unable to stand up for herself, and it was a massive interference with her mourning. It may also have been a re-enactment in the analysis of her family's problems with mourning. However, she wrote that she had enjoyed the discussion.

The analysis continued with only a brief, if sincere, acknowledgement of her grief. All that seemed to matter was that she had read her paper. Her wish to postpone its reading was interpreted as her envy of Sharpe's creativity, transferred from her envy of her parent's sexual relationship and creativity. In a chapter in her book (*ibid.*, p. 31) she disguised herself as a male patient with a male analyst, writing that the patient's mourning had been so inter-rupted by an inappropriate interpretation that he was not able to recognize his distress until two years later. She attributed the accep-tance of this interpretation to the analyst's non-differentiation from the patient, and to the failure of the analyst to have recognized his own unconscious countertransference to the patient.

The treatment was extended for a further sixteen months, with agreement to terminate it at the end of the summer term 1947. While Dr Little was away at a psychoanalytic conference, Ella Sharpe died unexpectedly, and she returned to the news of Sharpe's death. She felt that it was a repetition of the unworked through trauma of her father's death, recalling a similar occasion when Sharpe had prevented her from mourning the death of a loved aunt by interpreting something about a forthcoming analytic holiday. She was very distressed and sought assistance from Dr Payne and Marion Milner until she was able to enter analysis with Winnicott.

D. W. Winnicott

In the interval between leaving Ella Sharpe and starting with Winnicott, her housekeeper retired. She moved house, so that she no longer worked at home. She did not begin analysis immediately after her initial interview with Winnicott, because she had just begun a sexual relationship with a man. Winnicott agreed to keep the vacancy for her. When that relationship was in difficulties, she began her analysis, lasting from 1949 to 1955, and resuming in 1957. She wrote that she could not give a detailed account of her time with him, only of some of the incidents that happened.

In the first of her regular sessions, she experienced the same terror that she had felt in the first session with Sharpe. It was relieved when Winnicott spoke for the first time at the end of the session, interpreting that, although he did not *know*, he felt she was shutting him out for some reason. The crucial element was his admission of not knowing. In a later session, feeling desperate that she could not make him understand, as she wandered about the room, feeling suicidal, she smashed a vase containing a lilac. Winni-cott immediately left the room, coming back later to find her clear-ing the mess up. It was replaced with a replica the next day, and the incident was never mentioned again. It has been argued that Winnicott may have conveyed to Dr Little that he was afraid of her aggression and destructiveness, which resulted in its remaining unanalysed.

She experienced the same spasms of terror in a session some weeks later, and seized his hands until the spasms passed. Winnicott interpreted that he thought that she was reliving the experience of birth, and held her head as if she were a baby. She felt that she had been reborn into a relationship (*ibid.*, p. 34), and had been held both literally and metaphorically. The spasms were not repeated, and the fear only occasionally. The themes of holding and of regression to dependence were very significant for Dr Little. She described how she often lay silently and withdrawn, sometimes in distress, while Winnicott held her two hands clasped between his, "almost like an umbilical cord" (*ibid.*, p. 36), despite his boredom and the pain in his hands. It was possible to speak of these experiences only later.

Holding, Dr Little explained, meant that the psychoanalyst took full responsibility for the patient, sometimes restraining or controlling, and supplying ego strength until she could take it over herself. It included ensuring that there was somebody to be available in his absence, and even arranging hospitalization if he felt that there was a danger of self-harm or suicide. On one occasion, Winnicott took away her car keys in case she rushed from the room, and drove away dangerously (as she was inclined to do). She attributed all of this to his concept of the facilitating environment, particularly necessary for regressed patients in an infantile, dependent condition. It provided an opportunity for her to feel safe, when it had not been possible with her mother in her infancy or childhood. She believed that Winnicott's capacity to work in this way was derived from his understanding of infants, children, and their parents, as well as from his great empathy, and ability to allow her to work at her own pace.

She wrote that he gave very few verbal interpretations. When he did, they were usually apposite, expressed tentatively or speculatively, leaving her to accept or reject them. The verbal exchanges between them seemed less about interpretations than about other things. He commented, for example, that he really hated her mother, considering her unpredictable, chaotic, and organizing chaos around her (Little, 1981, p. 33). He made similar non-interpretive remarks at other times. She wrote that although she had not told him much about her family he seemed to understand nevertheless. Very much of their interaction seems to have been physical or verbal. Psyche and soma, for Winnicott, were not separated but were deeply interdependent. If she seemed unwell, he would check her physical condition with medical instruments kept in his consulting room. He was also ready to change his way of working if she was physically ill. Early in the analysis, when she was suffering from gastro-enteritis she felt physically exhausted and unable to go to her sessions, he came to see her at home for as often as five, six, or seven sessions per week for as long as three months.

There were periods when, in her daily life, she was acting in a very adult way, despite the underlying psychotic manifestations in her analysis. This may have been a repetition of her childhood and adolescence, when, performing well at school and in higher education, she developed a false self to conceal a very serious disturbance behind it. So, becoming the Business Secretary of the Institute of Psycho-analysis *faute de mieux*, as she was the Assistant Secretary when the Secretary unexpectedly died, was an example of this capacity to function in reality. She performed the task for two years under protest, feeling that she was not qualified. Her anxiety was intensified during the early months of this appointment because Winnicott was ill with his coronary problem, and was unable to see her for some time. When she fell ill with depression after two years, a professional Company Secretary was appointed in her place. She continued with her own psychoanalytical practice as well as writing some papers for publication. She was also able to mobilize her medical knowledge to recognize two occasions when Winnicott was suffering from a coronary illness. On the second occasion, she became very anxious about his depression, but they were unable to speak of it. It reminded her of a time in childhood when she was simultaneously in difficulties at school and anxious about her mother's pregnancy, none of which could be acknowledged.

Winnicott had divorced, remarried, and moved to a new home, when in reality she found it possible to explode with anger at her mother in the most hostile and acrimonious way, never seeing her mother again. Winnicott approved the spontaneous assertion of her feelings. While he was on his summer holidays, soon after this outburst, she went on a walking holiday in Scotland. Her mother wrote to her in Scotland, making what Dr Little called outrageous demands, as if the angry incident had never occurred. She stormed off up a mountain in fury. The next day, she fell on the wet grass outside her hotel breaking her ankle so badly that it needed a fortnight's treatment in hospital. She commented that if the accident had happened the day before she might not have been found in the mountains, and could have died from exposure.

She sent a card to Winnicott to let him know what had happened to her, and he responded with a telegram and a letter. With her leg still in plaster, she returned home, but was unable to see him for six weeks. When the sessions resumed, he interpreted her accident as a response to his holiday, describing it as a suicide attempt. She did not correct him about the misinterpretation of his absence on holiday. She knew that it was an attack on her mother that, in her guilt, she had turned against herself in the accident, while he was on his summer holidays. She wrote that she could not recall the content of the next year's sessions. She seems to have felt the same confusion that had accompanied Sharpe's transference interpretation, which had failed to recognize the primitive relationship between Dr Little and her mother, from whom she was unable to distinguish herself. In that relationship she had not known who she was. Winnicott seems to have made the same mistake as Sharpe in his interpretation.

There appears to have been some implied criticism of him in Dr Little's account of her confused state. Like Sharpe, she felt he was interpreting in accordance with the orthodox theory. She worked out for herself that something had to break to free herself from her mother and destroy the repetition.

Two childhood memories seemed relevant, involving some confusing sexual identifications, and of replacing her father in mother's bed when she was deliriously ill with *pneumonia*. Her mother had said that Margaret had clung to her night and day. Winnicott interpreted that her mother would not let her die. Dr Little rephrased it later that, "She would not let me *choose* whether to live or die. I *had* to live for her" (*ibid.*, p. 49). Her mother's reassertion of her hold over her during the holiday had made her feel that something had to break, and it was her own ankle. She concluded that her very confused state, following the rejected interpretation, was a repetition of the delirium when she could not distinguish herself from her mother. She was unable to make it clear to Winnicott how the condition had been precipitated, any more than she had been able to let her mother understand about the original trauma. She had only been able to fall ill and threaten to die. Neither her mother nor Winnicott had been able to let her choose between life or death. *He* might have understood that she had made her choice by falling at the hotel, and not in the mountains where she could not have been found. At the next summer break, Winnicott felt anxious about the possibility of another suicide attempt and wanted her to enter hospital to be safe. She wrote,

> I went for him, wildly; I think I hit him, though I am not certain. He caught my wrists and held me, and was not hurt. Eventually I agreed on condition that he would ensure that I was not given electro-shock, that I could have a private room, that I could discharge myself if I wished (make my own choice), and that he would take me there himself and bring me back—all of which he agreed and carried out. [*Ibid.*, p. 58]

At the hospital, she at first felt safe, but then forlorn, abandoned, weepy, and afraid, remaining in her room for ten days. One morning she asked to be left undisturbed (presumably she had been on some kind of suicide watch), and eight people came in to her room, one after another. The eighth was the ward maid, by whom she was so annoyed that she spanked her while she knelt cleaning the floor. She was immediately threatened with other treatment by the Deputy Superintendent, whom she reminded of the agreed ban on ECT. Her anger continued to grow, and by the evening she began to smash up her room. She was secluded feeling paranoid and delusional, seeing the attendant nurses as devils. She had two transitional objects to help her. In the morning, she was moved into an open room in a locked ward. In that ward, she felt cared for like an infant. It was like the same care that Winnicott had given in his treatment of her. In hospital, she could regress fully into dependence. Winnicott kept in touch with the hospital, and sent her postcards to let her know where he was. The hospital care was total; Dr Little took full advantage of it. In contrast to her parents in infancy and childhood, the hospital "went on *being*, and holding and looking after me, calm and apparently undisturbed" (*ibid.*, pp. 58–59).

She felt safe to be uncontrolled within its boundary, but not abandoned. Something again had to be broken, but not herself. She linked it to the breaking of the vase in Winnicott's consulting room, when she felt she had been abandoned when he rushed from the room, and the hospitalization was symbolically similar. This time he had maintained the contact with her through his postcards. She had only one suicidal impulse in the hospital when she saw some rope in the garden, but realized she had no need to act on it. She was able to come back from regression to ordinary life on discharge from hospital.

In the hospital Dr Little began to write poetry and to paint, which she regarded as playing in a way she had not been allowed to as a child. She developed the poetry writing and the painting after she left hospital, becoming quite accomplished in both. She worked through her hospital experiences when she resumed analysis with Winnicott. She talked with him about the meaning of her paintings and poems, and realized that she did not need his approbation to value her work. Its value lay in its creation. That realization importantly counter-balanced the annihilation she had experienced in infancy. In the terminal phase of the therapy, she especially valued Winnicott's interpretation, that her fear of annihilation belonged to the past, and that she had survived a psychic annihilation, emotionally relived in the present (*ibid.*, p. 60). She wrote that it was some time before she was able to assimilate this interpretation, but that it had been of value after the analysis had ended.

In the final stages, the frequency of the sessions decreased and became less fraught, allowing for playfulness and creativity as well as being more enjoyable. Winnicott revealed even more of himself through gossip, information, and more serious discussions about analysis itself. He was able to let her see the demand and distress he experienced in what he had offered her, as well as others. It was not necessary to sacrifice himself totally, but to survive the intensity of such a relationship it was essential to provide for his own needs through his marriage and leisure activities. She especially valued these revelations, making her feel safe and able to value herself.

After the analysis formally ended, she formed another sexual relationship, which ended unsuccessfully because it was based upon oedipal feelings. She then returned to Winnicott for weekly sessions for eighteen months, which he ended because it was "time I took over my own responsibilities and got on with my life" (*ibid.*, p. 62).

In the "Aftermath", 1957–1984, she wrote of her life after the analysis and of her achievements, both as a psychoanalyst and especially as a painter. She was able to continue the work of her analysis through self-analysis, applying the insights not only to herself, but also to others in her professional life.

In these three very different accounts of her analyses, it is interesting that in the first two, despite problems with each of them, she identified with both therapists to the extent of wanting to train as a psychotherapist at the Tavistock Clinic, then as a psychoanalyst at the Institute of Psychoanalysis. Might this have been a repetition of her original merged identity with her mother, but not seen by either of the two therapists who simply encouraged her to proceed? The wish to identify with them may have disguised her discordant agenda, which she could not bring into the two therapies. It is also possible that the same thing occurred with Winnicott, since she adopted his practice very wholeheartedly, publishing papers exploring his idea of the psychotic transference and countertransference. However, it was only in the analysis with Winnicott that she found it possible to begin to resolve her primitive identifications, and the fear of annihilation, continuing in her self-analysis. At one point, her discordant agenda with Winnicott was revived for as long as a full year. She could not explore it with him or remember the sessions, but it apparently resolved spontaneously at the end of that time.

The analysis with Winnicott also raises questions about the nature of therapy and what its healing quality might be. It contrasts with the classically remote analysis with Sharpe. With its introduction of personal matters and non-interpretative interactions, it can be compared with the analyses by Freud discussed in earlier chapters, as well as with Jung's analysis of Catherine Cabot. Another interesting difference from Freud, although not from Jung, is the amount of physical contact, as well out of session contact, that Winnicott made. This was not just an indulgence, but followed from the concept that the social, psyche, and soma were interlinked. For Dr Little's primitive disturbance, attention to all three elements was necessary in the treatment. A more significant difference from both

Freud and Sharpe was Winnicott's own corresponding regression to Dr Little's, while he was able to maintain his observing, healthy ego at the same time. Dr Little seems clear that it was these differences that contributed to her recovery from the psychotic disturbance she suffered, as well as her capacity to use and conceptualize these differences in her own psychoanalytic work. Both Sharpe and Winnicott acted out the transference of Little's feelings about her mother when the reality of her feelings was not recognized by them, and impeded her recovery.

CHAPTER FIFTEEN

Jeffrey Masson

Introduction

Jeffrey Masson was born in 1941 to a wealthy merchant family of Indian origin. His parents moved frequently within the USA and Europe when he was a child. His grandfather and father were both very promiscuous, and he followed their example, although his wide experience of women was ungratifying to him. He obtained his PhD from Harvard in aspects of Sanskrit poetry, and was then appointed as assistant professor in Sanskrit at the University of Toronto. After a few months, he was given tenure and felt that his career was settled. He began psychoanalysis after marriage, in the hope that he would be able to overcome his profound sadness (Masson, 1990, p. 11), as well as his promiscuity. This marriage, in which he had had a daughter, ended in divorce. He subsequently married again and had two sons with his second wife.

He had formed an ambition to become a psychoanalyst in 1962, after he had met by chance a psychoanalyst couple who had impressed him with their human curiosity, openness, and friendliness (*ibid.*, p. 12). His training analysis began in 1971 and continued until 1976, the year after his daughter was born. He became a graduate member of the Toronto Institute of Psychoanalysis in 1978, and a year later of the San Francisco Psychoanalytical society. In the same year, he was admitted to the International Psychoanalytic Association and The Canadian Psychoanalytic Society.

A charismatic, narcissistic, and forceful individual, he felt confident enough of himself, even while still in training, to present papers at meetings of the International Psychoanalytic Association. He formed a close relationship with Eissler, the Secretary of the Freud Archive, who, hoping to retire, thought of Masson as his successor. Masson preferred research to being an analyst with patients, and wished spend more of his time researching the life of Freud. He persuaded Anna Freud to allow him to have access to Freud's unpublished letters, translating them into English after he had spent six months in Germany learning the language.

Soon after this, the psychoanalytic community began to be disillusioned with him, when he published a critical work about Freud's theories (Masson, 1992). His contract with the Archive was terminated acrimoniously after a year, following which he gave up the profession of psychoanalysis in disgust. He has continued an academic and writing career.

The analysis

In the preface to his book, he clamed that nobody had told him what it was either to undergo training as an orthodox Freudian analyst, or what it was like to leave the profession (Masson, 1990). No one else has written in such disillusion about the analytical training process, the theory underpinning it and its organizational structure. Masson compiled the story of his analysis partly from notes made at the time, and partly from memory, recognizing that memory could be faulty but feeling that he had done his best to verify his recollections. He wished to use his own story to expose the injustices and corruption he believed to be endemic in the institutionalization of psychoanalysis and psychoanalytic training, which the post graduate process of acculturation of analysands made seem normal.

From the beginning of his analysis, in 1971, Masson felt critical of his training analyst, Dr Schiffer. He knew little about him, but was aware that Felix Deutsch had analysed him. Schiffer was the only one who could handle him, he was told. He arrived for his first appointment feeling apprehensive, and Schiffer's bad taste in furnishing surprised him. Schiffer was smoking a cigar and Masson was disturbed by the smell this caused, accentuated by the lack of ventilation. The ground rules were established, and the basic rule of psychoanalysis was explained. As he lay on the couch, a multitude of thoughts occurred about the situation, the room, and about Schiffer himself, but he could say nothing about them. Eventually he said that he would probably never know whether Schiffer was married or had children. Schiffer's reply surprised him. "Wrong. I am married, and have four children." Masson felt nonplussed by that, and cautiously said that he thought that Schiffer could not answer questions. The response to that was even more surprising. "What? Nobody tells me what I can and cannot say in my office. This is my office. I do what I goddamned well please in here" (*ibid.*, p. 24).

Masson continued to struggle with his problem about free association and whether he could really say whatever he liked without regard to social niceties. He ventured a criticism of Schiffer's furnishings. Schiffer's response was even more abrupt and demotic, rejecting his criticisms because the furniture had belonged to his recently deceased mother. Masson wondered if Schiffer was responding with his own free associations, and asked if that conformed with psychoanalytic rules. His analyst replied, "Well, welcome to Irvine Schiffer's office. As for analytic rules, it's all a bunch of flea fucking as far as I'm concerned. Here, I make the rules. I do whatever I please. I say whatever I please in here" (*ibid.*, p. 26).

Masson tested this by asking a number of questions about psychoanalytic colleagues; Schiffer replied frankly and scurrilously about them. Masson was bewildered by this, wondering about the concepts of the blank screen, and of the mirror. Schiffer continued to make it clear that he could do and say whatever he wished. Masson thought this was an idiosyncratic view of the analytic space. Both analysand *and* analyst must be completely and totally honest, and were obliged to say what they really believed. Truth was the only guide. He wondered at the end of this first session how Schiffer's idiosyncratic behaviour could be reconciled with what he understood about psychoanalytic therapy. Could Schiffer really say anything he liked, without regard to its hurtful or humil-iating consequences? At that time, he believed that Schiffer was wiser than himself, although uncertain whether he could really help him. He felt concerned and apprehensive about Schiffer's power over him, and how far he would be able to speak freely about himself, because what occurred in the sessions was not really private.

Somehow, he found it possible to overcome these anxieties and to focus on the difficulties of conveying, for example, the complex-ity of a dream, and of putting into words the pictorial image of the dream, as it was experienced. Whatever else he complained about, he never felt bored in his sessions. Schiffer's free associative responses to his own associations intrigued him, but he had some reservations about whether there might be something potentially abusive about this, since they were not two equal partners in the analytic experience. Schiffer certainly had his own rules about that, and Masson thought that this might possibly be true of other analysts who had their own private versions of theory and tech-nique not shared with colleagues.

Schiffer's technique included allowing his temper to be displayed in the sessions. Masson felt dazed by that experience the first time it occurred. It followed an occasion when Schiffer had been late; he was habitually late by as much as thirty minutes or more. Schiffer at first dealt with this by extending the time to make up for the lateness. As time went by, he was less meticulous, often ending a session after only half an hour. Although Masson had difficulty about being kept waiting, he was reluctant to raise it, believing it might be thought of "as stepping beyond the basic rule of free association". He tried to deal with it by coming late himself, and when Schiffer was late too, this worked. If he was not, then the session would be abbreviated, although sometimes the next patient might be kept waiting. Somebody always lost, except Schiffer, Masson commented cryptically. Generously, Masson thought that Schiffer was not trying to cheat him, but his erratic time-keeping suggested that he thought that Masson's time was not as important as his own. Masson felt he had to say something about it. He did so on the next occasion when Schiffer was even more than forty-five minutes late. Masson began reasonably to talk about it as a problem of his own anger. Schiffer replied by saying that his fifty minutes were from 12.30–1.20 p.m. and that if he chose to do other things then he had to pay for the time. Masson expostulated that the rule did not appear to apply to Schiffer himself. "Correct", said Schiffer (*ibid.*, p. 30). Masson continued by pointing out the inconvenience that Schiffer's habitual lateness caused him in respect of his own professional appointments at the University. He ended by complaining that he had the impression that he was not getting his full time from Schiffer. "Too bad", replied Schiffer. Masson then told him that he was fed up with being kept waiting and that ". . . he could bloody well be on time if I was expected to be on time."

Moreover, he had waited more than forty-five minutes that day, and was tired of it. The following exchange was recorded by Masson:

S: "You're a liar."

M: "I beg your pardon?"

S: "You heard me. You're a goddamned liar. You were forty-five minutes late. I was waiting for *you*."

Masson thought that Schiffer was lying and told him so.

S: (imitating Masson mockingly), "You have your appointments. Very important no doubt. *Dr* Masson. *Professor* Masson. Don't make me laugh. You're just a candidate, remember that." [*ibid.*, p. 33]

Masson, rather caustically, wrote that this might be a curious way of pointing out something about his grandiosity. But what of Schiffer's grandiosity? Who was to say whose time might be more important? Was Schiffer responding in this angry way to defend himself against Masson's bold attack on him? Masson thought the interesting issue was that they had stopped *talking* about something, but were doing it. But it had more to do with Schiffer than himself, and Masson was not paying to hear about Schiffer's vulnerabilities.

He continued to muse about the problem of Schiffer's erratic time-keeping, and his explanation that he (Schiffer) was not a slave to time, nor bound by society's silly rules about time-keeping. Masson compared this with what he had understood to be Lacan's practice of always charging the full fee, but varying the time depending on how quickly he believed the core had been reached. He thought such freedom often seemed to work exclusively to the analyst's own advantage. He argued with Schiffer about the issue in this session only to be abused again, whereupon he left. He wondered afterwards if this loss of temper had been a ploy. Was it a way of showing him something about his faults, and about his interactions with others? Perhaps it was an unorthodox device necessary to crack such a hard nut as himself (*ibid.*, p. 34). He consulted a friend who had been in a training analysis with Schiffer. He was hesitant to comment, perhaps because of his own continuing relationship with Schiffer, and his realization that Masson would be reporting the conversation the next day. In some notes following another session, after Schiffer had lost his temper and called him a filthy Nazi, he decided that he would tell Schiffer that he wanted to consult another training analyst about what was happening in the sessions.

He did so the next day. Schiffer responded by saying that if he did the analysis would be at an end; nobody had the right to judge, and in any case they were all a bunch of losers. If Masson did consult anybody else Schiffer would claim that he was paranoid, delusional, and inventing it all. He went on, "And whom, Masson, do you think they will believe? You, a first year candidate, not even a medical doctor, or me, Irvine Schiffer, training analyst, and an officer of the Toronto Psychoanalytic Institute?" (*ibid.*, p. 35).

Masson was acutely aware that this was no more than the exercise of power. He accused Schiffer of trying to save his own skin. Schiffer claimed that he was acting in Masson's interest to save the analysis; nobody else in Toronto could analyse Masson except himself. "I'm your only analytic friend. You are your worst analytic enemy. I will employ any means necessary to save you. Lie, cheat, steal, it's all the same to me, as long as you get better" (*ibid.* p. 39).

He went on to flatter Masson as having great psychoanalytical potential, that he had confidence in him, and was only doing what he did out of love. Masson wrote that he felt shamed by this, questioning of his own motives. How could he have believed that Schiffer had a political agenda? Schiffer had touched his narcissistic weak spot with these comments. Moreover, Schiffer explained to him that Masson was simply projecting his own defects on to the analyst. It would be better if Masson could take him as his ego ideal and pattern himself on Schiffer's greater maturity. It may be that Schiffer's agenda was not political but narcissistic, and discordant with Masson's agenda.

While Masson did not accept any of the theoretical concepts, especially of the ego-ideal, he realized that Freud had written in various places that analysis involved a superior, the analyst, and an inferior, the patient, so that the analyst could act as a model for the patient, as well as being a teacher. Masson had found great emotional resonance in these ideas, and Schiffer claimed that it came from his having had a weak father who had formed the nucleus of Masson's ego.

Masson coupled his problems of promiscuity with feelings of not being able to fit in, and believed that he either had to continue the analysis to resolve them, or quit. Hope lay in identifying with Schiffer, taking him as his own superego. He was especially concerned with his promiscuity and his ability to find his sense of common humanity only in promiscuous heterosexual relationships with different women. He hoped that Schiffer would be able to interpret the unconscious roots of this repetitious behaviour like a dream text to be deciphered, and it would then disappear. He wrote that he had a repetitive conversation with Schiffer about identifying with his promiscuous father, who in turn had identified with *his* promiscuous father. It was only natural to wish to go to bed with a beautiful woman, that he must have lovers and not let his wife know, and that if it was a disease he would be sick for the rest of his life. But he did want to get away from that model. Schiffer would interpret that his problem was that his father was no good, unlike Schiffer's own father who had been faithful so that Schiffer, himself, had always been sexually faithful. He had had a good father; Masson had not. Masson found this comment too simplistic. He was unable to get Schiffer to accept that his father had many loveable and valuable qualities.

Schiffer's concept of cure in psychoanalysis was to expect the analysand to imitate the analyst. "You have to learn to be more like me" (*ibid.*, p. 40), he repeated regularly. Schiffer considered himself to be a good person so he could do no wrong. As Masson was still an unanalysed, bad person, he could do nothing right. Freud, Masson wrote, had believed that he had never done a bad thing in his life, although he did not quote the source for this (Freud, E. L.,

1960, p. 308). This may have been an exaggeration of what Freud wrote,[1] but Schiffer, he believed, was identifying with Freud in this respect (Masson, 1991, p. 40).

Masson continued to be anxious about the implications their disparity of power might have for his status as a candidate member. Schiffer could easily have terminated him from the analytic programme. That might also involve the ending of his marriage, since he would not be able to control his promiscuity without Schiffer. It is not clear whether this was a threat from Schiffer, or a recollection of his own anxiety about the premature ending of the analysis. He was beginning to question the *bona fides* of his analyst, as well as of the process itself. He was uncertain whether he could be expected to change his character, if that was what was required, by having Schiffer's model to imitate. He was unable to think of anybody he could turn to in the Toronto Institute who could help him to resolve his doubts. He was concerned, too, about the amount of money he was spending on analysis. He concluded that if Schiffer thought he suffered from a narcissistic personality, he had to accept his help if his candidature was to be successful.

He thought that Schiffer often introduced extraneous topics in the session, particularly when Masson fell silent. He wrote of one such occasion when Schiffer told him he trusted neither Masson nor or his wife (he trusted another patient, not Masson). He was stunned by this random comment and thought that the problem was Schiffer's, not his own, since before he fell silent he had not been talking about issues of trust. He felt he had to respond, and the following exchange took place.

> M: "Dr Schiffer, I'm not sure how to say this—but while I think you have touched on something worthwhile, and even significant, perhaps this is your thought and your preoccupation, not mine. Anyway, you are here to analyse me. Whether you can trust me or not is irrelevant and shouldn't even come up."

> S: "Don't tell me what I'm here to do. I know my job. And don't tell me what should or should not come up. If it comes up, it is to be discussed. Period."

> M: "Yes, but it didn't come up. You brought it up. You, not me."

> S: "Because you're too chicken."

M: "How do you know?"

S: "Easy. Look at the way you're trying to worm out of this. "
[*ibid.*, p. 42]

Masson felt defeated and began talking about why he thought
Schiffer could not trust him. He was aware that several of the
analysts, including Schiffer, formed little coteries of their former
analysands that *he* had no wish to join. He said that Schiffer did not
trust him because when he left analysis and entered the world of
the Toronto Institute, he would not be on Schiffer's side.

Masson ended this part of the narrative of his analysis with
reflections about Schiffer's vulnerabilities, his defects, limits, and
his vanity. He felt comforted that Schiffer had so many, and easily
visible, defects, although they continued to feed his doubts about
psychoanalysis, but he felt more and more confused. "The more I
knew of the actual practice of psychoanalysis, the less I felt I understood," he concluded (*ibid.*, p. 44).

The narrative of the analysis continued in a later chapter, after
he had described his experience of being an observer in a psychiatric hospital. He compared the analytic interaction to the vicissi-
tudes of marriage (in real life) to the actuality of the analytic
marriage-like relationship with its highs (few) and lows (many). He
felt, too, that it resembled the relationship of a prisoner and his
guard; both were compelled to be there. However sad Masson felt,
Schiffer had to endure it with him, ascribing it to the intractability
of his sexual problems. Masson felt the need to provide Schiffer
with some pleasure to lighten the tedium because of that.

By now, because he was taking his own training patients, he was
cognizant of how the analyst might be feeling and thinking. He did
not want to imitate some of Schiffer's practices, such as taking telephone calls during Masson's hours, without apology or explanation. Masson felt, not unreasonably, that as he was paying for it the
time was his. Neither he nor Schiffer addressed the issue until
Masson exploded, complaining about it and comparing with his
own practice with patients with whom he did not take calls during
their hours. Schiffer was sarcastic about the idea of Masson's
comparing his work with patients with Schiffer's practices. On
another occasion, having been told by Masson that his parents were
visiting Toronto, Masson reported that he had had a phantasy they

would all meet for lunch. Schiffer then proposed that they all have lunch, dismissing the fact that it would be against the classical rules of psychoanalysis. Masson felt as if he was the uncomfortable subject of a parent–teacher conference when a lunch meeting was arranged. A comparison may be made with Jung's practice with Catherine Cabot of mixing analytic with social occasions of just this sort.

Masson was critical of what he felt was Schiffer's overuse of transference interpretations. Whenever a reference to an individual, male or female, old or young, occurred in Masson's associations, Schiffer always interpreted it in the transference as referring to himself. Masson did not find that credible. Moreover, writing after the therapy had finished, he felt that his transference to Schiffer had prevented him from seeing the reality of the relationship, dominated as it was by the power imbalance. If psychoanalysts treated patients in the same way that they treated candidates, the patients would feel abused and leave; the analyst would not take the risk of losing income. The candidate, on the other hand, could not leave without the loss of his candidacy as well as the loss of a financial investment. Masson often complained that he did not feel that he was getting value for the high fees he was paying, and could do nothing about it because of the undermining influence of the transference making him question his own reactions to Schiffer's abusiveness. In his old age, the Wolf-Man had made the same comments about the detrimental effects on his life of the overpowering transference to Freud (albeit with the financial dependence reversed).

Despite Schiffer's referring every reference to individuals, real or phantasied, to himself, Masson was never able to explore his complicated relationship with his mother. Schiffer always took up associations about his father, comparing Masson's father, in derisive terms, with Schiffer's own father. In respect of Masson's wife, Terri, he was even more derisive and insulting. He ascribed Masson's promiscuity to the fact that Terri was not beautiful, when it was not a result of his identification with his promiscuous father. "In fact, she looks like a horse's arse", Schiffer said, comparing her to his own wife whom he had married because she *was* beautiful, provoking his father's rejection of him because she was not Jewish. Masson's emphasis on Terri's intelligence was a compensation for her lack of beauty. Masson thought that there were three issues raised by these comments. They were the insult to his wife; that it came from his analyst; and he had been given information about Schiffer's private life he ought not to have had. How should he have used this information? He challenged Schiffer, who replied that he had simply voiced Masson's own thoughts that he was too scared to say for himself. He met Masson's further denial with a rationalization that all men wished to have a beautiful wife, it was only natural. Terri's intelligence was unnatural and Schiffer found it disgusting, as did normal women. They could tell she used her brain like a penis;

> ... because she is so filled with penis envy. She is so desperate for a penis that she has created one in her head. Her brain. Her huge brain is nothing but a substitute for her desire for a huge penis. Your wife has a cock for a brain, Masson, and you're getting fucked. [*Ibid.*, p. 75]

Masson felt that this was an over-simplistic interpretation of the concept of penis envy, combined with the worst of Schiffer's personal sexism. He did not say that, even if correct, it was highly inappropriate to make such an interpretation without some input from himself. Because of the inappropriately passionate way that Schiffer had advanced these views, Masson felt that he was helpless to deal with them. He often felt that Schiffer might have had a point about him, but that it had been impossible to disentangle it from Schiffer's biases. Schiffer thought he had none, and that his interpretations came from a deeper level than other analysts' interpretations because his own analysis had been so successful, although not really needed because his father had been so perfect. He had only entered analysis because of his war experiences, when, under orders, he sent men to their deaths.

In retrospect, Masson's view of Schiffer was not entirely critical. He could get some things from Schiffer, even if they were not why he had begun analysis. He had to take what Schiffer was capable of offering. He wrote,

> To me he was crude, and he was biased, and he was narcissistic, but he was not a stupid man, he was not without strong passions and a certain shrewd intelligence when it came to the unconscious, and

he had some insight into what was wrong with me even if that
insight might be just plain common sense. [*Ibid.*, p. 76]

Masson also wrote that Schiffer was quite shrewd in his interpretation of dream symbolism, even if he did not always agree with
him. He had talented free associations to Masson's associations that
were sometimes quite illuminating.

As the analysis drew to a close Masson felt that Schiffer was less
interested in analysing him than in securing his friendship. He did
not know if he wanted Schiffer's friendship, and did not want any
involvement in the disputes within the Toronto Institute. He again
pondered about the intensity of his transference to Schiffer, which
had led to his over-valuation of Schiffer's two books published
during Masson's analysis. After the analysis ended, he had realized
how inadequate they really were. His own sense of worth was tied
up with his need for Schiffer to be the man he claimed to be. The
inevitable disillusion began during the final year of the analysis,
when Schiffer was unable to empathize with the Massons' dilemma
about the treatment of their daughter, Simone, who was desperately
ill in hospital. Jeffrey and Terri were unable to decide whether she
should undergo a blood exchange with all the risks that entailed.
With no knowledge of the doctors involved, Schiffer urged them to
stop their horrendous acting out and trust the doctors because they
were medically qualified. After discussion with another paediatri-
cian, they decided that Simone should not have the treatment, and
she recovered. As Schiffer had been unable to behave with ordinary
human decency, Masson was no longer able to have any further
confidence in him.

At the end of the treatment, Masson felt no healthier than when
he had begun, but in order to graduate Schiffer had to be convinced
that he had been cured. Masson was successful in that endeavour
when Schiffer told him that he had graduated from his couch
having had a good analysis, and he would recommend him to the
committee. Leaving analysis was not traumatic, but there was an
element of sadness after five years. He felt ambivalent about
Schiffer, but he had a kind of archaic affection for him, mixed with
distaste. It was like leaving a parent with a certain pang; independence meant that he did not hate Schiffer, nor wish to take
vengeance.

There was a final disillusionment when the San Francisco Psychoanalytic Society asked him to give a paper. After discussion with Terri, they decided to write together about the sexual seduction of children and the origins of neurosis. When he met Schiffer over lunch, he told him about the proposed content of the paper in detail. Schiffer claimed that Masson had stolen *his* paper. If he was not acknowledged as a co-author he would retract his recommendation to the committee, telling them that Masson needed further analysis. Masson could not believe what he was being told, and did not know what to do. He took advice and it was suggested that he should agree with Schiffer to include his name, and then not do so. He took this advice and heard no more from Schiffer. It finally dissolved his idealizing transference to Schiffer. However, that paper was the beginning of his troubles with the psychoanalytic world.

According to Masson's account, this analysis can at best be regarded as idiosyncratic, but he thought it was not untypical of most training analyses. His view was based not just on his own experiences, but also on what he had learned in subsequent interactions with other analysands and experienced training analysts The imbalance of power, and the training analyst's influence over the future career of the analysand, ensured that there would always be an element of corruption. The training analysts he met subsequently were all deeply flawed, and unfit to offer themselves as models for the candidates. Some of his thoughts seem to presage the criticisms made in Kernberg's paper (1996) about the mistreatment suffered by candidates in their relationships with their training analysts and institutes. It was also a forerunner of the comments by Douglas Kirsner (2000) about the problems of the power of the training analyst in American psychoanalytic institutes. In respect of Masson's individual analysis, Schiffer's disregard of many of the basic principles of psychoanalytic practice, but also of the ordinary rules of courtesy and tact, makes it hard to believe that he could properly be described as practising psychoanalysis. It is far from clear within which psychoanalytic tradition he fell; certainly not in the classical tradition. For Masson himself, it seems to have done little to help him change what may have been deep-seated feelings of sadness, of being unable to fit in, or to modify his promiscuity. Schiffer's interpretations appear to have been formulaic, and not really to have been addressed to the individual problems that Masson presented. Almost certainly, analyst and candidate had very discordant agendas.

Discussions and reviews of Masson's account in *Final Analysis* have focused more on the man, and his views about the nature of psychoanalysis and its organization, and less on the account of his analysis. That analysis itself is the basis of my discussion. Masson's book ranges over a number of issues about psychoanalysis, including the controversy about the significance of phantasy or reality in the development of neurosis, and in the therapy, the power relationships in the interaction of the analysand with the analyst, and the institutional arrangements of the psychoanalytic community. Not surprisingly, these issues have attracted the attention of reviewers more than the account of the flawed analysis lying at its heart. Masson's attack on the value of psychoanalysis, and the baleful influence of its institutional arrangements, may well have evoked a counter-attack in personal terms. As Michael Sacks (1993) wrote, "it is fashionable to dismiss Masson by saying that he is a sociopath, misogynist turned feminist suffering from a personality disorder, etc. . . .".

What was not asked was why the analysis, by a respected training analyst of the Toronto Psychoanalytic Institute, did not help him to overcome some of his personal problems? If this was the case, how did the analysis come to be regarded as so successful that Masson could be admitted to the membership of the Institute, and eventually to membership of the International Psychoanalytical Association? There seems to have been no published enquiries into these matters. There has, however been some support for Masson's critique of psychoanalytic training and organizational structures, even if expressed in less extreme and personal terms. Two studies that tend to support his views have already been referred to, namely those by Kernberg and Kirsner. Kernberg, who is an eminent psychoanalyst, identified a large number of practices having a detrimental affect on the candidate's progress. Presumably, he would not have written in this way if he had believed that the practices he enumerated were not commonplace experiences. Many of them seem to be relevant to Schiffer's practice. Equally, Kirsner's studies of several American psychoanalytic institutes expresses, in measured language, some of the same problems criticized in

Masson's book. So far as I know there have been no *ad hominen* arguments against them.

Note

1. The comment by Masson seems to have been an exaggerated version of what Freud actually wrote, "... I can measure myself with the best people I have known. *I have never done anything mean or malicious, nor have I felt any temptation to do so ...*".

CHAPTER SIXTEEN

Harry Guntrip, John Hill, and Arthur Couch

G untrip, Hill, and Couch have each written short papers about their analytic experiences with more than one psychoanalyst. Each raises interesting, but different, questions about the meaning and therapeutic nature of psychoanalysis; and how it differs as between different analysts.

Harry Guntrip

Introduction

Guntrip was the elder of two brothers. His younger brother, Percy, died when Harry was three and a half years old. That event, described in his two analyses, was enormously significant in his psychological development. He described his mother as cold, unloving and a strict, almost sadistic disciplinarian (Guntrip, 1975, p. 453), who herself had been traumatized in childhood. His father, a Non-conformist Minister, was warmer and more reliable than his mother. She broke off their sexual relationship after Percy died. His father provided Harry with a good internal object, to some extent offsetting the internalized maternal bad object. It is noteworthy that Guntrip followed him into the ministry later in life. He subsequently trained as a psychotherapist and published important works on the object relationship theory. He was married and had a daughter.

The analyses

Guntrip wrote of his psychoanalyses with Fairbairn and Winnicott in a paper entitled "My experience of analysis with Fairbairn and Winnicott (How complete a result does psycho-analytic therapy achieve?)" (Guntrip, 1975). As the title suggests, he raised some very interesting questions about the nature of therapy in psychoanalysis. It provides a fascinating insight into the relationship of two analyses, with two analysts involved in developing the theory and practice of object relations. They were consecutive in time, and the second, with Winnicott, much briefer than the first, was plainly a completion of the first. Guntrip, rather like Little, found that a more traditional analysis, concerned primarily with oedipal factors, did not reach something much more primitive. Although his analysis with Winnicott was not as intensive as Little's, he had a similar experience of being able to be in touch with an early trauma, coupled with an even more primitive internalized maternal bad object. It did not, however, lead to the recovery of the lost memory of the trauma precipitated by his brother's death. He had to complete the story in his own time a few years later, at the age of seventy, after Winnicott's death.

Fairbairn

For some time before he contacted Fairbairn, Guntrip had been interested in the quality of the parent–child relationship, and the idea of object-seeking as the basis of psychological development rather than Freud's classical formulations of the instinct theory. He had experienced a repetitive symptom of falling prey to a "mysterious illness" on the death of a college friend, and later on the departure of a significant colleague. Subsequently he was alerted by a dream of a man buried alive, trying to get out, who was being threatened by Guntrip himself, who locked him in, and ran away.

He had become more psychoanalytically aware, and realized that the mysterious illnesses were like the one he suffered after Percy's death; that he had "lived permanently over the top of its repression", and that he had to solve the problem (*ibid.*, p. 454).

In 1949, Guntrip began analysis with Fairbairn because he was interested in his new ideas about "object-seeking". He found that Fairbairn was past the peak of his creative powers through failing health, but he had one thousand hours with him. As the analysis proceeded, he was surprised to find that Fairbairn gradually reverted to a classical technique. Guntrip felt the need to regress to the level of the severe infantile trauma. For his own purposes, he kept very full notes of each session (and of his sessions with Winnicott), and when he later came to study those notes, he found that neither analyst had resolved his amnesia for the trauma of Percy's death. They had, however, prepared for its post-analytic resolution.

The sessions with Fairbairn seem to have fallen into two parts. The first part of each session was slightly formal and orthodox. The second part was more relaxed, when they engaged in a theoretical discussion and Fairbairn became the understanding, good father. In the analytic transference, he was Guntrip's dominating bad mother, imposing exact interpretations like mother's stern regime. Guntrip's relationship with his mother was an anti-libidinal defence, Fairbairn said, to which Guntrip had a double, conscious resistance. First, because Fairbairn became the bad mother forcing her views on him; second, because he disagreed with Fairbairn, on the "genuine grounds" that his real problem did not lie in the oedipal complex after the death of Percy, but in his mother's failure to relate to him from his birth. Fairbairn's oedipal analysis maintained Guntrip's defence against the underlying schizoid problem, and prevented him from progressing in the therapy. Guntrip wrote that the oedipal analysis had not been wasted, but that it made him aware of how much he had repressed of Percy's death, and what had preceded it.

Fairbairn had insisted that the bad-object relations with his mother, post Percy's death, were the core of his psychopathology. For months, Guntrip had struggled to get his mother's attention by a stream of psychosomatic medical symptoms, puzzling the doctor, who could not understand either their equally sudden arrival or disappearance. They did have the effect of making his mother attend to him by arranging a bed in the kitchen adjoining the shop she owned, and popping in and out during the day. This was an unsatisfactory solution for the four to five-year-old Harry. As he grew bigger, he tried to get the same effect by becoming disobedient, enraging his mother, who punished him severely. Their stormy interaction was ameliorated as he became more independent through his school life, and mother became less depressed as her business improved, so he repressed nearly all the memories of the first seven and a half years of his life. Although this bad relationship with his mother after Percy's death was important, Guntrip thought Fairbairn was wrong to see it as the core problem of his psychopathology, since it did not take account of the pre-oedipal period. He acknowledged that the oedipal material did have to be analysed to open the way to the underlying schizoid material, which began to intrude more and more into his associations during the sessions. Fairbairn began to accept, in theory, Guntrip's concept of a regressed ego split off from the libidinal ego, but was too unwell to be able to deal with it in practice (*ibid.*, p. 450). He wrote to Guntrip, accepting that the theory he proposed was an advance on his own.

The human factor, that Guntrip believed was so important in therapy, was conveyed by the set-up of Fairbairn's consulting room, in his old family house in Edinburgh. The large drawing room, filled with precious antiques, served as a waiting room leading into the study Fairbairn used as a consulting room. Fairbairn sat behind a large flat-topped desk in a plush-covered armchair. His couch had its head to the front of the desk. Fairbairn was somehow sitting in state, reminding him of his father's situation as a Methodist local preacher in his Mission Hall. He wondered at the formality of the situation in an analyst who did not believe in the classical "mirror" function. It conveyed a sense of Fairbairn's aloofness, and lack of personal warmth in the conduct of the analysis. A dream of being in father's Mission Hall, lying on a couch with its head towards the front of the platform, where Fairbairn, with the hard face of Guntrip's mother, was presiding, led to some insight. Guntrip wrote that it was a thinly disguised version of Fairbairn's consulting room, showing that he wished him to be his supportive father, but that wish was overpowered by the negative transference of his dominating mother. Later, Guntrip realized that he had unconsciously chosen this position in the consulting room, and had not noticed that there was another settee by the side of the desk where he could have sat. It is noteworthy that, apart from being described as supportive, there is very little about Guntrip's father, who remains a rather undefined character by comparison with Guntrip's mother, in the analysis. Fairbairn could unbend and become his supportive father when Guntrip was sitting up, and "after the sessions we could discuss and I could find the natural warm-hearted human being behind the exact interpreting analyst" (*ibid.*, p. 452).

While he felt that he owed much to Fairbairn for the analysis of the years after Percy's death, he became convinced, after several years, that Fairbairn's analysis was keeping him in the world of bad object relationships. It was defending against the more primitive problems of the earlier period. That material kept pushing through, and two events occurred almost simultaneously. The first was the death of a close friend, precipitating another bout of the mysterious illness first experienced after Percy died. The second was illness of Fairbairn, who nearly died from influenza, and was unable to work for six months as a result. Unable to work through the recurrence of the mysterious illness, either alone or with Fairbairn, Guntrip felt he had had to reinstate the repression to survive.

When the analysis resumed and Guntrip talked about his friend's death, Fairbairn interpreted that since *his* illness *he* had become, in the transference, the dying Percy, and was no longer the good father or the bad mother. That interpretation made Guntrip realize that he could not resolve the problem *with* an analyst (a traditional analyst, whom Fairbairn had now become, would not be able to help further). He wrote to Fairbairn that he must end the analysis, but knew that then he would be re-presented with the full eruption of the problem precipitated by Percy's death. Fairbairn would be unable to deal with the transference involved. He then decided that he needed to approach Winnicott, because of his profound insights into the early infantile stage.

Through this time, Guntrip was writing publicly about his experiences. Winnicott and Hoffer thought that Guntrip's adherence to Fairbairn's theories was because he was not allowing Fairbairn to analyse his aggression in the transference. However, Guntrip wrote, they were not aware of the actual attacks he had made, consciously and unconsciously, on articles and books in Fairbairn's consulting room, or of his need to make reparation when he had been aggressive in reality.

At the end of the final session, he realized Fairbairn was letting him leave without a friendly gesture and that they had never once shaken hands. So Guntrip took his hand and noticed tears trickling down Fairbairn's cheeks. He felt that he had seen the warm heart of a shy man with a fine mind, but Fairbairn did not have the capacity for natural, spontaneous "personal relating", in contrast with what he found in his relationship with Winnicott.

Winnicott

Guntrip had previously had some correspondence with Winnicott, as well as reading his papers as they were published. He felt that Winnicott was the only person able to help him, but he could only visit London once monthly, when he had two sessions. He thought that his ability to benefit from such widely spaced therapy was a result of the previous long analysis. Winnicott was surprised that so much could be worked through in only 150 sessions, made possible by Guntrip's capacity to keep the analysis alive in his absence and Winnicott's profound insights into the early infantile period. Winnicott helped him to discover that his mother may have been naturally maternal for a brief period immediately after his birth. Her personality problems had caused its loss.

Winnicott began in a very informal way in a consulting room designed to help the patient feel at ease. After Guntrip had entered, Winnicott, in what has become an almost iconic image of himself, walked in holding a mug of tea and making a cheery greeting. He sat on a wooden chair behind the couch and Guntrip would sit or lie on it, as he felt appropriate. At the end of the session, Guntrip left with a friendly handshake. This was in marked contrast to the formality of Fairbairn within his sessions, and may have been an important element in the capacity for Winnicott to become, in the transference, Guntrip's very early and briefly experienced good mother. Very soon in their sessions together Guntrip felt that Winnicott had reached the heart of the matter. In the first session Guntrip talked about Percy's death, and that, in the analysis with

Fairbairn, he had not understood his earliest relationship with his mother, who had failed to relate to him at all. At the end of that session Winnicott made his famous interpretation that he had nothing to say, but that Guntrip might feel that he was not there if he said nothing.

In the next session, he made what Guntrip felt was the perfect object-relations interpretation. Winnicott said that Guntrip might feel that he (Winnicott) was not a person yet, and might go away feeling that he was not real. He related this to a possibility that Guntrip might have been ill before Percy had been born, and that mother may have left him to look after himself. Harry had identified with Percy as his infantile self, needing care, collapsing when Percy died. When later Guntrip identified a feeling of being static, unchanging, and lifeless, Winnicott interpreted that he had managed to go on living very energetically, repressing the feeling of being static and lifeless into an unconscious cocoon. In a later interpretation, Winnicott connected this repressed feeling to an unresolved illness of collapse, which meant Guntrip could not take his own existence for granted. He had to work hard to stay in existence, keeping active, awake, and talking, lest he might die like Percy, when his mother would not be able to save him. Winnicott linked this, in the transference, with Guntrip's fear that Winnicott would not be able to keep him alive, as his mother might not have been to save him, so he had kept up the link through his notes. He could not relax and feel that he was a going concern for Winnicott, without having to do anything about it. He was not able just to continue to grow, breathe, and sleep.

Guntrip felt that he was subsequently able to tolerate silences, but was relieved on one occasion when Winnicott interpreted silence as meaning being abandoned and forgotten by his mother, and that this had been relived in the transference. The repeating trauma of illness after Percy's death was a way of trying to recover from an earlier trauma. With that interpretation, he felt that Winnicott had come "right into the emptiness of my object relations situation in infancy with a non-relating mother" (*ibid.*, p. 459). When, towards the end of the analysis, Guntrip suddenly returned to his hard talking, without silences, Winnicott interpreted it differently; it was as if Guntrip was giving birth to a baby. He had to know that Winnicott could stand the concentrated talking, without being destroyed, while Guntrip was being creative in the production of something rich. "You are talking about 'object relating', 'using the object' and finding you don't destroy it," said Winnicott (*ibid.*). While he had been the good breast/mother to Guntrip, in place of the real mother who had lost her ability to mother and care for a live baby, he was also able to value Guntrip. He interpreted that Guntrip had a good breast too and that he was good for Winnicott, having given him more than he had taken. Guntrip had valued that interpretation, but had not appreciated its full import at the time it was made. Later, he realized that it had transformed his understanding of the trauma of Percy's death.

Guntrip differed from Winnicott when he fell back on the internal instinct theories of Freud and Klein to interpret Guntrip's sadism. Guntrip felt that it was an embodiment of his cold mother's failure to respond to him. His angry fight was not an expression of a sadistic attack on the object, but an attempt to extract a response from her. He felt that Winnicott was departing from his object-related stance of being "concerned with living persons, whole living and loving" (*ibid.* p. 460), characteristic of his difference from Freud's interest in curing symptoms. Fairbairn and Winnicott had together neutralized his earliest traumatic years, in spite of Winnicott's brief aberration. He was able to end his analysis with Winnicott, who had related to him in his deep unconscious. He had enabled him to feel that it was not just the loss of Percy, "but having been left alone with an internalized non-relating mother, who had not been able to keep him alive, and caused his collapse into apparent dying" (*ibid.*). He had internalized Winnicott, who counteracted the non-relating mother. His sessions with Winnicott ended in July 1969.

Post analysis developments

Only seven months later Guntrip was seriously overworked, and was advised to retire before nature would make him. He found this difficult, and whenever he took a rest, he found he was thinking of the loss of his ministerial, brother figure. Then in October 1970, he fell ill with pneumonia. After five weeks in hospital, he was again advised against being over active.

In February 1971, Guntrip learned the sad news of Winnicott's death, whose secretary rang to tell him. That night Guntrip dreamt that he saw his mother in black, immobilized, staring into space and totally ignoring him. He, too, stood immobilized and feeling frozen. In other dreams, his mother had always been attacking him, so this was different. He thought the dream meant that, having lost Winnicott, he was alone with the unrelating, depressed mother after Percy had died. He noted that he did not feel ill, as on previous occasions of loss. A sequence of dreams each night for two months took him back to his earliest days, through every place where he had lived. His parents, wife, daughter, and other relatives appeared in the dreams, but not Percy. He felt he was struggling to stay in the post-Percy period. Two dreams at last broke his amnesia of Percy's life and death. In the first, he dreamt that he was about three, holding a pram with Percy in it. Harry was looking towards their mother who was gazing into the distance, ignoring them. In the second dream, he was standing next to a man who was his double. Both were reaching out towards a dead object, when the other man suddenly collapsed in a heap. The dream then changed. Harry was in a lighted room where Percy was sitting on the lap of a woman who had no face, arms, or breasts, only a lap. Percy was looking depressed and Harry was trying to make him smile. He felt he had recovered the memory of his own collapse when he saw Percy dead. More than that, in the dream he had gone back to the time before Percy had died, and found the depersonalized mother who had failed to relate to either of them.

He continued to analyse these dreams by looking back at his notes made during his analyses. He realized that, while Winnicott's death had reminded him of Percy's death, it was not the whole story. His proposed retirement had activated the unconscious fear that his mother would undermine him at last. He had dreamt of the death of Percy, not Winnicott, together with the image of the depersonalized mother. He had been given the strength to face the basic trauma because Winnicott could not be dead for him. Unconsciously, he had linked up with his supportive father, who was still alive within him, enabling him to resist mother's later deadening influence. Winnicott had been able to relate to the earlier, lost part of Harry, who became ill because of his mother's failure. He wrote, "He has taken her place and made it possible and safe to remember her in an actual dream—reliving of her paralysing schizoid aloofness" (*ibid.*, p. 460) He felt that after this momentous dream series he had reaped the gains he had sought in the analyses. That was accompanied by a feeling of sadness for his mother who had been so damaged by her childhood; and by the discovery in analysis of the mental security provided by his father in the struggle to become his "true self". Finally, he paid tribute to both his analysts who, in their different ways, had enabled him to discover the resolution of his fundamental infantile trauma. However, without the understanding and support of his wife he would not have been able to undertake these analyses, nor achieved that resolution.

John Hill

Hill wrote in his paper (1993) describing his analyses, that he became interested in psychoanalysis at the age of fourteen through enthusiastically reading Freud's work, and began to develop a wish to become a psychoanalyst. Ten years later, he became interested in the ideas of Klein through his work at the Tavistock Institute of Human Relations, where he was concerned with the problems of labour turnover. He developed the idea of the induction crisis and the survival curve, replicating another study of metal fatigue in steel rods when he was employed by the British Iron & Steel Research Association. His study of accidents and absences of steel workers highlighted that the worker's relationship with his workplace presented an important opportunity to re-experience feelings associated with earlier parental ties. These studies convinced him of the importance of Klein's concepts of the schizoid and depressive positions (although it was unlikely that the behaviour of stressed steel could be explained by these concepts). His ambition to be analysed by a Kleinian was realized when he became employed by an engineering firm in a personnel-sensitive job; to be analysed was a condition of employment. It was especially valuable that the firm offered help to pay for analysis, since he was then able to afford analysis as well as a family. He chose to go to a training analyst, hoping he might train as an analyst himself.

The analyses

Dr Anderson

Although his experience with Anderson was helpful and enjoyable, he was uncomfortably aware of limitations of content and presentation in Anderson's technique. Anderson's time-keeping was erratic; he often arrived at least fifteen minutes late, thus creating problems for Hill's own employment schedules. To compensate, the end of the session might be delayed, but sometimes it was truncated. Hill could hear Anderson enjoying his breakfast with his family, in the room above, while he waited after the time to begin the session had passed. Mrs Anderson, and telephone calls, might also interrupt from time to time. His concern about these practices was interpreted as obsessiveness; Anderson himself was not obsessional. Hill's complaints were a result of his apparent belief "that patients should be treated as though they were porcelain" (*ibid.*, p. 465). Anderson would make jokes, and tell anecdotes about his family, and his own professional development.

When Hill discussed this behaviour with another senior Kleinian, he was told that some thought that Anderson was a ghastly analyst, but this person then hastily corrected himself, saying that others believed that he was a very good analyst. Hill agreed that he was not a good analyst, but quite liked him. Hill only discovered about an hour before his scheduled session was to begin that Anderson had died suddenly, so the analysis terminated. After a few weeks, it was suggested that he should go to Rosenfeld, but he had no vacancies. He was then recommended to apply to Mrs Bick.

Mrs Bick

Hill was grateful to be able to begin analysis with her quite soon so that he could work through the trauma of Anderson's death. With her, he successfully passed through the training process to qualify. Mrs Bick was quite different from Anderson; she was meticulous about time-keeping, and ensured that sessions were free from interruptions. While not without humour, she did not tell jokes, and her interpretations were much more precise and economical. He felt that he was now in a "genuine Kleinian" analysis. However, he began reluctantly to experience doubts about both his analysis with Mrs Bick and his experiences with her Kleinian colleagues, whom he met in the course of his training. Those doubts fell into four groups.

1.   The idealization of Mrs Klein by her followers, which he felt she enjoyed, resembled "a school-girl with a serious crush on the gym mistress" (*ibid.*, p. 406). It was an example of unanalysed positive transferences, and the difficulty of distinguishing between a good and an idealized object. He discovered that these doubts could not be resolved in analysis. When he raised them with Mrs Bick, her response was to threaten him with a reconsideration of his original application for training, a potent threat because of his heavy investment of time, money, and career development. Written in 1993, these comments echo similar thoughts expressed by Masson two years earlier.

2.   Hill had concerns about the attitude of Mrs Bick, and of her colleagues, to the issue of parental authority. Critical comments about parents made during the sessions were always interpreted as projections, and an attack on the parental object. He wrote, "The consistent idea conveyed was that one's parents were almost by definition angels and if for any reason they might just perhaps occasionally slip from this pinnacle this was entirely due to one's own inherent badness that had forced even them to this unwished for lowering of standards" (*ibid.*, p. 407). Effectively, this prevented him from examining the issues of his childhood, or considering the complexities of the human interaction between himself and his parents. The beginning of discordant agendas between the two can be seen here.

In the transference, there was a similar tendency to interpret his feelings about the analyst negatively. For example, he had bought himself a leather jacket, which he enjoyed, wondering if it might symbolize the skin. Mrs Bick interpreted that Nazis had worn leather jackets, and that in identifying with them he was attacking her Jewishness. He thought there was no evidence from his associations.

3.   He was concerned that the attitude of Mrs Bick, and her colleagues, was to treat patients as if they were naughty children.

This was a dilemma for patients if they wished to change their hours for any kind of reality reasons. They sometimes felt compelled to discontinue their analyses because of the intractability of their analysts, who seemed to regard their firmness and inflexibility with pride. Mrs Bick, on one occasion in a seminar, read out a poignant and sensitive letter from a patient written during an analytic holiday. The seminarians were implicitly invited to join in her laughter about it. Hill felt that she was holding a vulnerable patient up to ridicule.

4.   Any narcissism in the patient would be subjected to a severe put-down. If he expressed any satisfaction with himself, Mrs Bick interpreted that he was pretending that his shit was the same as his mother's good breast milk.

While in analysis, Hill suddenly experienced a disabling phobia that was very painful and affected his non-analytic work, without interfering with his personal life, or his analysis. It was related to the loss of some of the competence that he had enjoyed since his teens. He wanted to explore this in his analysis, but Mrs Bick refused to acknowledge that there had been any change, treating it as a negative hallucination. Parenthetically, Hill wrote that this might have been the point that Mrs Bick had begun to go mad, although he continued to believe that she must know what she was doing. Further symptoms began to appear, and a colleague, realizing that something was wrong, suggested that he might consult Rosenfeld about it. Hill mentioned this in a session, and Mrs Bick interpreted it as an attack on herself. Consulting Rosenfeld would be useless for two reasons. First, all Kleinian analysts were agreed on fundamental matters, and he would get nothing different from Rosenfeld; second, Mrs Bick knew that Rosenfeld had made a mess of the analysis of one of Hill's senior colleagues. He remained with Mrs Bick and his phobic condition continued to deteriorate, but she opposed his seeking help elsewhere. Eventually he did go to Rosenfeld.

Dr Rosenfeld

Hill wrote that Rosenfeld was not as meticulous about time-keeping as Mrs Bick had been, and was habitually a few minutes late as well as erratic about the ending of the sessions. From the beginning, Hill felt that there was a fundamental difference about the way that Rosenfeld worked, characterized by an open-minded empiricism, making the analytic process a search for, and the accumulation of, evidence. It resembled the scientific idea of successive approximation. The idea of discussion was also part of Rosenfeld's method. This contrasted strongly with Mrs Bick's authoritative pronouncements, not open to discussion or dispute. She denigrated the notion of discussion, referring to it as "mere discussion". Rosenfeld emphasized the need to understand the *patient*, and for the patient to feel understood. This led to a process of continual reappraisal, and consideration of any dispute about his interpretations. He believed that there was no such thing as "the correct interpretation", and if one did not work, another should be sought. This was in considerable contrast to Mrs Bick's rigid, dogmatic practice, and Hill found that Rosenfeld's analysis was enjoyable, enriching, and engaging him in a fruitful exploration. Outside the analysis, he learned from Rosenfeld that Mrs Bick had spoken to him about her work with Hill. She told Rosenfeld that she had made gross mistakes, without elaborating what they were. She said nothing to Hill about that, always insisting that any problems arose entirely from his own shortcomings.

Hill concluded his paper with a discussion of the question raised in its title. He did not find any commonality between any of the three analyses he experienced, beyond the use of the couch for the patient, the chair for the analyst, and an adherence to analytic reticence (in which he had been able to include Anderson, despite his comments referred to above).

Arthur Couch

Arthur Couch began his analytic training in the Boston Institute in 1963 with an analyst trained in Vienna in the 1930s, expecting to experience a classical analysis. He wrote, "Fortunately, these expectations soon succumbed to analytic realities . . ." (Couch, 1995, p. 157). He had anticipated that he would meet the stereotypical, rigid, orthodox analyst based on Freud's papers on technique taught in theoretical seminars. An altogether less rigid impression was conveyed in his analysis and clinical seminars. After the death of his analyst four years later, Couch decided to change his university career to become a clinical psychoanalyst. He was accepted for a new training analysis with Anna Freud in 1967, lasting six and a half years. He added to it a training in child psychoanalysis at the Hampstead Clinic. His account of his analysis in his paper (*ibid.*) is relatively brief. It is plainly intended to support his views about psychoanalytic theory and practice that he set forth in other parts of the paper. It is interesting in its own right, and his experience reported in it resonates with some of the accounts of other analysands reviewed previously.

Anna Freud

On his arrival at Maresfield Gardens for his first session, he was greeted by Paula, the maid, who had worked for Freud in Vienna. She showed him Freud's library, and talked about her memories of Vienna. She pointed out that hardly a word had been changed in the original hand-written manuscript of *Mourning and Melancholia* lying on the desk. Paula greeted him warmly throughout the years of his analysis, making him feel like a guest in a Viennese home. As he entered her consulting room, Anna Freud greeted him in a friendly way, too. After talking about his journey from America, and his living arrangements in London, they settled various administrative matters about the time of his sessions and fees. He was already aware of analytic procedure from his previous analysis in Boston. He began by telling her about his feelings of loss following the death of his Boston analyst. At the end of the session, Anna Freud reassured him about his anxieties at starting analysis again.

What had impressed him in the early months of the analysis was her naturalness, and the absence of a classical stance. She had felt free to talk to him briefly off the couch before and after the session, and was able to deal realistically with some matters on the couch. She was always herself, with no signs of a learned technique, or an imposed system of rules or technique; she answered direct questions. She did not leave her real self behind when she was in the consulting room. He often commented that she seemed not to have taken an Institute course in technique, and appeared not to know the orthodox Freudian rules of technique. She frequently talked with him about his adjustment to English culture, and of the different cultures of the British Institute and the Hampstead Clinic. He was surprised about her expression of her own opinions about some of these matters. She questioned his surprise, and he gradually adjusted to her "deviations" from Freudian technique. He found that her attention to the reality problems in his life became a valuable aspect of his analysis, and it did not interfere with the development of the transference, or with working through. He realized that his previous presumptions about Freudian clinical principles had been too rigid.

In the interaction between realistic communication and analytic work, Anna Freud maintained firm analytic boundaries. He did not meet her outside the analytic sessions, and she maintained a sense of personal reserve with an underlying attachment, but not a rigid barrier in the sessions. She had an evenly balanced focus on all aspects of the unconscious. Dreams were important, and she interpreted his defences in simple words. She paid much attention to the reconstruction of his childhood development, and, within the intense transference that developed, she was aware of both the maternal and paternal aspects of it. She did not, however, focus on the mother–child interaction, despite his frequent recollections of his childhood. Nor did she make direct transference interpretations, either in the "here and now" of their interaction or in relation to his account of external events. Nevertheless, her interpretations, expressed in ordinary words, making complex points simply, displayed accuracy and depth that he found astonishing. He felt that she had been listening quietly, but with a passive intensity, making him feel that she was taking in his every word. She encouraged him to gain insight without her intervention, demonstrating her faith in "the analytic process itself, as a silent but continuous curative factor" (*ibid.*, p. 158). Sometimes she would refer to her father's views about an interpretation she was about to make, and Couch took special note on these occasions, feeling that he had not only learned something profound about himself, but also about Freud. Her technique was sometimes unorthodox when, for example, she might put the analytic work aside for discussion of some important reality. On other occasions, she gave him advice about applying for another grant, or commented favourably about papers he had read, or presentations he had made. She thought it was

appropriate to praise his positive achievements. Once she recommended a psychoanalyst for a friend. These interactions had been
analysed later, thus integrating them into his analysis.

He once brought photos to a session, having asked her approval,
looking at them together as he talked about them. In another, he
brought a problem about a training patient, who was very softly
spoken and difficult to hear. He recounted the discussions with his
supervisor, and the ineffectiveness of the various interpretations
that had been suggested. He hoped that she would suggest an alternative interpretation to solve his problem. She said, "Tell her to
speak up" (ibid., p. 160). He did, and the problem was solved! Similarly, when, during the supervision of different patients with different supervisors, he had told her that he had found their approaches
conflicting and confusing, she had advised that he should accept
their ideas, but develop his own style. When he had criticized the
Kleinian influences at the Institute, she simply said that was the
way it was. Although he knew she held similar views, she did not
join him in his criticism.

He found that her involvement with the Hampstead Clinic
sometimes impinged on their sessions. He had contrasted the
furnishings and curtains at the Hampstead Clinic unfavourably
with his own taste in furnishings and felt particularly guilty when
her only comment was that she had made all those curtains herself.
He had been completely nonplussed by this personal comment, and
had fallen into a stunned silence until he had been able to say something about her dedication to, and pride in, her creation of the
Clinic. Although he did not say so, it illustrated Anna Freud's technique of not making transference interpretations in the analysis
about reality factors, even though such an interpretation might
have been appropriate on that occasion. In another session, the
sound of fire engines could be heard across the road at the Clinic.
He had continued talking, but she soon got up to look out of the
window, and had asked him if he would go and find out what was
happening. He did so, and discovered that the fire was a minor
kitchen fire and that it had been dealt with. He wrote, rather baldly,
"We then continued the session" (ibid., p. 161).

There were negative phases in the analysis when Couch had felt
frustrated, and others when their disagreements were intense,
because of what he described as "contentious feelings". Anna Freud

openly conveyed her disapproval of his wish to be married in a Protestant church, and of the complex preparations that had to be made. Religion, she said, was an illusion, and most intelligent and aware young people married in a register office. As he continued to speak of the various pre-nuptial problems in successive sessions, she had suggested that he should bring some dreams, as those concerns "were hardly material for analysis" (ibid.). He had been disappointed at her lack of empathy with his underlying anxieties and his preoccupations with the wedding arrangements. This seemed to be a lapse from her usual collaborative way of working to reach the depth of the meaning of things, and from the importance of the working alliance. There may have been a countertransference issue for Anna Freud, but he made no other comment about it.

He approved her approach to analysis, which was that inter-pretations of "here and now" interactions between them in the sessions would have been foreign to the atmosphere of their work together, which was to be strictly focused on the process of under-standing his past and present. Any deviation from that focus would have violated the integrity and authenticity of their analytic task. Any reference to her countertransference, even though it may have been relevant to the material about his wedding, would have been equally undermining of the authenticity of the analysis. Couch felt that her concern was to make a determined effort to understand his childhood development and his unconscious reactions to it. He ended his direct account of the analysis by expressing his gratitude to Anna Freud for having freed him from the influence of his past.

He continued with a critique of modern analysis, by which he primarily meant Kleinian analysis, tracing its development over the years since Strachey's 1934 paper. He added a section on Anna Freud's views about the issues of classical and modern analytical practice and technique, and was supportive of her views about them. Except for the one occasion he felt that she could not under-stand his anxiety, there was no indication of any conflict between their analytic agendas.

CHAPTER SEVENTEEN

Discussion

The analyses considered in this section have covered a long period in the history of psychoanalysis and psychotherapy from 1920 until the late 1970s. Some of the later accounts were not published until the final decade of the twentieth century. In that context, what is interesting about them is that, in many, what was most helpful were the departures from the stereotypical, classical, impersonal stance of the analyst. Little, Guntrip, and Hill all refer to the way in which a relatively informal approach had enabled them to gain more from their analyses and to reach more profound levels of unconscious material than from the classical, formulaic approaches of other analysts. Couch also preferred the less orthodox approach of Anna Freud, although he believed that she had practised the classical style of analysis, as defined by her father. She must, however, have been influenced also by Freud's sometimes unorthodox practices. Couch felt that she was able to allow the introduction of realities without the loss of analytic rigour. He did, however, record an occasion when an external reality, in the shape of a fire at the Hampstead Clinic, interrupted the session most dramatically. Her request to him to leave the session to find out what was happening, and his feelings about it, were not brought back into the session when he returned. It was remarkable that he did not refer to such a dramatic interruption in the process in his paper, beyond simply marking it as an experience. It may be compared with HD's account of the dog-fight in one of her sessions with Freud, which she had recorded as an incident that had occurred, but which apparently had no further exploration in her analysis.

The analyses of Little and Guntrip have been criticized by a number of people (Eigen, 1981; Glatzer & Evans, 1977; Hopkins, 1998; Newman, 1995; Padel, 1996), who have tended to be critical of the outcomes, largely on the grounds that Winnicott had failed to deal with their aggression. Newman claims that Little was the most imperious person he knew even after analysis. Marion Milner is cited by Hopkins as saying that Little was too grandiose to have been totally analysed. Both are making assumptions about the possible outcomes of psychoanalysis, as if there is a condition of completed analysis to be achieved by anybody. Additionally, Hopkins wrote that although Guntrip's suffering may have been relieved by the analysis, he remained hard-driving, omnipotent, and off-putting, as well as being left with other defects. Is the relief of suffering to be regarded as being of less significance than the achievement of that state of grace in which all defects have been removed? It is as if the analysand's feelings about the outcome of the therapy are to be dismissed in favour, not of the analyst's view, but the view of analytical critics. How many analysands fall short of this idealized condition while nevertheless feeling gratitude for the benefits they have received? Perhaps the increasing length of analyses is an outcome of the vain hope of achieving this utopian result.

Freud had analysed both Kardiner and Blanton. In 1920–1921, when Kardiner was analysed by him, Freud was at the height of his powers, and had recently published his seminal paper about the Wolf-Man. He was in the process of drafting other important papers. Freud was already ill when Blanton first met him, and the later stages of his illness were of great significance in the review sessions that followed. Despite the time interval, a very similar image of Freud, as an analyst and a person, was conveyed in both their accounts. They were both very respectful and admiring of him, and felt that he had been very insightful about their problems.

Both described how Freud provided information about his family, and talked about other analysts, sometimes quite critically.

Kardiner was critical of Freud's technique, particularly when Freud was using theory dogmatically, as when he insisted on the universality of a homosexual phase in masculine development, and when he felt Freud had made an incorrect transference about his father. At that point, the emergence of a discordant agenda could be discerned. Kardiner's account of the differences, identified in the informal discussion with Strachey and Rickman about Freud's practice with them and himself, is intriguing. What might account for Freud's reported silence with them, and his apparent garrulousness with Kardiner, as well as with some of the analysands discussed in Part II? It is difficult to tell whether the differences were a result of something about the patients, or of some conscious decision made by Freud himself, or whether there were unconscious interactional factors between analyst and patient, which might explain them.

There is a notable absence of any reference to the transference with Freud's patients. Kardiner, indeed, had specifically criticized Freud for failing to be aware of his transference to him of the fear of the dominating and angry father. He blamed that failure for the lack of further progress in the analysis. He believed that the problem with his father should have been dealt with in the present, through the analysis of that transference, rather than having been relegated to the inaccessible past as a repressed unconscious factor to be raised to consciousness. Freud's technique reflected that. That belief is borne out by the Wolf-Man's report of a remark by Freud that analysis could be regarded as a success when the repressed became conscious, although that did not automatically bring about the patient's recovery (Gardiner, 1973).

Although Freud had considered the idea of working-through (1914g), the relative brevity of his analyses reported here did not allow very much time for it. The accounts of both Little and Guntrip offer another view of working-through in so far as, for them, the final working-through of their problems did not take place until after their analyses had finished. For Guntrip it was very much later, after Winnicott's death, with the recurrence of some basic symptoms and the self-interpretation of some dreams. Blanton's repeated return to Freud, after his main sessions had been completed, might also be seen as an example of an attempt to work-through some of the issues he had been unable to complete during his analysis. He failed to achieve this outcome because of his wish to consult Freud about his own patients. It did not stop him from feeling that his work with Freud had been the most significant experience of his life.

Masson is the odd one out in this group, with his analyst by far the most unorthodox, observing no rules of technique as they were usually understood. His analyst kept no consistent boundaries of time, context, or reticence, according to Masson. All of that was in stark contrast to all the other analyses described in this section. Winnicott's practice, as described by Little, often transcended the recognized boundaries, by visiting her at home when she was unable to attend his consulting room, by having other contacts with her away from the consulting room, and by organizing spells in hospital for her when he was away. In those examples, he could be seen to have been acting in the interest of the principle of "holding" and of the principle of the unity of social, psyche, and soma, that Little felt had been so important in her recovery. In that way, it was possible to understand the underlying reason for Winnicott's departure from accepted practice. For Schiffer, Masson's training analyst, there seemed to be no similar rationale in his glaring departures from conventional practice. Masson attempted to justify them, believing that the particular difficulties that his psychopathology presented may have made orthodox practice with him ineffective. However, Schiffer's practice was so idiosyncratic as to have been beyond rhyme or reason to the disinterested commentator. With Winnicott, Little experienced a lengthy period when there were discordant agendas between them, especially in the year long failure to recall anything about her analysis; for Masson the whole of his analysis showed very little sign of accord between himself and Schiffer.

One impression conveyed in these accounts is that the personality of the analysand, or patient, may be a significant factor in the way that the therapy is transacted. The differences between Blanton, Wortis, and HD seem to have had much more to do with the way that their individual resistances were manifested than by any difference in Freud's technique with each of them. However, for Little, Guntrip, and Hill, their varying experiences seem to have had much more to do with the different analysts they encountered.

Both Little and Guntrip were much more conforming in their inter-actions with their different analysts and, as has been suggested, Little may have been compliant to the extent of identifying with each of her three successive analysts. Kardiner actively disliked Frink, his first analyst, whose technique made him feel uncomfort-able; some of Frink's interpretations disconcerted him, but that may have been due to his unfamiliarity with what might be expected in psychoanalysis or psychotherapy. What may be common to all is the feeling that they were disturbed by the application to them of concepts that did not seem to fit with their essential, if unconscious, sense of themselves. With the exception of Masson, they had been able to accept very marked departures from orthodoxy when those unorthodoxies were concordant with some fundamental aspects of themselves. What can also be seen in these analyses is that some of the resistances of otherwise compliant clients occurred when they resisted openly or silently if they felt that their agenda was discor-dant with their therapist's agenda, specifically where it seemed as if the therapist was pursuing a theory which did not deal with the problem as experienced by the patient.

All these accounts raise issues about the object of psychoanaly-sis and psychotherapy. Are they concerned with helping the patient to achieve some relief from distress and a more gratifying life, or with a pursuit of self-knowledge to which a therapeutic objective is not relevant? Can psychoanalysis only be conducted within the strictest of boundaries, and with the absolute minimum of personal interaction and intrusion of the analyst's countertransference? These questions will be discussed, with others, in the conclusion.

PART IV
TWO UNGRATIFIED PATIENTS

CHAPTER EIGHTEEN

Prelude

Some patients have expressed their dissatisfaction with their psychoanalytic or psychotherapeutic treatment in general terms, offering a broad critique of their therapy rather than a specific example of their own experience (e.g., France, 1988). Two have been more specific, and have described the particular reasons for their dissatisfaction (Godley, 2001; Sutherland, 1987). For one, Wynne Godley, there can be little doubt that his experience was actually abusive and an example of malpractice. For Stuart Sutherland it is possible that the choice of psychoanalysis may have been inappropriate, either for himself or for the symptoms from which he suffered.

Godley, after a very distressing childhood and adolescence, had successfully completed a degree course at Oxford and was rising in the senior ranks in the Treasury. He was happily married, with no children of his own when he began his analysis, although his wife had a daughter by a previous relationship and became pregnant during the course of his analysis. At the age of thirty he began to experience anxieties he could not deal with without help. His account of the subsequent treatment with Masud Khan was made several years later, after he had found a much less flamboyant psychoanalyst in Canada, where Godley worked in a senior research post with an institute for economic studies. He wrote his story of the first analysis in the *London Review of Books* in 2001, when it caused a considerable stir in psychoanalytical circles, and resulted in an eventual adoption by the Institute of Psychoanalysis of a process to deal with instances of malpractice. It should be said that the model it adopted falls far short of what is needed for a modern model of ethical practice supported by a public complaints procedure.

Sutherland, who was a distinguished professor of psychology, describes his very severe, agitated depression with panic attacks, physical and psychological withdrawal, and suicidal feelings, alternating with hypomania, in his book entitled *Breakdown*, first published in 1976 and revised in 1987. Although he ascribes his breakdown to discovering his wife's affair with his best friend, and possibly to a mid-life crisis, there are a number of factors in his account of his life suggesting that there were incipient problems that might have made him susceptible to breakdown. He was very resistant to psychoanalysis, and as a result of his psychological studies, he was sceptical of its therapeutic efficacy. He found that two brief experiences with different analysts bore out his sceptical views, and he abandoned the treatment rather angrily and abruptly. His depression was the precursor of a bipolar disease, which continued for several years after the agitated depression had abated. From his account of his life before his breakdown, he may have been in a very manic phase for some time before the depressive attack. The illness was eventually controlled by a permanent prescription of Lithium. After many crises during this period his marriage broke down completely, and he ascribed his ability to deal with this trauma without further serious depression or mania to the Lithium regime. Despite that treatment he eventually committed suicide. Some of his conclusions about the relevance of psychoanalytic treatment to depression and bipolar illness are endorsed by Lewis Wolpert who also suffered from severe depression. Wolpert did not write about his individual therapy but made a general critique of it in a review of all the treatments available for depression and bipolar illness.

CHAPTER NINETEEN

Wynne Godley and Stuart Sutherland

Wynne Godley

Introduction

Wynne Godley is an eminent and distinguished professor of economics, whose childhood in a dysfunctional English aristocratic family in the Home Counties is well described in all its awfulness in the preface to the story of his treatment with Masud Khan in the *London Review of Books* (Cooper, 1993; Hopkins, 1998, 2000). He was the youngest of three children with an older brother, John, whose achievements he wished to emulate; the eldest, a half-sister, was mentally disturbed. His account of his childhood discloses a mixture of neglect, abuse, and premature exposure to adult sexuality. At the age of thirty he was suffering from terrible distress and realized that he needed more help than could be provided by friends. On the advice of one of them he consulted Winnicott, without knowing that he was a leading psychoanalyst, or that he was the President of the British Institute of Psycho-Analysis. In his turn, Winnicott suggested that Godley should go to Masud Khan for treatment.

Godley describes his symptom as having an artificial self that cut him off from social life and made him feel as if he was in a state of dissociation. With that false self he was able as a young man to benefit from his education at Oxford, and he said of his university years that they were supremely happy. He owed his success in higher education to Isaiah Berlin, who influenced him academically. Berlin was severely critical and challenging, so that he was spurred to make what he calls a "stupendous effort". Following that experience, and by the time he felt the need to seek treatment, he had become an economic adviser at the Treasury. Although he had been quite confused about sexuality and sexual intercourse earlier in his life, he had married and was happily settled with his wife. The splitting that had enabled him to flourish intellectually and to make a marriage was beginning to break down as he reached the age of thirty.

In his brief consultation with Winnicott he felt he had been able to reach a very primitive part of himself, baby to baby. Since Winnicott had no vacancy, he referred him to Masud Khan, without telling Godley that Khan was his current analysand. Godley then began his treatment without knowing that it was psychoanalysis, or anything about Khan. As a child he had not been kept informed about important family matters, or about impending changes in the family circumstances, although sometimes he was over-exposed to intimate and sexual experiences from which he ought to have been shielded. The beginning of his treatment apparently unconsciously replicated that early experience.

The analysis

The first session with Khan was a disaster and, perhaps with hindsight, he wrote that within minutes the therapeutic relationship had been completely subverted. It never recovered. From the very first moments of their meeting, Khan evidently felt the challenge to his narcissism from Godley's aristocratic background and intellectual status. Khan had to assert his own credentials by enquiring whether Godley had read anything about him in the newspapers, and especially about his pending marriage to a ballerina of the Royal Ballet. He also indicated that he already knew something about Godley's wife (that she was the daughter of Jacob Epstein, the sculptor) that he had not been told by Godley, who felt that this was an unwelcome intrusion. He was also concerned by Khan's need to assert his own narcissistic image by offering him a lift home in a prestigious make of car, and informing him that he kept a book of James Joyce's poetry in it to read while stuck in traffic jams. As in his childhood, Godley was being given completely inappropriate information, and it had the same effect of making him anxious and completely disconcerted. Already both the frame of the analysis and the reticence of the analyst had been broken.

In the ten days' interval before Khan's marriage and honeymoon, Godley became increasingly subject to quasi-hallucinations and storms of emotion, which, surprisingly, affected neither his working life in the Treasury nor his domestic life. During these disturbing events he gained a completely new insight, "that he hated his father", which generated an outburst of infantile rage. He hallucinated a sentence floating in the air—

UNLESS HE JUSTIFIES HIMSELF I MUST SAVE HIM.

He understood this to mean that unless parents are perceived as strong and self-sufficient the caring process would be catastrophically reversed. He believed that this experience was a breakthrough to a state of feeling that had been blocked for as long as he could remember. He hoped that on the renewal of his sessions with Khan, after his honeymoon, that another such recovery of genuine feeling would occur. It never did.

The remainder of his analysis, he wrote, was "a spiral of degradation". Khan never undid the reversal of roles that had characterized the early sessions, and he could not create the conditions that would have made Godley feel safe in the expression of anger and aggression. The analysis became a bitter struggle between them and, at one point, Khan told him that, unlike his colleagues, he believed in returning aggression for aggression. It was evident that something in Godley's background and ancestry made Khan feel denigrated by comparison, so leading him continually to reassert his threatened narcissism by disparaging Godley's status, at the same time admiring his achievements at the Treasury as if they reflected credit on Khan himself. Since Godley was at that time unfamiliar with the techniques of psychoanalysis, he believed that every unkind, hurtful thing that Kahn said to him was justified. He

244 THE ANALYSAND'S TALE

had to accept these painful home truths as the essence of good analysis.

Much of what occurred was simply bad practice, when it was not abusive. In some ways it replicated symbolically the events of Godley's childhood, as he himself recognized. When Khan took phone calls during the sessions so that Godley could often hear both sides of the conversation, or when Khan told him of his various social encounters, he realized that he was being made inappropriately aware of information as he had been in his infancy by his mother. Khan told him in some detail about another patient, Marian, whom he thought Godley should marry, although he was already happily married. He induced Godley to take her out to lunch on several occasions, and at a later stage joined them himself. He arranged social events for them both with himself and others, when he behaved spectacularly badly towards his guests. Despite being in five times a week analysis Godley was sometimes invited to Khan's flat to meet his wife. On one occasion both Khan and his wife were drunk, and had a physical fight in front of him. After that Godley told Khan that he "might, at some stage, have to say that things had got so far out of hand that I would have to break off the analysis". Khan responded that if that were so he would break it off first.

Subsequently things went from bad to worse. Khan, with his wife, visited the Godleys at home, which was a particularly flagrant intrusion and breach of psychoanalytic practice. During that visit he mimicked and teased Godley's stepdaughter, who was in analysis with Winnicott. On other occasions he had initiated events at various restaurants with Godley and his wife, and at other times with other celebrities known to Khan and his wife. After one such meeting, when Khan had behaved particularly badly in the restaurant, he telephoned Godley's pregnant wife. She described Khan as having "torn into her", leaving her with a sharp pain in the womb. Godley felt that this was a painfully distressing attack on their unborn child, and upon himself. He spoke to Winnicott immediately, asking if Khan was mad. Winnicott replied that he was, and came to Godley's home the same day to tell him that he had forbidden Khan from communicating with him again. Khan did, however, try to get Godley to continue the analysis. He refused and ended it at once.

Ten years later, and after Khan's operation for cancer of the throat, Khan phoned Godley at home and, speaking hoarsely, asked Godley to visit him Even after ten years Godley could not resist, and when he arrived Khan was drunk. Although he was ravaged by his illness, his grandiosity and narcissism were not diminished. He was entertaining guests who Godley described as sycophants. From time to time he pointed to Godley and drunkenly said to the guests, "He and I the same. Aristocrats." So Khan's narcissism had never ceased to be challenged by Godley's aristocratic status.

Stuart Sutherland

Introduction

Sutherland was born to a middle-class family, and in infancy was subject to a rigorous and unvarying routine of infant upbringing. When he was two a younger brother was born, and his mother was advised not to see her first-born for two weeks. Although she was at home with the baby, she followed this advice to the letter. Sutherland could not remember this event but he was told later that he had sat outside his mother's locked bedroom door and "howled for fourteen days" (Hopkins, 2000). He thought that such an experience might or might not have been harmful. He described his parents as upright, Calvinistic, dutiful, and self-sacrificing, and his upbringing as normal and conventional, without any dark Freudian passions or sibling rivalry. In adolescence he became introverted, shy with girls, and with a mild phobia of train travel. He was clever and good at rugby, but disliked the rowdy behaviour associated with rugby players. He succeeded in repressing his introverted self, and forced himself to be confident and outgoing despite his underlying feeling. Eventually, he wrote, the mask became the man, but he gave up listening to music and reading poetry because it was emotionally upsetting.

After graduation he became an academic at Oxford, but felt unable to fit in with what he describes as the pretentious, shallow life at High Table, becoming rather intolerant of the petty-minded and snobbish attitudes of his colleagues. His appointment as Professor of Experimental Psychology at Sussex University provided some relief from that atmosphere, but he was plunged into the hive of activity, entailing both his research and bureaucratic activities, required in managing a university department. With his research time swamped by bureaucracy he began to feel that he was not being sufficiently productive, and possibly was no longer capable of producing satisfying, first-class research results. Additionally, although he was married and had children, he was unable to devote very much time to family life, even at the conventional holiday times. He had a low tolerance of boredom and family celebrations, with social events making him restless, preferring the pub to the home. He described himself as a less than ideal husband and father, taking his wife and children for granted. He had other, casual, sexual relationships, and was aware of his wife's affair with another man. He was undisturbed by it until he learned that it was a close friend of his, when he was hit by very primitive feelings of sexual jealousy, precipitating his breakdown. He had evidently been functioning with a false self, manically keeping his depression at bay until he was precipitated into it by learning of the identity of his wife's lover.

The analyses

His accounts of his two encounters with psychoanalysis are contained in a brief chapter of his semi-autobiographical book. In distress he sought, with his wife, advice from his GP about how to save his marriage. He was advised to seek help from a psychoanalyst who specialized in working with discordant marriages. He did this, despite his scepticism about psychoanalysis, and was seen with his wife by the analyst for a few sessions, and then alone. The joint sessions were intended by the analyst to take "the steam out of things", rather than as an attempt to understand the shared unconscious meanings of the relationship. After a few sessions Sutherland was told that his problems were too complex to be treated in joint therapy with his wife. So individual sessions with Sutherland alone replaced them. It seems that this analyst's way of working with couples may, in fact, have been a method of treating an individual patient in the context of the relationship, rather than treating the pair as an entity containing both sexual promiscuity and a sick, driven partner. In his individual sessions Sutherland felt the analyst was rather bored, allowing him to ramble incoherently, making a few interpretations while looking at his watch, or out of the window at his children. These interpretations were not only Freudian in content but also sometimes just common sense, except for one occasion, when he appears to have supported Sutherland's wish to beat up his wife's lover. Sutherland's scepticism led him to feel critical of the analyst's treatment and interpretations. The analyst had accepted him as an acute case, hoping that a few sessions might alleviate the problem, but recognizing that it had not, he referred him to another local psychoanalyst who was unable to take him but in his turn referred him to another, younger London colleague.

The train journey to London activated Sutherland's railway phobia, exacerbated by the fact that the terminus was the one used by his wife in keeping her assignations with her lover. These factors made Sutherland panic and he arrived for his session shaking with terror. The analyst was late getting to his consulting room, so his wife showed Sutherland into what he described as rather a squalid room. Lying on the greasy couch while he waited, he began to cry for the first time in many years. The analyst found him in this state and, without any preliminaries or enquiring why Sutherland was crying, asked if Sutherland thought that he had deserted him. Sutherland does not record his response to that rather rash, premature interpretation. On another occasion he was shocked by the analyst's asking him, in response to an association to a childhood memory, "Did you not feel then as though you wanted your father to fuck you until the shit ran out?" (Sutherland, 1987, p. 20). What had become of analytic tact and timing?

He felt critical of the analyst's youth and student-like attire, and that while he may have wanted to be helpful he was rather clumsy in the way he went about it. Sutherland believed that the analyst may have been threatened by his status as a well-established professor of psychology. That feeling may have been fostered by Sutherland's launching at once into a critique of analysis in an attempt to be honest. He added to that by suggesting to the analyst that he thought he was only recently qualified and had not been very successful, judging by the poverty in which he lived. The analyst responded defensively, telling Sutherland that he had a large house elsewhere in London and many patients waiting to see him.

As the sessions proceeded, Sutherland felt that the interpretations were both bizarre and irrelevant as well as sometimes being rather stereotypical interpretations of repressed homosexuality seeming to proceed from theory rather than from his associations. The analyst's understanding of the depressive breakdown as an opportunity to change his life was not appreciated by Sutherland, who felt that to break down from the trivial reason of being jealous of his wife's affair was demeaning. He did not, however, grasp that feelings of guilt and attacks on, and denigration of, the self were themselves symptoms of depression. One aspect of Sutherland's behaviour that distressed him most was that at home he sat like a small baby, holding his head and moaning. He could not stop, despite upsetting his wife and children. The analyst evidently had very little knowledge of Sutherland's infancy, and had he known about Sutherland's distress at the birth of his brother he might have linked his current behaviour with that event. As it was he gave him some "good" advice to try to sit in a chair like a baby without giving any outward expression of his feelings. Sutherland could not, of course, do that, and felt that there must be something false about his behaviour if it was intended to gain sympathy and attention. He wondered if there was anything genuine about himself, which may again have been a manifestation of low self-esteem generated by his depression.

Mrs Sutherland attended one of the sessions on the advice of the analyst, who felt that she might be feeling jealous of the analysis. His evidence for this was not clear and was not recorded by Sutherland, although he complied with the analyst's suggestion. In the event Mrs Sutherland was as dismissive of the analyst as her husband, and refused to come again. One might wonder how this intervention could have been helpful when offered at such an early stage by an analyst without experience of the problems of couple relationships. As it is, the reason offered for it must have been spurious before the therapy had had a chance to be established.

After a few sessions Sutherland felt that he was deteriorating and that the treatment was responsible for it. He wondered about seeking an admission to a psychiatric hospital, to the horror of the analyst, who seemed prejudiced against mental hospitals. In the end Sutherland decided not to return after his analyst's holiday, taken only a few weeks after the therapy had begun. He left without paying the bill for his sessions because he felt so mal-treated. On hearing from the analyst's solicitors, seeking payment, he told them that he would claim that the analyst was incompetent and had made his problems worse; he also claimed, among other things, that the analyst had fraudulently asserted that he could be cured in six months, and therefore he had entered the analysis under a false pretence. He heard no more about it.

That was not quite the end, because he was in just as bad a state after a holiday in Italy with his wife and family and he decided to consult his GP again. The GP was convinced that psychoanalysis could be helpful and persuaded him to seek an assessment from the first psychoanalyst he had seen. He did so, reluctantly, and was advised that he should continue analysis "in the hope of learning a new set of emotional responses". He asked some questions about this process but the answers only distressed him more, so he abandoned psychoanalysis for treatment in a psychiatric hospital.

None of the various treatments he endured was very effective, including several abortive efforts to work at the problems of his marriage, and he continued to suffer from bipolar disease until, after several alternating bouts of depression and hypomania for some years, he was treated with Lithium, which enabled him to stabilize his mental state but not to resolve his marital difficulties. Despite these treatments, he eventually committed suicide.

CHAPTER TWENTY

Discussion

T he two accounts presented in Part IV offer very different experiences from most of those considered in the rest of this book, with the exception of Rosie Alexander and Jeffery Masson. These patients did not gain anything from their analyses, and, so far as Godley was concerned, not only did he not gain but may well have been damaged by the erratic behaviour of Masud Khan. It is surprising that Godley did not lose confidence in psychoanalysis, but later in his life found a more orthodox experience with another analyst in Canada that may have repaired the harm done in his first analysis.

The work of Masud Khan has been discussed by others (Hopkins, 2000), although all before 2001 when Godley's account burst on the world. Hopkins (2002) asserts that Khan's work in his prime period until 1971, when Winnicott died, has to be separated from his subsequent work. However, his analysis of Godley began in 1956, some six years after Khan's first qualification, fifteen years before Winnicott died, and when Khan was making his first bid to become a training analyst (accepted in 1959). His conduct of this analysis could hardly have been more eccentric than those he undertook after 1971.

Throughout this early period both Khan and Winnicott were moving towards a different process in the management and treatment of patients. It relied on encouraging the *use* of the object (the analyst), and modified play techniques of child therapy to gain access to unconscious layers of the mind, rather than on free association alone. Khan's behaviour with Godley at this very early stage could hardly be described as a model for this technique. He abandoned the discipline of observing the boundary of the analytic session by engaging Godley in all sorts of inappropriate, extracurricular social activities, which included not only Godley and his wife but Khan's wife, and many of the celebrities known to Khan. On those occasions Khan's flamboyant behaviour often went far beyond the bounds of social acceptability. That behaviour may have become more prevalent after Winnicott's death, but how many other examples may there have been during that early period? And when Godley told Winnicott of a particularly serious breach of professional behaviour, leading Winnicott to forbid Khan from having any further contact with Godley, why did he not ensure that the British Institute of Psycho-Analysis dealt with it as a disciplinary matter? Perhaps, because at that time the Institute had no formal disciplinary process or complaints procedures, there may have been no formal action that could have been invoked. However significant the use of a play technique may have been, it could hardly have included most of the activities in which Khan indulged with this patient. Even unorthodoxy has to respect some boundaries, and additionally has to be capable of intellectual justification. Drunkenness and boorish behaviour cannot be said to approach that justification.

From a psychoanalytic point of view, it may be important to think about how, in his countertransference, Khan succeeded in re-enacting the abuses of Godley's childhood, as Godley himself noted. Was Khan so sensitive to the unconscious transference from Godley that he was readily able to tune in to that repressed infantile turmoil, which may have been near the surface as Godley sought treatment? Was the benefit that his sensitivity might have brought to the therapy disrupted by Khan's narcissistic rivalry with Godley, and his consequent inability to control his countertransference in a way that would have advanced the treatment? In one of his papers, Khan wrote that taking a patient into analysis involved a responsibility demanding "... vision, skill, intellectual acumen, concern and *a disciplined sensibility*" (Khan, 1974, p. 112, my italics). Could those important characteristics of psychoanalytic therapy have been so disrupted by Godley's transference that Khan was unable to gain control of his countertransference, or was this a manifestation of Khan's profound characterological disorder, beyond the capacity of any of his three analysts to have resolved?

Talking to Robert Boynton (2002–2003) about Masud Khan and his analysis of Godley, Peter Fonagy is reported as saying that without a firm and good theory the personal encounter in the analytical session may be so powerful that the analyst may be washed away. Was this the case for Masud Khan? He almost certainly had a good theory, as his theoretical writings testify, but plainly the theory was not enough to be a bulwark against his fragile narcissism.

So far as Sutherland was concerned, he was persuaded by his enthusiastic GP to seek psychoanalytic treatment against his own judgement. His studies of psychology had made him very sceptical of analysis, and he would have been a difficult patient even for a very experienced therapist. Neither of his analysts seem to have behaved very skilfully. Their interventions, as reported by Sutherland, often seemed tactless and sometimes inappropriate. Both attempted to engage Sutherland and his wife in some form of couple therapy, but little evidence is provided that they understood anything about working with couples even if it had been appropriate. The involvement of Mrs Sutherland in the treatment seems to have been ill-considered, and the reasons for it either unexplored with Sutherland himself, or, on the second occasion, simply wrong.

Although there were problems in Sutherland's life, as he describes it, that may have been accessible to psychoanalysis or psychoanalytically based couple therapy had Sutherland been less sceptical about analytical treatment, it is not evident that his major presenting problem, the agitated depression, was either related to those matters or would be responsive to analytic methods. He tried a number of other treatments for it without success until he was offered a permanent prescription of Lithium, which succeeded in controlling the swings of mania and depression, suggesting that they might have been a consequence of a chemical malfunctioning in his brain. What precipitated that malfunction is not clear, nor whether it could have been prevented by other treatments, but

Sutherland himself believed that there was an interaction between neurological and psychological processes such that each could be affected by the other. He wrote, "One's psychological state affects the body's hormones and the body's defences against illness. It would be surprising if it did not also affect the neurotransmitters in the brain, which are much akin to hormones" (Sutherland, 1987, pp. 81–82). This perhaps raises the unanswered question whether, in the interaction between psychology and neurology, the psychological factors cause the neurological changes, or the neurological changes cause the psychological condition. In either event Sutherland did not believe that psychoanalysis had anything to offer in understanding or treating that interaction.

Lewis Wolpert, a professor of Biology as Applied to Medicine, raised some of the same issues in his book (Wolpert, 1999) describing his own depressive breakdown. While he referred very sceptically to psychoanalysis, he did not give any account of his experiences in analysis, although he claimed that it did not work for two reasons. First, because his analyst's claim that Wolpert would not get better without his help would, immorally and intolerably, trap him into years of treatment; second, that he found nothing new or correct in the analyst's diagnosis or interpretations; even if true, they gave no indication of how he could be cured beyond lying on the couch several times per week and paying £94 per session (*ibid.*).

His scholarly discussion of the causes of depression is wide ranging, and he made use of Freud's study of "Mourning and melancholia" (Freud, 1917e) and object loss, as well as attachment, neurological, physiological, and genetic theories to gain some understanding of the illness. He thought that the causes of depression were multi-factorial, but his major conclusion was that depression, in the form of illness as he experienced it, was related to, but not the same as, sadness, as Freud suggested. He thought that it could be compared with the development of cancer resulting from a malignant form of the natural growth processes, and in this sense depression is a malignant form of sadness, as his title suggests. By contrast, he suggested that mania might be a malignant form of happiness. He accepted that three factors identified by Freud were all significant in the development of depression (Wolpert, 1999, p. 88). These were: a belief in the powerful influence of parents on infant personal and social development; that their influence begins early and provides a lasting mental model for their children: and that experiences that shape this mental model include anxiety provoking experiences involving the loss of love or of a loved person. Despite his approval of Freud's thinking about mourning, and awareness that some of these factors might be unconscious, he did not endorse their exploration psychoanalytically. He believed that the two other forms of psychotherapy that would be most therapeutic, in conjunction with some drug treatments, were cognitive behavioural therapy and what he described as "inter-personal psychotherapy".

Wolpert was much less dogmatic and more thoughtful about therapy than Sutherland and did not believe that the causes of depression were exclusively somatic, but they both raise issues about whether psychoanalytical treatment is relevant to profound depression or bipolar illness. They question whether the exploration of historical antecedents of these illnesses is in any way helpful, and claim that it may even be harmful to recovery. These are quite cogent comments, raising questions about whether psychoanalytical explorations are therapy at all, or are simply ways of exploring the foundations of personality without any therapeutic consequences.

PART V
FINALLY

CHAPTER TWENTY-ONE

Concluding

Review of case material

The patients' stories presented here, while not representative of the client population for psychotherapy or psychoanalysis as a whole, nevertheless provide a range of experiences with a variety of analysts from Freud, Jung, and some subsequent practitioners, which offer illuminating possibilities for comparison and contrast. They include a number of those who were themselves training to become therapists, as well as those who were simply seeking help for their distressing symptoms. What emerges quite strongly is how different the accounts of analysands are from those usually written by therapists, even when the analysands were themselves therapists. Might this support the view that the patient's view, while different, is as relevant to the story of the process as the analyst's? Many were gratified by their treatment and were able to express their gratitude to their therapists, while others felt that they had not gained from their therapy, and were very dissatisfied with their experiences. What also emerges quite strongly is the considerable variation between analysts in the way that they function in the clinical setting. Sometimes those variations can be seen in the same analyst with different patients. Kardiner's account of Freud's differences with himself and with Strachey and Rickman is simply anecdotal even if the story rings true. Evidence of Freud's variability can also be found in his change of location for a session with HD and Wortis; in his willingness to see Blanton's wife in part of a session in place of Blanton himself; in his engaging in discussion about his family with the Wolf-Man and HD, and about other matters and other patients with the Wolf-Man, HD, Kardiner, and Blanton. Freud's changes to what has become known as the "frame" has been followed by others, notably Winnicott, Anna Freud, Masud Khan, as well as Jung. Hill's questions, "Am I a Kleinian? Is anyone?", could as well be asked of others who adhere to particular theoretical positions. It is not evident if these many variations are primarily related to the analyst, to the analysand, or to the idiosyncrasies of the particular clinical pair. But strict observance of the same conditions or technique by all analysts with all analysands is not to be found in this collection. Wallerstein has discussed these issues arising from this variability of practice, and has concluded that uniformity in psychoanalytic practice cannot be found.

Discordant agendas

In several accounts, there appears to have been what I have called "discordant agendas" between patient and therapist. By this I mean that the analysand and the therapist may be pursuing different, and sometimes contrary, agendas in the treatment, a discordance that may be overt or sometimes covert. It may lead to resistance to the interpretations of the therapist as being irrelevant to the process the patient is trying to follow. It differs from the resistance arising from unconscious sources, although it may become related to them, and tends to be a conscious rejection of the analyst's stance.

Kottler and Carlson (2003), although not writing primarily about psychoanalytic therapy, introduce the notion of the therapist's narcissistic attachment to a theoretical agenda as a source of bad therapy. My view is that the discordant agendas of therapist and analysand may be a source of therapeutic difficulty and failure. Sometimes the discordant agendas appeared only briefly in the treatment. Kardiner and Couch provide examples of this in what were otherwise satisfactory therapies. Kardiner thought that both Freud and Sachs had interpreted his homosexuality in a way that did not resonate with anything in him and was a manifestation of their adherence to a theory they believed to be universal, applicable to all analysands, without relating it to the analysand's reported accounts of particular experiences or memories of infancy. Couch found it difficult to accept Anna Freud's dismissal of his concerns about his approaching marriage when she claimed that those in the psychoanalytic world had long since abandoned the idea of forming relationships through traditional weddings and marriage. He felt quite hurt by her inability to take his anxieties seriously.

Others gave evidence of much greater discordance, although not always related to bad outcomes. HD is the prime example of this, as throughout her analysis she secretly pursued her own way of understanding her unconscious processes without losing either her respect for Freud, or incorporating his concepts uncritically. Others, such as the Wolf-Man, Wortis, and Blanton were at odds with Freud, much to their own disadvantage. The Wolf-Man is a particularly interesting example of the discordant agenda between himself and Freud, as he only gave up his own agenda when Freud announced the termination of the analysis as a way of bringing him into conformity. Freud referred to this process as a "blackmailing device" (Freud, 1937c, p. 218) and claimed that it had produced all the material that confirmed his agenda. But, as his reminiscences demonstrate, the Wolf-Man never really acceded to Freud's agenda, wishing that he could have "wrenched Freud out of him" at the end of the first analysis, despite his trading on the special position he subsequently occupied in the pantheon of psychoanalysis. Although he had read many of Freud's papers, he never mentioned the one about himself in his published memoirs, although adopting the soubriquet. Freud claimed that he had given consent to its publication. In his conversations with Obholzer, the Wolf-Man specifically rejected Freud's construction of the primal scene, and never recovered any conscious memory of it.

Dr Little is an even more interesting example, since she undertook three different analyses. Neither of the first two, with Dr X and Ella Sharpe, proved to be very satisfactory to her. She stayed with them, repressing her discordance by seeking to identify with them, first through training for psychotherapy as proposed by Dr X, and then by finishing a training analysis with Ella Sharpe while remaining completely at odds with her throughout the analysis. Although she successfully identified with Ella Sharpe by becoming herself an accredited psychoanalyst at the British Institute, she was left unsatisfied by that process, and critical of the way that Sharpe applied the classical concepts of Freud's libido theory to her without acknowledging her protests that they did not explain or relieve her basic distress. Winnicott's unorthodoxy and his capacity to function therapeutically outside the conventional boundaries of the psychoanalytical session seem to have facilitated her capacity to discover the source of her psychotic disturbance. She felt that her analysis with him was more satisfactory, and except for one period lasting for a year when she felt herself to have been completely misunderstood by him, she identified with him, and became an advocate for his ideas.

The same seems to have been true for Guntrip. He experienced Fairbairn's correct and rigid application of theory as helpful, but unable to expose the deeply unconscious cause of his psychological problem, for which he needed the supplement of Winnicott's different concepts. To be quite fair, although Guntrip felt that Winnicott's unorthodoxy had taken him further, building on the foundations laid by Fairbairn, it also left him feeling uncompleted. The denouement came after he had ended his work with Winnicott, who had died before Guntrip had a number of very significant dreams precipitating the emotional condition that enabled him to recover the memory of his basic trauma.

Winnicott's analyses of both Little and Guntrip have been criticized as being unsatisfactory in various ways (Hopkins, 1998). Most argue that Winnicott was unable to deal with the destructiveness and aggression of either of these two analysands. Neither of them, it is claimed, finished their analyses with him with their characters radically modified. I have suggested that this belittles their claims to have had their suffering relieved by him. The critics dismiss the analysands' stories in favour of an idealized vision of what psychoanalysis might achieve. If Winnicott was at fault in not producing this outcome, were either Fairbairn or Sharpe any less culpable with their classical approaches? No mention is made by Hopkins, or other critics, of the contribution of either of them to this less than satisfactory outcome. It should be recalled that Sharpe's analysis was believed to be so satisfactory that Little was admitted to membership of the British Institute. Nobody commented that Little's character had changed insufficiently, so making her unworthy of that membership. Equally, nobody has commented on Fairbairn's analysis of Guntrip as having failed to produce any radical change in his character, even though Guntrip was in analysis with him for much longer than with Winnicott. It is as if the shortcomings of the classical approach need not be examined, while Winnicott's new approach carried the whole responsibility for whatever defects remained in these two analysands, despite their own belief that it had reached levels of unconscious material that the others had not..

Discordant agendas between analysand and therapist seem often to arise when the therapist appears to be more interested in the theory of psychoanalysis or psychotherapy than in the unconscious realities of the patient. This may have led to the patients feeling that they were being used as examples of a theory that they did not feel was appropriate to them. Sophie Freud, Sigmund's granddaughter, commented on the importance of recognizing and respecting, and not denying, the patient's own construction of his reality (Freud, Sophie, 1993). Although she may have been referring to the way transference implications were read into real world events in the patient's life, it may also be true that the patient's unconscious agenda, differing from the analyst's, should be respected by the analyst or therapist. Sigmund Freud claimed that he was more interested in theory than he was in therapy, and was convinced that he had found the veritable cause of neurosis.[1] He was less interested in the process of cure in the analytic setting, and confessed that he often felt bored when working with patients. The story of the Wolf-Man, as told by Freud, was intended to illustrate how his concepts could provide a definitive explanation of the Wolf-Man's psychological problems, thus providing some evidence for those concepts. Sergei himself was interested first in replacing his lost sister with Therese, claiming that Freud described this as "the break through to the woman", although that idea does not appear in Freud's paper. Second, he wished to find a replacement for his dead father who would love him for himself rather than as a replacement for his sister, Anna. In Freud he found such a replacement, believing that he was being treated as a junior colleague of Freud's rather than a patient. He claimed that Freud had told him that he understood psychoanalytical ideas better than some of Freud's students, a confirmation indeed of Sergei's privileged position. As the subject of Freud's paper he may also have found confirmation of his special status, emphasized by the subsequent interest in him of the whole psychoanalytic community. It is possible that Freud was so captivated by the intensity of Sergei's wish for him to be the father who really cared for him unreservedly that his paper unconsciously demonstrated his very special feelings for Sergei in response to that wish, and conveyed that message to him. However, Sergei was not able to give up lightly his discordant agenda until his failure to comply with Freud's agenda led to the announcement of the termination of the analysis,[2] threatening his position as Freud's favourite. It may be simply coincidental that Freud subsequently wrote his paper as an argument against Jung, who had been his favourite son and had fallen from grace, and, during this analysis, the Wolf-Man was seeking to compensate for not having been the favourite of his father by becoming Freud's favourite son. It is as if the dethroned favourite son, Jung, was in some sense being replaced by the Wolf-Man in Freud's triumphant paper.

Hill was similarly at odds with Mrs Bick's interpretations. He felt that they were dictated by her rigid theoretical stance, sometimes seeming to have little or no relevance to his associations. It was difficult to discuss this with her. The idea of discussion of any of her interventions was anathema to her, and she dismissed any attempt that he made to do so. When he tried to find an alternative analyst she thwarted him by threatening to terminate his training analysis, so that he would lose the investment of time and money he had made. This was similar to Masson's experience with Schiffer, whose threats to cancel his candidate status kept him in therapy until he was able to conclude the analysis and proceed to qualification without Schiffer's opposition. These two examples draw attention to the vulnerability of the analysand in training to the unscrupulous use of the analyst's power, to which others have also referred. They also illustrate the danger presented by the narcissistic identification of the analyst with the theory, although it might be difficult to identify the theory to which Schiffer was attached.

Perhaps it was simply his basic narcissism that created the discordant agendas between himself and Masson. Hill's eventual escape from Mrs Bick allowed him to find a much less dogmatic successor, whose careful technique allowed him to experience their interaction as completely concordant.

Wortis and Blanton were also discordant with Freud, although for different reasons. Wortis had plainly misunderstood what Freud would offer him by way of a "didactic analysis". He could not grasp that being analysed was a part of the learning experience, and seemed to understand very little about the process. He regularly tried to turn his sessions into seminars on Freud's concepts, although he continued to lie on the couch. He avoided introducing personal material about himself as far as he could, and did not want to examine any personal issues about homosexuality. Ostensibly, he had come to learn about it academically. He persisted in his belief that homosexuality was socially constructed and was not related to unconscious factors. Much to Freud's horror, he believed that there should be no sanctions against homosexuality. Freud told Wortis that the repression of homosexuality was absolutely essential for the maintenance of modern civilization, although his evidence for this proposition seems to have been rather eccentric. So, Wortis left without belief in psychoanalysis as a science or as a treatment, except as a preliminary to other organic methods. After leaving Freud he practised as a psychiatrist, confining himself to organic methods of treatment.

Unlike others who had written about their work with Freud, Wortis was unable to value anything about the experience. Blanton, on the other hand, was keen to become a qualified analyst and, despite what looked like a rather arid experience with Freud, he insisted that it had been the most gratifying event of his life. His powerful transference to Freud had not enabled him to form a concordant agenda with him, and there seemed to be occasions when Freud may have conveyed unconsciously that he did not believe that Blanton could be analysed. Twice Freud commented on the difficulty that Americans had in accepting his ideas, and perhaps, in the analysis, that was a displacement of his feelings about Blanton, with whom he was discordant. Although Blanton returned three times between 1935 and 1938, ostensibly to seek further analysis, he succeeded in turning those sessions into opportunities to present some of his cases for Freud's comments rather than to explore any of his personal problems. Since these included a period when his wife had left him for a year, and that she too met Freud on two or three occasions during some of Blanton's sessions, it is surprising that he did not bring that relationship to his sessions with Freud. Mrs Blanton attributed the breakdown in their marriage to his analysis, and to the way that Freud had taken her place in her husband's mind. Although she returned to live with her husband after a year's separation, their relationship was no longer what it had been before Blanton's analysis. It is as if Blanton's agenda with Freud was to avoid as far as possible anything of a problematic nature. The meetings between Freud and Mrs Blanton, and their separation, were never mentioned in Blanton's sessions Equally, Blanton's resistance never seems to have been directly interpreted by Freud or related to the work of the analysis. In these two analyses it can be seen that something regarded as essential to their success was missing: the interpenetration of the subjectivities of analysand and analyst.

The account of Masson's analysis and subsequent career in psychoanalysis has been criticized by Malcolm (1984), Young (1998), and Sophie Freud (1993). According to Masson's story, it became quite clear at an early stage that Schiffer's agenda was discordant with Masson's; he seemed to be unable to hear Masson's agenda. Young approaches Masson's description of his analysis with some scepticism and ambivalence, though not denying that his tale of his experience of the analysis was authentic, if hyperbolic. Some others have been rather less caustic or vituperative than Young. Sophie Freud is much more sympathetic, and, with reservations, inclined to believe Masson's story. If Masson's account of Schiffer's behaviour is only partly true, it describes gross abuse and professional malpractice that, although not approaching Masud Khan's abuse of Godley, was inexcusable. It is not reasonable to ascribe the failure of the analysis only to Masson's difficult, damaged personality. Psychoanalysis lays claim to being able to help modify and improve the personalities of such patients, through their interaction with the personalities of their analysts, but here it is as if the two personalities of Schiffer and Masson were at war rather than in accord. Sadly, some of the responses to Masson's story follow the characteristic of many psychoanalysts, and their institutes, to treat such failings as manifestations of the analysand's unresolved transference rather than a problem of the analyst, or of psychoanalysis. The fact that Masson's analysis with Schiffer was believed to have been adequate for admission to professional status, not only by the Toronto Institute but also the San Francisco Institute and the International Institute of Psychoanalysis, has been overlooked by his critics. How had that come about if it was later so obvious that Masson had been inadequately analysed, bearing in mind that this was a *training* and not simply a therapeutic analysis? His subsequent troubles with the psychoanalytic world, and in particular with Eissler and the Freud Archive, have been ascribed to Masson's character defects rather than to the defects of his training analysis. It suggests that there may also have been an institutional problem about accepting the analysand's story of the analysis. In pursuing the goal of becoming a psychoanalyst, Masson had hoped that it would provide a remedy for his "almost congenital sadness". That outcome was to be denied.

Jung's analysis of Catherine Cabot is more difficult to evaluate, despite her lengthy description of it, because it was co-terminous with her other analysis with Toni Wolff, about which little is known since no record of it was made. Jung's work with Catherine throws up some interesting differences with Freud's technique. The practice of using of two analysts was introduced by Jung at that time, but is not normally practised by Jungian analysts now. So far as Catherine's notes go, and despite what seems to have been a very unorthodox interaction between them, there is no suggestion that Catherine felt in any way discordant with Jung. If anything, the discordance was with Toni Wolff, and she complained to Jung about it in her sessions with him. Although never interpreted by Jung, there may have been something very significant for Catherine about not only the use of two analysts, but also in the context of the Zürich Psychological Club, where Jung, Wolff, and Catherine mingled freely with other Club members.

I have suggested that the interaction between the two analysts and Catherine, together with their socializing at the Psychological Club and elsewhere, may have been therapeutically significant for her as a way of re-experiencing her parents' interaction, and a reversal of her mother's neglect of her during her childhood and adolescence. Unconsciously, Jung and Toni were turned into herself, while she became the abandoning parent leaving the deserted child. This was unlike a Freudian analysis, where the transference–countertransference interactions are expected to be confined within the boundary of the analytic sessions. It is evident that at this time Freud sometimes crossed this boundary, but not as promiscuously as Jung. As time has passed, the need to observe the boundaries of the analytic frame, as well as the boundaries within the session between analyst and analysand, have become important criteria of good practice, observed by both Jungians and modern psychoanalysts of different theoretical allegiances. Jung, in his early period, and Winnicott, much later, have both presented challenges to those ideas, which I will consider later in this section.

It is evident from Catherine's account of her analysis that Jung had a very different way of understanding the meaning and practice of analysis than Freud and the psychoanalytic world in general. Jung's theory of the unconscious diverged considerably from Freud's and Klein's theories. In the analysis of Catherine, he seems to have had very little interest in relating her early experiences in infancy and childhood to her problems in her present relationships, or in tracing how her unconscious fantasies of those experiences may have shaped her psyche. On one occasion, Jung did interpret her anxieties in the funicular to the conflicting wishes to be contained as well as to be free, the conflict between claustrophobia and agoraphobia, as a possible outcome of the experience of being inadequately contained by her parents. On another, he interpreted that she was unable to "see" with her ears because of her father's bad language. But these examples were very few in a meticulously recorded account of the analysis lasting several years. His advice to her to keep to the impersonal, and to try to stop Wolff from concentrating on the personal, indicate that his ideas about the effect of her unconscious conflicts on her present problems were very different from Freud's way of understanding. Jung's method seems to have been to try to help her reach an awareness of her unconscious processes in her current interactions with others, and to increase her knowledge of those processes through the technique of amplification, of which there are abundant examples in Catherine's account. Additionally, he introduced ideas about the archetypes, especially the animus and the anima, to help her understand her interaction with her various male partners, including de Trafford.

Jung seemed to be prepared to comment freely on the psychological state of her partner, and Wolff went so far as to advise her to get married to him, although the difficulty about that lay with de Trafford, who seemed unwilling to proceed with the divorce from his first wife.

What is particularly surprising in Catherine's account was the interaction between Jung and Toni Wolff. It is not evident that she knew that Wolff was sexually involved with Jung and in a *ménage à trois* (McLynn, 1996) with him and his wife, Emma. Although this may have been common knowledge in the Jungian community, Catherine made no overt reference to their relationship in her analysis with Jung. It is not known what she may have said to Wolff about Jung. However, Jung talked about Wolff's psychopathology in response to Catherine's complaints about her, and generally advised Catherine how she should manage her relationship with Wolff. Nor is not known whether Jung and Wolff discussed their concurrent analyses with Catherine to try to avoid being at cross-purposes. In fact, Jung often seemed to be siding with Catherine against Wolff, as well as frequently giving Catherine quite derogatory information about Wolff's psychopathology as he saw it. Catherine clearly regarded her analysis with Jung as the more significant of the two.

Both analyses were very interrupted by Catherine's frequent absences on her trips abroad, and even during wartime, when she was unable to leave Switzerland, she often spent time away in different parts of the country and out of immediate contact with either Jung or Wolff. These interruptions appear to have passed without comment or analytic exploration, and it is not clear what the nature of the contracts with Jung or Wolff may have been about regularity of sessions. It sometimes seemed as if no appointment had been made to resume at a particular time after a break, even after traditional holiday breaks. On one occasion following a Christmas holiday (and it may have been that Jung was unwell during that time), Catherine wrote to Jung to ask for another appointment as she had heard that he was seeing patients again. Was it a normal practice to require patients to reconnect with their analyst after a break, or was Catherine's life so haphazard that no regularity from her could be relied upon? No reference to the meaning of the irregularity of the sessions appears in what must have been almost verbatim notes made by Catherine in each session.

The role of the Psychoanalytic Club in all this was quite important. It provided some kind of container for what may have been rather disjointed experiences. Many of the patients of the Jungian analysts practising in Zürich attended to hear lectures and join in discussions and seminars about Jungian ideas and practice. In some senses, there may almost have been an element of group therapy as patients shared their experiences, not only within the confines of the club, but in the streets and cafés around the meeting place. All of that may have made for a sense of common membership, and of concordance. This must have been of particular significance for Catherine, whose life in all its stages had been very uncontained and fragmented. Members and attenders at the Club were very like a group of siblings, with attachments and disagreements between them that Catherine discussed with Jung. He gave her advice about how to deal with those matters and also interpreted that the faults she was finding in others were probably a projection of her own. Jung described the Club as an analytical collectivity, and in Catherine's writing it certainly seemed to function in that way. It has been described as a cult, and the argument about it can be found in Noll (1996) and Shamdasani (1998). Whatever the truth of these counter claims, for Catherine the Club combined together with her two analysts to form a container where she seems to have been able to come to terms with the legacy of her parents' fragmented nurturing. Her account of the therapy raises questions about the nature and effectiveness of more orthodox treatments.

Of the remaining stories, Marie Cardinal, Rosie Alexander, Wynne Godley and Stuart Sutherland, only one can be described as successful, that of Marie Cardinal. Her un-named therapist's self-confidence established the framework in which, in her own time, she was able to discover the unconscious source of her symptoms and to recover from them. Her analyst's reticence and his belief in his technique enabled Marie to make these discoveries in safety. Her negative transference during part of the process was not the outcome of a discordant agenda, but a consequence of her unconscious resistance to more deeply held unconscious factors, which then made their appearance once her resistance was resolved. The story of the analysis as told by herself seems to be a beautiful account of psychoanalytic treatment at its best.

The other three analysands were not relieved from their suffering, and in Rosie Alexander's case her treatment seems to have left her in a worse condition than when she entered it. The intensity of her transference to each of the therapists seems to have overwhelmed them. The first two had not been analytically trained, and perhaps, unaccustomed to meeting such an intensity of feeling, they were unable to deal with it. For the analyst, Luc, a number of factors were responsible for the difficulties he had in working with her. The most serious was his failure to establish a boundary between his private and professional life, and she was able to fantasize about it from her actual observations of his personal space in his home, where he also practised. He also failed to make clear how her absence, so soon after the treatment had begun, was to be handled, so that she was unable to understand why he did not respond to her messages. The difficulty with boundaries was manifest not only in his inability to create a safe container by indicating the terms on which they would meet, but in also allowing infringements of the internal boundaries between them. There was inappropriate, erotic touching and holding in the sessions, and some of his transference interpretations could only have aroused the expectations that he might be ready to enter a physical sexual relationship with her. Her fantasies were acted out, short of actual sexual intercourse, by both of them, and there were few if any appropriate interpretations of them that might have linked her present experiences with him to former and formative relationships. Finally, he often failed to take up leads in her associations that might have led to some insight into her difficulties. It is hardly surprising that Rosie failed to benefit from his treatment when her agenda of forming an infantile dependent relationship with him was not interpreted in the transference. It may be that Rosie was suffering from an extreme version of the problems that Little and Guntrip had brought to Winnicott, and may have needed something more than interpretations, but Luc's technique could not encompass it.

Luc's laxity in the observation of boundaries was far surpassed by Masud Khan in his analysis of Wynne Godley. That involved less an omission in the observance of boundaries, but more an active violation of them even as the treatment began. The agendas of analysts and patient became instantly discordant as Khan violated the frame of the therapy in the very first session by giving Godley information about himself during it, and at the end of the session by driving away with him in his prestigious car. Other multiple boundary violations of all kinds followed until, after one particularly blatant intrusion, Godley consulted Winnicott, who brought the analysis to an end by forbidding Khan to see Godley again. He also confirmed to Godley that he thought Khan was mad. Khan had just been elevated to the status of Training Analyst when his work with Godley had begun, and he continued in analysis with Winnicott for the duration of it. It is therefore surprising that, as Winnicott must have had knowledge of what Khan was doing, he did nothing about it until Godley appealed to him directly. Nor did he take it any further with the British Institute. By the time Godley wrote his account in 2001 Khan had died, but before his death had been stripped of his membership of the Institute in 1988 because of the anti-Semitism evident in his final publication. Following Godley's revelations, investigations were begun in the British Institute to understand how these flagrant breaches of psychoanalytical protocol had come about, and what might be done to prevent any further occurrences. Anne-Marie Sandler's paper (2004) describes in detail these investigations, and of the anxiety aroused both personally and institutionally about the knowledge of such violations, often leading to disbelief at all levels. To her credit, she makes no reference to the way in which the idea of transference may be used to suggest that the analysands' accounts of improper behaviour of their analysts or therapists might be ascribed to transference-generated fantasies rather than being accounts of actual behaviour of the therapists. In her recommendations to the Institute she eschews that explanation and draws attention to the danger of regression and self-gratification for the analyst, and to the unconscious desire for exploitation of the analysand against which safeguards should be erected.

Much of the discussion has focused on Winnicott's analysis of, and colleagueship with, Khan, lasting over many years. The concept of object usage introduced by them has also been criticized. There is an issue about whether the concept is sound, or whether Winnicott's and Khan's use of it was flawed, which will be considered below. However, Winnicott was not Khan's only analyst. He began a training analysis with Ella Sharpe, who died nine months after it had begun, and he continued with Rickman to complete that training leading to his admission to qualified membership of the Institute in 1950. Rickman continued with the analysis after Khan's admission to qualified membership of the Institute, but he died a year later in 1951, when Khan transferred to Winnicott. Sharpe and Rickman were classical analysts, and although nothing is known about Khan's training analysis with either of them, they were evidently regarded as having been successful by the standards prevailing at that time. Willoughby (2005, pp. 28, 30–31) has suggested that both Sharpe and Rickman may have been unable to maintain clear analytical boundaries with Khan, and that his relationship with Rickman may have been more of a mentorship than an analytical one. Despite that, his application for membership of the Institute went forward.

There was, however, some disquiet about the recommendation for Khan's admission to Associate Membership, since almost one third of those present at his reading-in voted against it, although on what grounds is not known. Apart from Willoughby's, no criticism has been levelled at the work of these two analysts who, like Winnicott, had been unable to modify Khan's deep psychotic hostility, aggression, and profound narcissism. Winnicott may have been very remiss in having Khan in analysis as well as using him as an editorial assistant and partner for his publications, but while in this problematic relationship with him Khan was approved as a Training Analyst (after three applications). Was nobody else aware, not only of his inappropriate behaviour with Godley, but also his other infringements of analytic protocol with other patients, which had begun long before Winnicott's death? While fault legitimately may be found in Winnicott's professional and personal relationships with Khan, does no blame attach to Rickman, who must have been satisfied that his analysis of Khan was good enough to allow his application for Associate Membership to proceed? Was there an implication that any analysis conducted on classical lines must be satisfactory, regardless of the actual outcome? This assumption seems to have prevailed for Margaret Little's application too, despite her belief that her fundamental psychological problem had not been resolved. Winnicott himself had had the same experience in his two analyses with James Strachey and Joan Riviere, which had not reached an important "element of his psychology" (Newman, 1995, p. 261), despite anything else he had gained from them.

Sutherland's description of his abortive encounters with analysis might suggest that either he was unanalysable, whatever condition he was suffering from, or that his illness was not treatable by analytic methods. As he describes them, none of his analysts was particularly skilful in their interactions with him. If the account of his first encounter with the London-based analyst is accurate, he was assailed by a premature transference interpretation, given even before any formulation of the context of the analytic method had been made, and before any words had been spoken by Sutherland. Even if the assumption that Sutherland was distressed because of feelings of abandonment by the analyst, who was late for the session, was correct, it might have been tactful to have waited for some other confirmation of it in Sutherland's associations. Later in the analysis, he made a crudely insensitive interpretation. Inclined to be sceptical before any treatment began, Sutherland found these interventions not only unhelpful but reinforcing his basic hostility to the practice of psychoanalysis. He and this un-named analysts never formed a therapeutic relationship and their agendas were discordant from the outset.

I now turn to the relevance of all these stories to the development of ideas of the therapeutic frame, boundaries, boundary crossings and violations that have been the subject of much recent discussion.

Therapeutic frames, boundaries, boundary crossings and violations

Much has been made of the concept of the Therapeutic Frame since it was first proposed by Marion Milner in 1952. In it, she made the distinction between the rigid frame of a picture and its contents as a metaphor for boundaries of the psychotherapeutic process. Her assumption seems to have been that the frame would remain a constant throughout the length of the analysis. Although there might be variations these were to be regarded as boundary violations, detrimental to the continuing therapeutic work. Gabbard and

Lester (1995) added to this idea the concept of internal boundaries between therapist and patients within the sessions, which may also be subject to crossing and/or violation. Many others have taken up the discussion, extending or refining the ideas. The frame is usually taken to mean the initial stage-setting by the analyst or therapist of the terms on which the process is to be conducted. These may include: times; length and frequency of sessions, which may not be varied nor interrupted by telephone calls to the therapist or other intrusions; fees to be paid; the place where the sessions are to be held, which should contain few or none of the therapist's personal objects; the withholding of personal information by the therapist, usually referred to as the anonymity rule; confidentiality; and the prohibition of social contacts, which may prove difficult when the analysand is in training to become an analyst or therapist and attends professional meetings of the training institution. As far as possible, most of these conditions are to be kept constant through the course of the treatment, so that a safe container is created and maintained, enabling the analysand to feel secure enough to be able to bring to the process painful, distressing, or repressed, frightening memories or experiences. It is claimed that the frame also serves to protect the development of the transference and countertransference interactions, through which it is believed healing may be promoted. The constant frame is believed by some to be the *sine qua non* of the psychoanalytic process, without which the emergence of the unconscious sources of the analysand's problems would not occur. Some (e.g., Young, 1998) have added many more characteristics to the list defining the frame, so that it becomes almost impossible to distinguish it from the content.

Although many of these conditions may seem to be uncontentious and factual, they are subject to interpretation by the analysand in the light of the transference, or, as Greenson (1973) has claimed, they may also be understood as being outside the transference in the real relationship. So, for example, the apparently neutral, anonymous stance of the analyst/therapist may be experienced by the analysand not as a benign unobtrusiveness but as a frightening absence, indifference, or fear of intimate involvement with another. The setting of a fee may be understood as an expression of greed, particularly if it is announced as the amount to be paid without any reference to the analysand's ability to pay, or to the therapist's varying observance of time and place. This was certainly how Masson felt about Schiffer's frequent lateness, which did not affect his demand for payment in full. So, can the conditions constructing the frame be taken simply as objective matters of fact? They may convey something about the image of the analyst/therapist in the analysand's mind not necessarily having its root in the repressed unconscious or the transference. Freud, in the cases discussed here, frequently varied some of these requirements of time and place, and usually presented himself as a warm human being having no need to shelter behind the principle of anonymity. In the summer, patients were sometimes seen at Freud's holiday home in the mountains. The use of the couch with himself sitting behind it was ascribed by Freud, not to the need for anonymity, but to his dislike of being gazed at directly for several hours daily. To this extent it was a defence for Freud's vulnerability rather than a required technique.

By contrast, Jung's analysis of Catherine Cabot seems to have been conducted without the benefit of a frame of any kind. Sessions were irregular, interrupted by the frequent absences of Catherine. Letters were exchanged, social as well as other kinds of meetings occurred between Jung, Toni Wolff, Emma Jung, Catherine, her partner, and her daughter. Sometimes these meetings were around social meals and events, such as the wedding of Catherine's daughter. References to these occasions were sometimes made in the analysis, and sometimes not. Within her sessions with Jung her relationship with Toni was discussed, and although some of this might have been expected where the treatment was shared with another therapist, Jung's comments, as reported in Catherine's notes, were often very partisan and critical of Toni. In addition, there was the social interaction with the members of the Psychological Club. Jung was very free in his comments about those members with whom Catherine came into conflict. It may be that this amount of freedom from constraint could be exercised where the therapy seems less concerned with uncovering deeply unconscious past experiences and fantasies than with exploring how Jung's psychological concepts could be used to understand current relationships and contemporary problems. Jung did not seem concerned with the interaction of transference and countertransference as an essential part of the process, and little reference to it can be found in

Catherine's notes of her sessions. In broad terms, and in contrast to the relatively enclosed experiences of Freud's patients, it is as if the world somehow swept through Jung's work with Catherine, and in an untrammelled way, it enabled her to gain something from her work with him.

Was she changed in any fundamental way by Jung's work with her? It seems almost impossible to tell, but at least no harm was done to her, and, as I have argued, her acting out, within the analysis, of her uninterpreted childhood experience may have been the therapeutic factor. It is possible that Winnicott, who believed that interpretation in some cases might be insufficient, was functioning in a similar way in his treatment of Little and Guntrip.

Without going as far as Jung in dispensing with the concept of the frame and the inviolable boundaries of the session, the idea of the frame may also be seen as importing an aspect of excessive rigidity and inflexibility, especially in a time of considerable social and economic change, and it might imply a fear of a changing social world against which the therapist seeks protection. There were considerable social changes since Freud's first formulation of his technical concepts in early twentieth century Vienna until the period when Marion Milner offered her ideas. Since that time, in the second half of the twentieth century there have been even more substantial changes in the way people live their lives, and they, both patients and therapists, have become less able to sustain an unchanging arrangement over several years. Even pictures themselves may no longer be contained in an inviolable frame. Some artists have continued their pictures on to the frame so that it no longer forms a discrete boundary. Others, like Jackson Pollock, have declined to have their pictures framed at all; they have an edge, but no frame.

Arguments have been made for providing less rigidity in the construction of the basic conditions for the therapy, notably in recognition of the circumstances that make unchangeable regularities of time and place impossible to maintain or unhelpful, not only for he patient but also for the therapist. Less rigid concepts might be found in the idea of a flexible container, responsive to life and reality changes for both therapist and patient, and in the concept of object constancy, implying consistency in the therapist's capacity and person to maintain the therapeutic process despite inevitable changes to the frame and other boundaries. It might also be the case that the adherence to rigidity, not subject to changes in the social world, either for the analysand or the therapist, could transgress the notion of there being two equal interacting subjects in the therapy. Hence, although the patient's circumstances may change, nothing else, in the analyst or the situation, will change correspondingly. This may account for the therapists' reports of the process resembling the story of an objective other observed objectively, in accordance with medical tradition, and contrary to the notion that they should be accounts of interacting subjectivities.

Gabbard and Lester contrasted the internal boundaries of the session with its frame. According to them, the frame is expected to be constant and unvarying, but the boundaries in the session between the analysand and therapist might be more flexible since the sessions are principally concerned with the fluctuating, interpenetrating subjectivities of the participants, representing the interplay of transference and countertransference. The fantasies of the analysand would almost certainly resonate with those of the therapist, and, more importantly, the countertransference of the therapist might often be echoing the transference, so the observance by the analyst of the boundary between the awareness of feelings and acting them out might be difficult, although essential. Acting out countertransference through interpretations might not always be harmful in itself. Casement (1985) provides an interesting example in the account of his interaction with Mrs B over her wish to relinquish one of her five daily sessions. In his detailed description of the transactions, he illustrates how he was unconsciously acting out his wish not to replicate her absent mother at the time of a traumatic incident in infancy. His capacity to recognize this led to the patient's re-experience in fantasy of some aspects of her original trauma, in the analysis, with the difference that he was able to be present at the re-enactment of the trauma in a way that her mother failed to be. It may represent what Gabbard and Lester call a *boundary crossing* rather than a *boundary violation*. The difference lies in the avoidance of inappropriate action; that may be illustrated by the examples of Luc, in the case of Rosie Alexander, and Winnicott with Margaret Little. Luc's behaviour was undoubtedly a violation of boundaries that was verging on a breach of the most serious kind, i.e., the sexual abuse of the patient. In contrast, Winnicott seems to have crossed boundaries consciously rather than violating them, guided by his theory of object use. His unorthodox methods proved more success-ful than had had been possible in Little's more orthodox analysis with Ella Sharpe. The same could be said of his work with Guntrip in contrast with the analysis with Fairbairn, although there is some controversy about it.

Anxiety about the possibility of inappropriate acting out by the analyst, particularly in sexual terms, is what may have given rise to fear that boundary crossing might become a violation. The destruc-tiveness of sexual activity between therapist and patient is acknowledged to be a consequence of the repetition in the analysis of "incestuous" feelings and experiences, which should be under-stood rather than re-enacted. Institutions as well as individual ther-apists are made anxious and uncomfortable when they become aware of colleagues' sexual transgressions. The concept of the slip-pery slope, with non-sexual boundary crossings leading inevitably to the initiation of sexual relations between therapist and patient, lies behind much of the exploration of the possibility that those boundary crossings might become violations of a gross kind. Freud expressed the same anxiety when he was reported as saying that the first generation holds hands (with the patients) and the next generation goes to bed with them.

The sample of patients' accounts I have discussed does not illus-trate the inevitability of a sexual outcome of unorthodox behaviour. While in some there were quite surprising departures from ortho-doxy, especially in Jung's analysis of Catherine Cabot, in only one case did it lead to any sort of physical sexual exchange. Luc, in his treatment of Rosie Alexander, came very close to acting out an incestuous relationship with her, but this was not a consequence of escalating, inadvertent, minor boundary violations but of his gener-ally poor technique and lack of skill. Because the possibility that such flagrant violations *may* arise from minor infringements earlier in the treatment, the emphasis on the rigid frame and the signifi-cance of internal sessional boundaries may, in this sense, be an attempt to impose a professional superego with the hope that this will prevent such violations, rather than just being a requirement of a professional technique.

For some practitioners of psychoanalysis, nothing but the strict observance of the frame and the boundaries within the sessions will ensure that the work of the analysis is being properly carried out (Langs, 1976; Bollas & Sundelson 1995); anything else would subvert the process. Theorists like Langs, Bollas, and Klein make much of these aspects of technique. Langs asserts, and attempts to demonstrate in his use of supervised case material, that the patient, when confronted by the analyst's violation of boundaries or boundary crossings, will attempt to correct the "errors" of the therapist in associations following them. He went on to claim that Freud's boundary crossing with the Wolf-Man resulted in the failure of the treatment (Langs, 1980). This view depends upon a very purist version of psychoanalysis, concerned only with the discovery of deeply unconscious fantasies, whose objective validity is not easily demonstrable as superior to less extreme versions. Some of these issues are explored in Luca (2004), where a variety of professional frames and methods of containment are shown to be feasible and, sometimes, a necessary consequence of different therapeutic objectives in a number of settings and in situations that do not allow for the strict observance, or sometimes of *any* observance, of the formal requirements of the frame. Some divergences from the rigid classical position may contain the wish to avoid the cold, impersonal image that can be created by the observance of rules of anonymity. The tradition of the anonymous and passive psychoanalyst is seen by some as meaning that the analyst may be experienced as an inauthentic figure in what should be an interaction between equal participants. It is noteworthy that some of the analysands considered here (e.g., Little, Guntrip, Hill, and Couch, as well as some of Freud's patients) welcomed the less rigid application of concepts and techniques by their analysts, as well as being able to enjoy a warm personal relationship with them. The examples of Freud's patients show that he was quite capable of entering into a more personal exchange with them than has become standard practice since, and most of them valued that aspect of the relationship they felt they had experienced with him.

Winnicott made the departure from his observance of the requirements of a rigid frame, the abandonment of anonymity, and the crossing of boundaries within the session into a new technique he called *object usage*, to be employed with patients whose neurotic symptoms were masking a psychotic core, unreachable through the interpretation of the transference. It was a condition he suffered from himself and which may have made him particularly sensitive to it in others. The concept is defined by him in his paper "The use of an object and relating through identifications" (1971). He distinguishes between "relating to an object" and "finding an object". The process is summarized as follows:

> (1) Subject *relates* to object. (2) Object is in process of being found instead of placed by the subject in the world. (3) Subject *destroys* object. (4) Object survives destruction. (5) Subject can *use object*. [*ibid.*, p. 94]

In his work with Little and Guntrip, it is clear that Winnicott allowed himself to be a real person, and became for them the object in their lives who could replace the one with whom they had had a disastrous and destructive relationship. This seems to be in accordance with step (5), above. The interaction in the therapy was akin to the playful and real interactions he used in his work with children in the paediatric clinic.

There are some problems about this concept of object usage as defined by Winnicott. One is that although he uses the term "object" throughout, in step 1 the object appears to be internal and different from those in steps 2 and 3. Another problem is the transition from steps 3 to 4. If the object survives the destruction in step 3, the attack can only have been in fantasy. But Winnicott seems to imply that the object was *really* destroyed because it was outside the subject's area of omnipotent control, thus it could also survive as a result. He lays emphasis on the real, and not fantasy, destruction of the object. It is difficult to understand how the object, in this paradox, could at the same time be both really destroyed and not destroyed. In a review of Jung's *Memories, Dreams and Reflections*, Winnicott returned to this problem (1989, p. 482). The review prompted a dream in which his head was being split open to remove something that had not been reached in his analysis. Winnicott analysed the dream into three parts. First, he was part of the world which was being *absolutely* destroyed. Second, he was the agent of the absolute destruction. Third, in the dream he awoke, and knew while still dreaming that he had dreamed both the first and second parts. By using the difference between waking and sleeping states he could solve the problem. He knew that he had dreamed of both being destroyed and of being the destroying agent. As there was no dissociation the three Is were all together in touch with each other. He remembered dreaming I(2) and I(1). Waking, and suffering from a headache, he realized the importance of the number 3, his three essential selves. "I(3) could remember dreaming in turn of being I(2) and I(1). Without I(3) I must remain split". The solution seems to lie in a recognition that the I(1) and I(2) are either part objects or split-off aspects from the integrated whole I(3),and so can survive within the integration of I(3).

It has been claimed that Winnicott had very great difficulty in dealing with aggressive and destructive behaviour. Most notably, he was unable to deal with Khan's openly aggressive behaviour towards him, and when Little smashed a delicate vase containing some flowers in one of their sessions he immediately left the room, returning only as she was clearing up the mess. The next day the vase had been replaced with another exactly the same as the broken one and containing the same flowers, providing some evidence that restitution could be made even for very destructive behaviour, but no reference was made to the incident by either of them. Equally, when Little became angry with Winnicott, feeling that he was not understanding her but was insisting upon *his* interpretation of events, she could not challenge him but withdrew into an unresponsive silence for a year. It has also been claimed that he failed to deal with Guntrip's hostility and aggression, who remained as difficult a personality as he had been before Winnicott's work with him. Marion Milner made the same observation about the unchanged grandiosity of Margaret Little (Hopkins, 1998, pp. 16, 18). If Winnicott had difficulty with the aggressive hostility of patents, he may have also had problems with his own hate and aggression, despite his identification of the importance of hate in the countertransference, and of the interacting aggressiveness between analysand and analyst in his theory. In respect of object usage, and of himself being the object used in the analysis, he seemed much more identified with the qualities of the caring mother who would replace the defective or abusive mother. The analysands could then incorporate him into their unconscious fantasy in place of the demonized image at the root of their split off psychosis. This seems to have worked with Little and Guntrip, but to have failed disastrously with Masud Khan.

There are no other published examples by analysands of this method of object usage by other analysts and therapists. The concept depends on the relative significance of the difference between the idea of inner, inborn objects, with which the infant constitutes its relationship with the world of reality, and the idea that those objects are introjected in the first instance in the form that the infant experienced them as mediated by the mother. Winnicott differed from Klein in the concept of objects and what they represent. Without denying the existence of inborn aggression, Winnicott asserts the importance of the differences in the actual experience of infants in their relationship with their mothers, which account for their varied capacity to manage aggression. The necessary destruction of the object, which nevertheless survives and continues to survive, creates the externality of reality. In that reality, the surviving mother becomes the dependable object, enabling the feeling of object constancy. Although this was Winnicott's thinking about the idea and technique of object usage, his intellectual construction was not able to be embodied by him in his practice. He could not survive his analysands' destructiveness; he avoided or ignored it, but despite that, two of the analysands who have described their experiences with him valued his work with them and felt it was sufficiently different from their more orthodox experiences to have enabled them to reach the source of their problems, notwithstanding the absence of a radical change in their personalities. The validity of Winnicott's theory of object usage seems not to have been challenged, despite the difficulty he had in applying it to his own analysands, because, as Hopkins (*ibid.*, p. 37) suggests in her discussion of his analysis of Masud Khan, the heart problems from which Winnicott eventually died left him particularly vulnerable. She believes that work of this kind, where aggressive and dangerous interactions may be involved, requires the analysis to be conducted within a firm and consistent frame for the protection of both analyst and analysand.

Even without the example of Winnicott, and his special examples of encapsulated psychotic elements, there seems to be evidence in several of the other stories of the therapists' flexible attitudes to the observance of a rigid therapeutic frame; they may even sometimes have varied the internal boundaries of the sessions, without there having been any apparent harm to the patient or analysand.

Couch cites the example of being invited to find out about the presence of the fire brigade at Anna Freud's Child Therapy Clinic across the road from her consulting room in Maresfield Gardens, as well as her advice to him about his whispering patient. Freud himself invited HD to see his collection of antiques; he met Mrs Blanton at least once in her husband's hour, while Blanton remained in the waiting room. Hill contrasts Mrs Bick's rigidity and conceptual purity, to her detriment, with Rosenfeld's greater relaxation and conceptual moderation, which allowed Hill to explore his psychopathology with less restraint. Where there has been evidence of adherence to the observance of stern boundaries and application of theoretical concepts, the analysands have protested. Perhaps the crucial question is whether therapy can be advanced or hindered by conceptual or technical rigidity.

What is the nature of psychoanalysis and psychotherapy?

Is the purpose of psychoanalysis to provide treatment for specific mental conditions such as neuroses, from which it first developed? Or is it rather of an exploration of the psychopathology of the subject, with particular reference to unconscious dynamics without therapeutic implications? Freud favoured the latter, and professed little interest in therapy for its own sake. Subsequent psychotherapists and psychoanalysts have been prepared to make claims for its therapeutic significance for a number of mental conditions and illnesses. In the UK, analysts and psychotherapists are increasingly practising in the National Health Service, and consultant posts in psychotherapy have been created. Some of the more purist schools of thought, such as the Lacanian, the Classical Freudian, and the Kleinian, seem less concerned with therapy and more interested in the exploration of the deep psyche. In her introduction to her studies of patients' stories of their experiences of psychotherapy, Rosemary Dinnage (1998) asks the question "Does psychotherapy work?" By "psychotherapy" she meant all the various talking therapies that had come into existence since Freud's original pioneering work, not just psychoanalysis. By using the term "work" in her question, she may be asking if it is a cure for anything, or whether it has some other functional outcome. Dinnage refers to the Wolf-

Man's comment (Gardiner, 1973) that Freud had said that the experience of psychoanalysis is like purchasing a ticket for a journey, and that at its end the patient has to decide whether or not to take it. The Wolf-Man pointed out the error of this idea in his discussions with Obholzer, when he said that if everything had been cleared up Freud would have had to say that the patient would have no option but to become well. Few psychotherapists, or psychoanalysts, would now claim that they could clear up everything about the patient's mental and emotional disturbances and symptoms, although there is an idealization of the perfect analysis which would have that outcome. There is a suggestion in some of the stories told in this book (Chapter Seven, HD; Chapter Fourteen, Dr Margaret Little; Chapter Sixteen, Harry Guntrip) that something important may have happened after, sometimes long after, the active treatment had been concluded. For many patients the important thing may be the experience during the therapy itself; to have reached its end and to have emerged with some greater understanding of themselves, similar to the experience of "good-enough parenting". In that way, psychotherapy and psychoanalysis may differ from orthodox medical treatments of physical illnesses, where cure may be defined, if not always achieved.

Dinnage suggests that the word "cure" may have become taboo among contemporary therapists of all kinds. It may, of course, be related to the idea that, in a medical sense, a diagnosis dictates what action is to be taken to bring about the restoration of the status quo, or the removal of the symptoms by attacking their underlying cause, representing the cure of the illness or condition. The restoration of the status quo can rarely be the objective of psychotherapy, since many patents are suffering from the consequences of experiences in infancy with enduring effects, and are seeking relief from what may be profoundly handicapping conditions whose origins are obscure. Those origins may be the hidden cause of the condition complained of, be it a psychosomatic condition, a neurotic or psychotic state, or a problem about forming or sustaining a mutually gratifying relationship with another or others. The exploration of them may be helpful in bringing about the sought after relief, but nobody knows quite why that process may have that effect, or why, in other cases, it may not. What is it that enables change in the analysand or patient? Is it, as Freud thought, gaining insight into the unconscious trauma or fantasies? Is it the process of gaining understanding through the interaction of transference and counter-transference in the analytic or psychotherapy session? Or, since it is claimed that psychotherapies of all kinds have about the same degree of success, is there some other process common to all, and independent of the various theories and practices? Is the essential ingredient for the "success" of psychoanalysis or psychotherapy the willingness of the patient to change, and to bear to relinquish previous "solutions" in order to explore other avenues of understanding and development? Do the stories presented here provide any insight into the problem?

Marie Cardinal, Rosie Alexander, The Wolf-Man, Wynne Godley, Stuart Sutherland, and Jeffery Masson were all suffering from conditions that might be properly described as illnesses. Others were concerned with anxieties that seemed to fall short of illnesses in that they were not substantially disabling but involved greater or less inconvenience. HD, for example, was suffering from writer's block, which, since she was a poet, caused her some distress. Yet others were seeking training, and did not initially want to be relieved of any symptoms, but to learn how to become psychoanalysts and to explore their own unconscious depths. Jung was the first to propose that candidates should experience psychoanalysis themselves as a significant part of their training. This requirement was adopted, and it continues to form a part of the training of all psychotherapists wishing to practise the psychoanalytic method. Although those seeking training may be found to have neurotic conditions, these are not necessarily the overt reason for undertaking psychoanalysis. Some of those in training (Kardiner, Little, Guntrip) did discover something about early experiences of which they had no conscious memories, but whose retrieval from unconsciousness helped them to feel differently about themselves. Blanton apparently made no such discoveries about himself, but felt warmly about his relationship with Freud. Hill and Couch do not describe themselves as discovering any powerful insights into deep neurotic conditions, but both benefited from a warm, consistent and interested relationship with Rosenfeld and Anna Freud, respectively, that had not been characteristic of their previous analyses. Might the establishment of such a relationship in itself be the essential therapeutic element in all psychotherapies, including psychoanalysis?

Of those whose presentation arose from their need to be relieved from disabling conditions, only Marie Cardinal can be regarded as having been substantially healed from her very distressing psycho-somatic condition. Her physical symptom was "cured" almost at once, when none of the physical interventions had had any effect on it at all. The lasting cure came from the eventual tracing of the problem to its unconscious sources, and from the understanding of the psychosomatic condition as a re-enactment of a deeply uncon-scious infantile experience of a destructive interaction with her mother, perhaps beginning while she was still in the womb. It is an example of psychoanalysis at its best, revealing what could not have been consciously known by therapist or patient until it was allowed to emerge, over many years, in the course of unforced free associations prompted by some careful comments of the analyst. These interventions, as reported by Marie, hardly seem to be inter-pretations in the classical sense, but often facilitated further associ-ations leading to developing understanding of the profoundly unconscious experiences that had led to her symptom.

In respect of the Wolf-Man, Freud exaggerated his incapacity before he entered treatment, and although claiming that he had cured some of his symptoms, such as his constipation, the Wolf-Man's subsequent memoirs show that they had not been changed. But "our Wolf-Man", as Anna Freud called him, remained close to the heart of the psychoanalytic community, thus fulfilling his wish to be the favoured son, although not delivering the relief from his distress that he had sought. Freud's paper about him was really concerned to show not the therapeutic effectiveness of psycho-analysis, but the correctness of Freud's theories of infantile sexual-ity, thus refuting Adler's and Jung's theories.

HD wrote warmly about her relationship with Freud, despite maintaining her own way of understanding her psychological world. Neither her writer's block nor her war phobia disappeared immediately after the end of her analysis with Freud. She had another analysis during the mid-1930s with another analyst, but wrote nothing about it, so it is impossible to assess the contribution it made to the removal of the two conditions she suffered from until they were relieved during the Second World War. To that extent, this provides support for Freud's view that the analysand must make the journey after the analysis has ended, although it is, of course, impossible to be certain that the outcome was a result of the analysis.

Neither Godley, Sutherland, nor Masson reported any alleviation of their conditions. The first two were plainly worse at the termination of their sessions than they had been at the beginning. All three suffered under analysts who were unsatisfactory, but there may be a question about whether Sutherland's depression would have been amenable to psychoanalytic methods even if he had not been so sceptical about psychoanalysis. Wolpert (1999), who suffered from a similar condition, had an analysis which was not successful in relieving it, and he argued that psychoanalysis could only have a part to play in its treatment. It should be supplementary to other kinds of treatment, rather than the major contributor. Classically, psychoanalytical theory ascribed depression to the repression of anger and hostility, which consequently become focused on the self, producing loss of self -esteem as well as depression. This formulation does not seem to fit Sutherland's or Wolpert's conditions. Both found relief from their symptoms through drugs, although vulnerability to depression remained, and eventually Sutherland committed suicide.

So, from the limited case material summarized here, it is, of course, not possible to find conclusive evidence of the interaction between neurology and psychology, but Sutherland's and Wolpert's experiences raise the question as to whether their symptoms were primarily neurological rather than psychological in origin. Were their psychological conditions a result of neurological malfunctioning, or were their neurological states caused by their psychological difficulties, which preceded depression? Sutherland had marital problems and a particular aspect of them (the discovery that his wife's lover was a close friend) was immediately followed by the symptoms of depression. Was this discovery the cause of his depression, or did it simply act as a catalyst for the depression? In some ways, he manifested the characteristics of what is now called a bipolar disorder in that his life, until the depression, had been rather manic, so that many of his difficulties may have been a consequence of that. It may, however, be appropriate to wonder whether, if he had consulted a competent couple therapist rather than psychoanalysts, whose skills in that area were deficient, there might have been a different outcome.

It could be argued that psychoanalysis is primarily a theory or a conceptual system for whose ontological foundation there is scant evidence, and for which little direct and consistent application in its immaculate form to psychotherapy can be found, as a number of these stories illustrate. Wallerstein's work (1992, 1995, cited by Eisold, 2005) also shows that examples of psychoanalysis uncontaminated by other processes are rare or non-existent; this despite the fact that all psychoanalysts in training are required to undergo lengthy psychoanalyses by approved practitioners and themselves are required to "treat" under supervision patients (who may be psychotherapists in training in different institutions) several times per week for many years. What is missing from this concept of psychotherapy is an objectively established account of the patient's condition at the outset that may be compared with the outcome at the end of treatment. Freud's account of the Wolf-Man's state of dependence at the beginning of his treatment was almost certainly wrong, and it was disputed in the Wolf-Man's own story. Nor was there any objectively established outcome of his treatment by either Freud or Mack Brunswick. Both claimed to have cured him of his various neuroses, and that, too, was denied by the Wolf-Man in his discussions with Obholzer. So, if the pure gold of psychoanalysis is almost impossible to practise, what can be said about it as a therapy?

In recent years a number of courses have been established in which psychoanalytical theories of all kinds are studied independently of practice. The students are not required to be in therapy themselves, although they may be. Nor do they treat patients under supervision. These courses, usually known as Psychoanalytical Studies, demonstrate that the concepts can be understood, taught, and criticized independently of practice. This contrasts with the established view in the formal psychoanalytical institutes that they cannot be understood in isolation from practice. It also casts doubt upon Eisler's claim that the Wolf-Man's story in analysis could only be understood by the cognoscenti.

Additionally, the concepts of psychoanalysis, with special reference to its symbolism, are frequently used in the critique of artistic productions, as well as in social, cultural, and anthropological studies, often far removed from the world of treatment and practice. Most psychoanalytic institutes mount events in which art and culture, rather than practice, are the focus. Thus, there is a sense that psychoanalytical ideas can be applied to other fields of thought and study. So, might there be value in thinking about Applied Psycho-analysis as being relevant to practice with patients as well as in other ways? Luca (2004) and her co-authors show how variable such applications may be, depending on the kind of patients being treated—children, couples, expectant mothers, individuals and groups—as well as upon the settings in which they are encountered. They might be hospitals of all kinds, social services' departments of Local Authorities, or every kind of residential facility. All might benefit from being helped to comprehend the problems of their patients, clients, and residents through a psychoanalytical under-standing, not only of the subjects of the care, but of the situation in which they found themselves. Such applications might be consid-ered an extension of the alloy of Applied Psychoanalysis being prac-tised privately with individuals who had signed on for some form of psychoanalytical treatment of whatever frequency or duration.

Finally, whatever may be claimed for analysis and psychother-apy, most of the stories related here show how differently analys-ands and patients record their experiences from the way they are typically described by practitioners. One of the significant differ-ences is that the analysands consistently tell their stories in terms of whole object relationships, rather than in the more esoteric terms typically used by analysts and therapists. Only one of the accounts in this book, that of the Wolf-Man, can be directly compared to the analyst's story. Freud's paper remains as an exemplar of those professional stories, and it is noteworthy that few of the Wolf-Man's words or responses to Freud's interpretations appear in it. Equally, although in modern professional accounts there may often be refer-ences to the interaction between analysand and therapist, the "plot" is almost entirely the practitioner's. The claim to specialist expertise and knowledge is thus subtly enhanced and the lay account subtly diminished. The accounts of the analysands reported here seem to me to demand as much respect for their authenticity as do those of their therapists.

Notes

1.   "A single case can never be capable of proving a theorem as general as this one: but I can only repeat over an over again—for I never find

it otherwise—that sexuality is the key to the problem of the psycho-neuroses and of neuroses in general. No one who disclaims the key will ever be able to unlock the door" (Freud, 1905d, p.115).

2. Under the inexorable pressure of this fixed limit, Sergei's resistance and fixation to the illness gave way, and now in a disproportionately short time the analysis produced all the material that made it possible to clear up his inhibitions and remove his symptoms (Freud, 1918b, p. 11).

REFERENCES

Alexander, R. (1995). *Folie à Deux: An Experience of One-to-One Therapy*. London: Free Association.

Bair, D. (2004). *Jung: A Biography*. London: Little, Brown.

Barnes, M., & Burke, J. (1991). *Mary Barnes: Two Accounts of a Journey Through Madness*. London: Free Association.

Blanton, S. (1971). *Diary of My Analysis with Sigmund Freud*. New York: Hawthorn.

Bollas, C. & Sundelson, A. (1995). *The New Informants: Betrayal of Confidentiality in Psychoanalysis and Psychotherapy*. London: Karnac.

Boynton, R. S. (2002–2003). The return of the repressed: The strange case of Masud Khan. *Boston Review, 27*(6):

Breger, L. (2000). *Freud: Darkness in the Midst of Vision*. New York: John Wiley.*

Caine, L., & Royston, R. (2003). *Out of the Dark*. Random House.

Cardinal, M. (1984). *The Words to Say It*. Pat Goodhart (Trans.). London: Pan (Picador).

Casement, P. (1985). *On Learning from the Patient*. New York: Tavistock.

Carotenuto, A. (1886). *The Spiral Way: A Woman's Healing Journey* John Shepley (Trans.). Toronto: Inner City.

Chisholm, D. (1992). *H.D.'s Freudian Poetics: Psychoanalysis in Translation*. Ithaca, NY: Cornell University Press.

Christopher, E., & Solomon, H. M. (Eds.) (2002). *Contemporary Jungian Clinical Practice*. London: Karnac.

Cooper, J. (1993). *Speak Of Me As I Am: The Life and Work of Masud Khan*. London: Karnac.

Couch, A. S. (1995). Anna Freud's adult psychoanalytic technique: a defence of classical analysis. *International Journal of Psychoanalysis*, 76(1): 153–171.

Dinnage, R. (1989). *One to One: Experiences of Psychotherapy*. London: Viking.

Douglas, C. (1993). *Translate this Darkness. The Life of Christiana Morgan, The Veiled Woman in Jung's Circle*. Princeton, NJ: Princeton University Press.

Eigen, M. (1981). Guntrip's analysis with Winnicott—a critique of Glatzer & Evans. *Contemporary Psychoanalysis*, 17: 103–111.

Erikson, E. (1958). The nature of clinical evidence. *Daedalus*, 187(4).

Esman, A. (1973). The primal scene. *The Psychoanalytic Study of the Child*, 28: 49–81.

Ferro, A. (1999). *The Bi-Personal Field. Experiences in Child Analysis*. London: Brunner-Routledge.

Fordham, M. (1993). *The Making of an Analyst*. London: Free Association.

France, A. (1988). *Consuming Psychotherapy*. London: Free Association.

Friedman, S. S. (1981). *Psyche Reborn: The Emergence of H. D.* Bloomington, IN: Indiana University Press.

Friedman, S. S. (Ed.) (2002). *Analyzing Freud: Letters of H. D., Bryher and their Circle*. New York: New Directions.

Freud, E. L. (1960). *Letters of Sigmund Freud*. T. & J. Stern (trans.). New York: Basic Books.

Freud, S. (1905d). *Three Essays on the Theory of Sexuality*. S.E., 7. London: Hogarth.

Freud, S. (1905e). *Fragment of an Analysis of a Case of Hysteria*. S.E., 7. London: Hogarth.

Freud, S. (1914b). *The Moses of Michelangelo*. S.E., 13: London: Hogarth.

Freud, S. (1914d). On the history of the psychoanalytic movement. *S.E.*, 14. London: Hogarth.

Freud, S. (1914g). Remembering, repeating and working-through. *S.E.*, 12. London: Hogarth.

Freud, S. (1918b). *From the History of an Infantile Neurosis*. S.E., 16. London: Hogarth.

Freud, S. (1920g). *Beyond the Pleasure Principle*. S.E., 18. London: Hogarth.

Freud, S. (1925d). An autobiographical study. *S.E.*, *20*. London: Hogarth.

Freud, S. (1930a). *Civilization and Its Discontents*. *S.E.*, *21*. London: Hogarth.

Freud, S. (1939a). *Moses and Monotheism*. *S.E.*, *23*. London: Hogarth.

Freud, Sophie (1993). Review of Masson's 3 publications on psychoanalysis. *Journal of William Whyte Psychoanalytical Institute*, 1–15.

Gabbard, G. O., & Lester, E. P. (1995). *Boundaries and Boundary Violations in Psychoanalysis*. Washington, DC: American Psychiatric Publishing.

Gardiner, M. (Ed.) (1973). *The Wolf-Man and Sigmund Freud*. London: Penguin.

Glatzer, H. T., & Evans, W. N. (1977). Guntrip's analysis with Fairbairn and Winnicott. *International Journal of Psychoanalytical Psychotherapy*, *6*: 81–98.

Godley, W. (2001). Saving Masud Khan. *London Review of Books*, 22 February, pp. 3–7.

Greenson, R. R. (1973). *The Technique and Practice of Psycho-Analysis*. Hogarth Press and The Institute of Psychoanalysis.

Guntrip, H. J. S. (1975). My experience of analysis with Fairbairn and Winnicott (How complete a result does psycho-analytic therapy achieve?). *International Review of Psychoanalysis*, *2*: 445–487.

Hazel, J. (1991). Reflections on my experience of psychoanalysis with Guntrip. *Contemporary Psychoanalysis*, *27*: 148–166.

H. D. (1944). *Writing on the Wall. Tribute to Freud*. Manchester: Carcanet.

H. D. (1948). *Advent. Tribute to Freud*. Manchester: Carcanet.

H. D. (1970). *Tribute to Freud*. Manchester: Carcanet.

Henderson, J. L. (1975). C. G. Jung: a reminiscent picture of his method. *Journal of Analytical Psychology*, *20*: 114–121.

Hill, J. (1993). Am I a Kleinian? Is anyone? *British Journal of Psychotherapy*, *9*(4): 463–475.

Hopkins, L. B. (1998). D. W. Winnicott's analysis of Masud Khan. *Contemporary Psychoanalysis*, *34*(1): 5–47.

Hopkins, L. B. (2000). Masud Khan's application of Winnicott's "play" techniques to analytic consultation and treatment of adults. *Contemporary Psychoanalysis*, *36*(4): 639–663.

Jones, E. (1970). Back cover, *Tribute to Freud*. Manchester: Carcanet

Jung, C. G. (1945). Medicine: Psychotherapy. *C.W.*, *16*: 84. London: Routledge.

Kanzer, M., & Glenn, J. (Eds.) (1980). *Freud and His Patients*. New York: Aronson.

Kardiner, A. (1977). *My Analysis with Freud: Reminiscences.* New York: W. W. Norton.

Kernberg, O. F. (1996). Thirty methods to destroy creativity of psychoanalytic candidates. *International Journal of Psychoanalysis, 77:* 1031–1040.

Kirsner, D. (2000). *Unfree Associations: Inside Psychoanalytic Institutes.* London: Process Press.

Knight, S. (1950). *The Story of My Psychoanalysis.* New York: McGraw Hill.*

Kottler, J. A., & Carlson, J. (2003). *Bad Therapy: Master Therapists Share Their Worst Failures.* New York: Brunner-Routledge.

Langs, R. (1976). *The Bipersonal Field.* New York: Aronson.

Langs, R. J. (1980). The misalliance dimension in the case of Dora. In: M. Kanzer & J. Glenn (Eds.), *Freud and His Patients* (pp. 58–71). New York: Aronson.

Little, M. (1981). *Transference Neurosis and Transference Psychosis.* New York: Jason Aronson.

Little, M. (1990). *Psychotic Anxieties & Containment: A Personal Record of an Analysis with Winnicott.* North Vale, NJ: Jason Aronson.

Lohser, B., & Newton, P. H. (1996). *Unorthodox Freud: The View from The Couch.* New York: Guilford.

Luca, M. (Ed.) (2004). *The Therapeutic Frame in the Clinical Context: Integrative Perspectives.* Hove: Brunner-Routledge

McLynn, F. (1996). *A Biography of Carl Gustav Jung.* London: Bantam.

Magid, B. (1993). Self psychology meets the Wolf-Man. In: B. Magid (Ed.), *Freud's Case Studies: Self-Psychological Perspectives* (pp. 157–187). Hillsdale, NJ: Analytic Press.

Malcolm, J. (1984). *In The Freud Archives.* New York: Knopf.

Mahony, P. (1984). *Cries of the Wolf-Man.* New York: International Universities Press.

Masson, J. M. (1990). *Final Analysis: The Making and Unmaking of a Psychoanalyst.* Reading, MA: Addison-Wesley.

Masson, J. M. (1992). *The Assault on Truth.* London: Fontana.

Milner, M. (1952). Aspects of symbolism and the comprehension of the not-self. *International Journal of Psychoanalysis, 55:* 181–185.

Newman, A. (1995). *Non-compliance in Winnicott's Words: A Companion to the Writings and Work of D. W. Winnicott.* London: Free Association.

Noll, R. (1996). *The Jung Cult: Origins of a Charismatic Movement.* London: Fontana.

Obholzer, K. (1982). *The Wolf-Man: Sixty Years Later.* M. Shaw (Trans.). London: Routledge & Kegan Paul.

Padel, J. H. (1972). The contribution of W. R. D. Fairbairn. *Bulletin of the European Psycho-Analytical Federation*, 2: 13–26.

Reid, J. C. (2001). *Jung, My Mother and I*. Daimon Verlag.

Sacks, M. (1993). Review of *Final Analysis*. *Journal of the American Psychoanalytical Association*, 41: 306–309.

Sandler, A.-M. (2004). Institutional response to boundary violations: the case of Masud Khan. *International Journal of Psychoanalysis*, 85: 27–44.

Scott, B. K. (1995). *About H. D.'s Life and Career. The Oxford Companion to Women's Writing in the United States*. Oxford: Oxford University Press.

Shamdasani, S. (1998). *Cult Fictions: C. G. Jung and the Founding of Analytical Psychology*. London: Routledge.

Spence, D. P. (1982). *Narrative Truth and Historical Truth: Meaning and Interpretation in Psychoanalysis*. New York: W. W. Norton.*

Spence, D. P. (1997). Case reports and the reality they represent. In: I. Ward (Ed.), *The Presentation of Case Material in Clinical Discourse* (pp. 7–93). London: Freud Museum Publications.*

Spurling, H. (1977). Using the case study in the assessment of trainees. In: I. Ward (Ed.), *The Presentation of Case Material in Clinical Discourse* (pp. 67–76). London: Freud Museum Publications.

Strachey, J. (1934). The nature of therapeutic action in psychoanalysis. *International Journal of Psycho-Analysis*, 15: 127–159.

Sutherland, S. (1987). *Breakdown: A Personal Crisis and Medical Dilemma*. London: Weidenfeld & Nicolson.

The Wolf-Man and the Freud Archives (1957). Letters pertaining to Freud's *From a History of an Infantile Neurosis*. Two letters from the Wolf-Man. *The Psychoanalytical Quarterly*, 26(4): 447–460.

Ward, I. (Ed.) (1997). *The Presentation of Case Material in Clinical Discourse*. London: Freud Museum Publications.

Willoughby, R. (2005). *Masud Khan: The Myth and the Reality*. London: Free Association.

Winnicott, D. W. (1971). *Playing and Reality*. London: Tavistock.

Winnicott, D. W. (1989). *Psychoanalytical Explorations*. London: Karnac.

Wolpert, L. (1999). *Malignant Sadness: The Anatomy of Depression*. London: Faber & Faber.

Wortis, J. (1954). *Fragments of an Analysis with Freud*. New York: Simon & Schuster.

Young, R. M. (1998). Review of *Final Analysis*. Human Nature, Internet publication.